ST ANDREWS

DOUGLAS YOUNG

St Andrews

Town and Gown, Royal and Ancient

CASSELL · LONDON

CASSELL & COMPANY LTD
35 Red Lion Square, London WC1
Melbourne, Sydney, Toronto
Johannesburg, Auckland

© Douglas Young 1969
First published 1969

S.B.N. 304 93376 7

Printed in Great Britain by
The Camelot Press Ltd.,
London and Southampton
F.369

CONTENTS

ILLUSTRATIONS

For David and Mary
C. and B.,
with best wishes
for many more happy years
to enjoy and embellish
the Kingdom of Fife.

WEST SANDS

1. BIG DOO CRAIG
2. WITCH HILL
3. ROYAL & ANCIENT CLUBHOUSE
4. MARTYRS' MONUMENT
5. WITCH LAKE
6. CATHOLIC CHURCH
7. UNIVERSITY HOUSE
8. HAMILTON HALL
9. ST KATHERINES SCHOOL
10. ST SALVATOR'S COLLEGE
11. CASTLE
12. ALL SAINTS CHURCH
13. ST REGULUS'S CAVE
14. DEAN'S COURT
15. QUEEN MARY'S
16. ST MARY'S OF THE ROCK
17. LONG PIER
18. ST RULES TOWER
19. THE PENDS
20. ST LEONARD'S SCHOOL
21. SITE OF NEW INNS
22. COTTAGE HOSPITAL

THE SCORES
NORTH STREET
MARKET STREET
SOUTH STREET
ARGYLE STREET

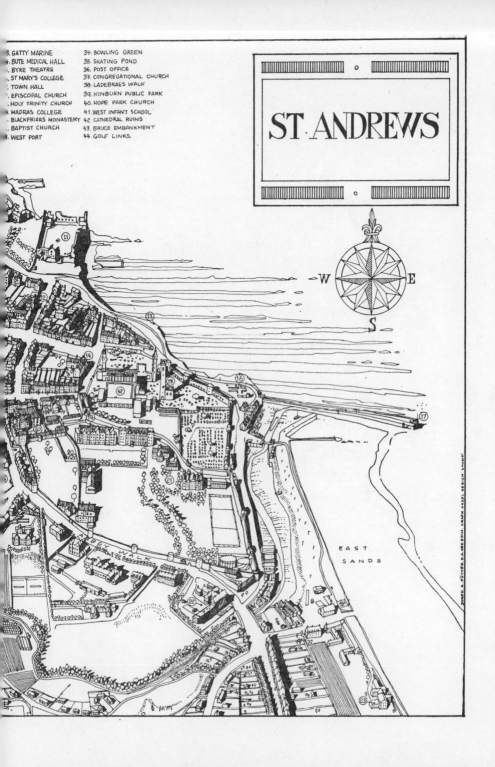

ST. ANDREWS

3. GATTY MARINE
. BUTE MEDICAL HALL
. BYRE THEATRE
. ST MARY'S COLLEGE
. TOWN HALL
. EPISCOPAL CHURCH
. HOLY TRINITY CHURCH
. MADRAS COLLEGE
. BLACKFRIARS MONASTERY
. BAPTIST CHURCH
. WEST PORT

34. BOWLING GREEN
35. SKATING POND
36. POST OFFICE
37. CONGREGATIONAL CHURCH
38. LADEBRAES WALK
39. KINBURN PUBLIC PARK
40. HOPE PARK CHURCH
41. WEST INFANT SCHOOL
42. CATHEDRAL RUINS
43. BRUCE EMBANKMENT
44. GOLF LINKS.

EAST
SANDS

FOREWORD

To attempt a biography of a city fourteen centuries old is doubtless rash for one who has been acquainted with it for a mere half-century. There were things about St Andrews that puzzled me when I was a wee laddie in a sailor suit towards the end of the Kaiser's War, and in the 1920s when I became a devotee of the golf-links, and later when I wore the student's red gown, and still during two decades when I served on the academic staff. It was therefore a pleasant challenge to accept the invitation from the House of Cassell to write a book about the place, and explain how there came to be, on a remote part of the Fife coast, a town which is at the centre of three great facets of Scottish life—learning, religion, and golf.

The effort to clarify matters for myself, after many years of desultory reading and talking about aspects of St Andrews, has resulted in the following chapters, which are designed for readers who may never have read a line about Scotland before, and never heard of the city except as a place of international pilgrimage for the great and growing congregation of devotees of golf. If at times I may seem to have written light-heartedly, and without excessive reverence for institutions old or new, the reader must excuse me: I was born light-hearted.

March 1968   *Douglas Young*

ACKNOWLEDGEMENTS

For most helpful advice over the whole field I am extremely indebted to my colleague Mr R. G. Cant, historian of the University and of much else, who benevolently and perspicaciously read two whole drafts in typescript. For a like service in regard to a draft on the Roman period I am most grateful to my colleague Dr Geoffrey Rickman. For further help with regard to illustrative material I have to thank Mr Stewart Cruden, H.M. Inspector of Ancient Monuments for Scotland, Mr George M. Cowie, Mr David Dorward, Mr W. F. Douglas, Mr James Gerrard, Dr David Jack, and Mr R. N. Smart. On particular points I was happy to be able to consult Mrs Marjorie O. Anderson, Professor Francis J. Byrne, Dr Nora K. Chadwick, Professor Gordon Donaldson, Dr Richard Feachem, Professor Kenneth Jackson, Mr R. L. C. Lorimer, Dr Euan MacKie, Mr Terence Bruce-Mitford, Professor Stuart Piggott, Dr Kenneth Steer, Professor A. C. Thomas, and Dr Donald Watt. I was much helped by Dr Isabel Henderson's generous gift of her book on *The Picts* and Professor Geoffrey Barrow's of his on *Robert Bruce*, and by my brother John's loan of rare books on golf. Many of the matters discussed, especially for centuries up to the twelfth, are obscure and controversial, and none of the consultants above mentioned is to be taken as necessarily sharing any particular view adopted by me here.

Douglas Young

1

PICTISH KINRYMONT

'Grand place, St Andrews,' said Thomas Carlyle. 'You have there the essence of all the antiquity of Scotland, in good and clean condition.' It was a casual remark by the Victorian Sage, then aged eighty-five, to the gossip-scribbling parish minister Dr A. K. H. Boyd; but there is truth in that reflection about 'the essence of all the antiquity of Scotland'. Unfortunately, the 'good and clean condition' is sadly to seek, especially for the earlier centuries, where the condition of the antiquity is woefully murky and fragmentary. Yet one must grapple with it, if only in the hope of making sense of the coming to be of the cathedrals and the castle, the university, and even the Royal and Ancient Golf Club.

The first precise date concerning St Andrews is AD 747, under which year the eleventh-century Irish monk Tigernach of Clonmacnoise records the death of Tuathalan, Abbot of *Cendrigmonaid*. Variously spelt, this Gaelic word means 'the headland of the king's hill'. A twelfth-century version of the Legend of St Andrew tells how the cult of the apostle arose in 'the region of the Picts, which is now called Scotland', when the monk Regulus, from Constantinople, brought relics of the saint to 'the summit of the king's hill, that is *Rigmund*'. The name survives still in the farms of Easter and Wester Balrymonth, along a ridge about a mile south of the cathedrals. The upland continues southwards into the King's Muir, where there was a King's Seat, known from charters of the twelfth-century priory. The whole area must have belonged to some Dark Age king of the type outsiders called a *Pict*—that is to say, a Celtic Briton who resisted Roman imperialism.

There had probably been a sizeable population in the St Andrews area from before 2000 BC. Between the estuaries of the Eden and the Tay there are abundant relics of Middle Stone Age settlement. Hunters and food-gatherers would make their way northward up the coast, in dug-out canoes or wicker-framed coracles covered with hides. Sailing towards the Eden from Fife Ness, they would have on their left hand slopes covered with swampy forests of oak and pine and beech, with

I

wild boars and deer and wolves and bears. Then they would come to the East Sands, at the outflow of the Kinness Burn, and beyond that the 'headland of the king's hill', where later were built the cathedrals and the castle; passing the cliffs with the cave called 'St Regulus's' they would reach the two miles of the West Sands, fringing the links where now are the four golf courses, and find safer ground to beach their boats in the tidal Eden, where most of the ships put in that brought traders to the medieval fairs held in the priory after Easter.

When grain-sowing began to be practised ridges were preferred for the farms in British conditions, such as the ridge of Balrymonth, 'village of the king's hill or upland'; and further up the slope to the south the folk of the second millennium BC built a stone circle, near the present parish church of Dunino, 'the fort of uniting'. On an adjacent rock, the Bell Craig, is a pothole, about three feet deep and four and a half across, which may have been a ritual pit for some sort of pagan antics.

South-west of St Andrews about three miles is the long *dun* of Dunork, a stone-walled fort some hundred and fifty yards long by fifty wide, on the top of a rocky hill. It has the same element as the tribal name in Orkney, known from around 300 BC. The Orkoi tribe may have had as their totem animal or heraldic emblem an *orc*, the Celtic word for a young boar. The promontory on which St Andrews stands was called *Muckross*, 'the headland of swine'; and the original lands of the eighth-century Pictish monastery consisted of the 'Boar's Raik', or run, ending at the village of Boarhills.

The earliest metal found in the area is some bronze knives in a cemetery of urns at Lawhead on the Kinness Burn, far enough along it to avoid the worst of the spring east winds. The people burned and buried there were probably Celtic-speakers from the Urnfield culture of northern Europe, who reached Fife soon after 1000 BC, maybe sailing direct from the Elbe mouth in Germany. Their prudent choice of site anticipated those Victorian and Edwardian gentlemen who built their villas and mansions westward from the medieval walled city along the Lade Braes. Their society would be run by a warrior aristocracy, with a *ri* or tribal king, head of a royal clan dominating a small *tuath* or tribe of maybe three thousand people. South of Dunork there was a round stone fort on Drum-carrow hill, of one of the types sometimes termed *broch*. Near it was found a thin silver breastplate.

It is not known how thick on the ground the pre-Celtic New Stone Age inhabitants were, taking Scotland as a whole. But the main exploitation of the land seems to have been done by metal-using Celtic-speakers who came in during the first millennium BC, probably in comparatively small bands, each carving out for itself an area of grazing and ploughing, with hilltop fortresses as strongpoints in disputes with neighbouring clans about grazing rights. Similar Celtic warrior aristocracies were to be found, in the centuries around 300 BC, from Bohemia to central Italy and from Galway in western Ireland and Galicia in north-west Spain to Galatia in Asia Minor. They sacked Rome about 390 BC, and traded with the Greeks, some elements of whose civilization gradually penetrated Celtic lands, as they also educated the uncouth Romans. Towards 50 BC the Romans, with their Greek-speaking ruling class, conquered the most powerful Celtic area, modern France and round about, and in AD 43 they began to try to conquer all Britain, greedy for metals and slaves and pearls and glory, and reluctant to leave unsubdued any focus of Celtic resistance from which the Gauls on the Continent might get help to rebel.

About AD 80 the peninsula of Fife first felt the tread of Roman legionaries and their auxiliaries. A camp of some thirty-five acres was recently found at Bonnyton, near Dunino, about three miles south-east of St Andrews. At Auchtermuchty, seventeen miles west, there is a sixty-acre camp, built by Julius Agricola, the first Roman general to try to conquer the Celts in what the Romans called *Caledonia*, north of the Forth–Clyde isthmus. His son-in-law Tacitus tells how, in the summer of 84, Agricola took an army to a hill called Mons Graupius (the Meikle Balloch hill in the Pass of Grange, in Banffshire) to fight over 30,000 Britons raised by a confederation of tribes under a general named Calgacus, which is Celtic for 'swords-man'. The Romans had some 3,000 to 8,000 legionaries, 8,000 auxiliary infantrymen, and between 3,000 and 5,000 cavalry. The battle lasted a day. The Roman propagandist

3

claimed a victory, and the Romans marched off south again, sending a fleet to ravage the coasts.

The great legionary fortress built by Agricola at Inchtuthill, on the Tay above Perth, was abandoned about 87. In 122 the Emperor Hadrian began his famous wall from the Tyne to the Solway, eighty miles long and twelve feet or more high. Then in 142 the Romans built the Antonine Vallum, from Forth to Clyde, thirty-seven miles long. Towards 180 the imperialists had to keep about 10,000 soldiers along Hadrian's Wall and a further 17,500 in the territory north of it to the outpost forts beyond the Vallum. Yet in 180 the Picts beyond were able to defeat and kill a Roman legionary general. In 209 a particularly bloody-minded Roman Emperor, the arthritic old Berber Septimius Severus, came up with a strong amphibious force, and built a new legionary fortress at Carpow on the Tay, near Abernethy, where the Venicones of Fife had a strong timber-laced fort. He and his son Caracalla claimed victories, but suffered heavy losses. In 210, thanks to the encouraging resistance offered by the Caledonians north of the Vallum, the confederacy of tribes between the Vallum and the Wall, called the Maiatai, rebelled; and the Romans eventually cut their losses and settled for a frontier on Hadrian's Wall, with a shadowy authority beyond it to the Vallum. How little the tribes between the walls had to do with the Romans in the next generation is indicated by the gap in the Roman coin finds from Traprain Law, the chief town between the Tweed and the Forth. Trading had obviously decreased since the hostilities.

In 306 the Romans ventured again to the far north, under Constantius, who went south again with nothing accomplished. His panegyrist wrote that he did not deign to acquire for the Empire 'the forests and swamps of the Caledonians and other Picts'. *Picti* is a Latin participle meaning 'painted', and was applied in the first century AD to Britons generally, all of whom practised painting or tattooing. The very name *Britanni* (or *Brittones*, Greek *Pretanoi*, Irish *Cruithni*) means 'the people of the patterns'. One may take it that the Celtic warrior nobles embellished their epidermises with animal and other designs, either for magical protection or as insignia of rank. As the Britons of the Lowland zone of England abandoned their ancestral ways

4

for the Roman toga, the epithet *Picti* was reserved for the free Britons of the north who totally rejected Roman ways. The form *Britanni* was used for the romanized Britons of the Lowland zone, and the slightly contemptuous variant *Brittones* for the tribes of north England and south Scotland, who had more to do with Rome in the way of trade than the Picts.

In AD 360 we first hear of the Scots, or *Scotti*, as a people raiding the Roman province along with the Picts. In the next few years they are joined by the Saxons, from the German coasts, and the Attacotti. It may be that the Scotti and Attacotti were two sorts of Cotti, a Celtic tribal group. Count Theodosius came to fight this barbarian coalition, and in 369 marched and sailed to the far north, again with no permanent conquest. But he enlisted the Attacotti into four regiments to fight as Roman mercenaries on the Continent. St Jerome encountered them in Gaul, and deplores their partiality for devouring shepherds' buttocks and women's breasts. (The Attacotti were only one of many barbarian tribal groups who took pay to fight somewhere. When the first Christian Emperor, Constantine I, was proclaimed at York in 306, the lead was taken by a German mercenary, Crocus, leader of the Alamanni. Scots from Ireland were settled in Wales and Cornwall by the Romans as *foederati*, military allies, on the same principle as the Romans had adopted on their Danube frontier, hiring one German tribe to fight off the others. Reformed poachers make the best gamekeepers.) Count Theodosius also made deals with three tribes in southern Scotland: the Votadini along the east coast from Tyne to Forth; the Damnonii (people of the mines, as in Devon) on the Clyde; and the Novantae in south-west Scotland. Some of their aristocracies took up Christianity, which was the Roman official religion by now, instead of their old Celtic cults of horned gods and horse-goddesses and the like. Enough of the Novantae were Christian by about 397 for the authorities at Rome, or in the British province, to appoint one of their tribesmen, St Nynia, as bishop. He built a stone church at Candida Casa, later called Whithorn, on the Solway, which radiated its influence to the Picts further north and to the Scots in Ireland.

In St Nynia's time the Romans made their final invasion of

the far north, under Stilicho, the barbarian who was running the western half of the Roman Empire after the east had split off with its centre at Constantinople. The poet Claudian writes at this time of a Roman legion 'bridling the fierce Scot and studying the iron-printed designs losing their animation as the Pict dies'. No doubt, when the Pict was operating in full vigour, the tattooed animals on his chest and arms would look quite lively. Celtic élite warriors used to rush to battle naked but for a belt, and a helmet, and maybe elaborate twisted necklets and armlets, sometimes of gold. When they went out to dinner-parties they dressed down, not up, to display their tattoo designs. The best idea we can form of them is from animal tattoo designs that survive on deep-frozen corpses from Pazirik, at the south Siberian end of the steppe region that was the home of the roving Scyths, from whom the Scots claimed to descend, for example in the Declaration of Independence sent to the Pope by the Scottish Parliament from Arbroath in 1320. Tattooing is not necessarily a mark of untutored barbarity, for even today, among the highly civilized Scandinavians, there is a popular monarch who has allowed photographs to be published of his elaborately tattooed royal epidermis.

The art-loving Picts also painted their ships with camouflage sea-green and raided far down the coasts of England, from Fife. At Norrie's Law, some nine miles south of St Andrews, a man found in 1819 a stone coffin with a complete suit of silver armour, with helmet, shield, swordhilt, and scabbard all of silver, a silver finger-ring in the form of a snake, and a circular silver plate: also some silver coins with Pictish designs. A local laird secured some of the objects, but the finder had sold most of them to a travelling tinker, who crushed them up to sell to jewellers in Cupar and Edinburgh. It seems there were at least four hundred ounces of pure bullion. This probably represents loot taken by a Pictish chief in Fife from some rich villa in south England or Gaul. To cope with the piratical Picts the Roman Government on the Continent gave leave, in 410, to the aristocrats of the Roman towns in Britain to organize their own army. It could not cope. So about 425 one Vortigern, the president of the Romano–British aristocratic republic, hired some Saxons and settled them in Kent. Before long they

6

mutinied, through lack of their promised rations, and began to conquer the romanized Britons on their own account.

About 425 also the romanized Britons arranged with the chief called Cunedda and some of his people, the Votadini, to defend Wales against further attacks of Scots from Ireland. Cunedda's pedigree starts with six Pictish names, and then has three Latin names, suggesting that his immediate ancestors had been Christians and *foederati* of the Roman authority in the Lowland zone. His great-grandson was a powerful king named Maelgwyn, who died in the yellow plague of 548 after ruling the Isle of Man, Anglesey, and the area of Gwynedd in North Wales. Maelgwyn was probably father of the important Pictish High King Bridei, whom St Columba visited near Inverness.

The first bishop we hear about in Ireland was St Palladius, who was sent in 431 to the Scots believing in Christ. More famous was his successor, St Patrick, who wrote an angry letter, about 455, to Ceredig, King of Strathclyde, complaining about slave-raids made on Ulster by 'apostate Picts'. It seems that whatever christianization had been carried out by St Nynia and others was only skin-deep among the Picts, like their traditional tattoos. But among all the barbarian peoples, and indeed among the Greeks and Romans too, Christianity did not make unimpeded progress. It was liable to relapses. However, the monastic centre founded by St Nynia flourished more or less for some generations, and about 525 a Pictish princess named Drusticc was sent there for education, much as today young ladies go to St Andrews to learn hockey and other things at St Leonard's School.

Just when Christianity reached St Andrews is unknown. In the Kinkell cave, two miles east, there were found Roman pottery of the second century AD and slabs incised with crosses, including the saltire cross of St Andrew. But these latter may well be later than the Roman pots. Yet it is not unlikely that some Roman trader, going to an authorized fair on the Tay, put in one day at the outflow of the Kinness Burn, and preached to the inhabitants the good news about Jesus.

The first named Christian mentioned in connection with St Andrews is an Irishman, St Kenny or Cainnech, who

7

founded Kilkenny and is said to have had a hermitage (*recles*) at Cendrigmonaid or Kinrymont, later called St Andrews. He was also patron of the parish of Kennoway, in central Fife. Kenny was a friend of the more famous St Columba, the most influential among the efflux of religious Irishmen to which Pictland was subjected from the later fifth century. St Buite of Monasterboice, County Louth, founded a monastery at Kirkbuddo in Angus, in a Roman camp-site given him by a Pictish High King, Nechtan, whose castle was at Dunnichen near by. A man from Munster, St Fillan, carried out propaganda in Strathfillan, where the Clan Macnab descend from his nephew, and probably at St Fillan's cave at Pittenweem, a dozen miles from St Andrews. Just across the Eden estuary is Leuchars, where the church was founded by one St Athernase, probably the St Ethernascus who was patron of Lathrisk (now Kettle), a dozen miles west. His day in the Scottish Calendar of Saints was 22 December, on which day the Irish commemorated St Iotharnaisc of Clane, County Kildare. The name Leuchars derives from Gaelic *lùchairt*, seen in Loch Luichart, originally from Irish *longphort*, fortified ship-harbour. Remains of a castle survive near the fine Norman church at Leuchars.

Among contemporaries of Columba who founded monasteries in Scotland were St Brendan the Navigator, of Clonfert, with a house on Tiree; St Comgell of Bangor, also there; and the Irish Pict St Moluoc or Lugaid, on Lismore. An Irishman who went further afield was St Columbanus (543–615), who founded abbeys at Luxeuil in Burgundy, St Gall in Switzerland, and Bobbio in Italy. He was learned in Greek as well as Latin, and was the main promoter in Europe of the practice of frequent private confession of sins. Compared with him, Columba (522–97) was unadventurous, but his houses in Scotland, with Iona as their head, were eventually the chief influence in establishing Irish Gaelic as the main medium of the aristocracy and intelligentsia of the Picts, who had hitherto spoken a kind of Welsh but without cultivating a written literature.

Columba came from Donegal, and belonged to the clan of the High Kings of Tara; but he also had relatives in the minor kingly house of Dalriata, which held small portions of land both in Antrim and in Argyll, on both sides of the Irish Channel. By the time of Columba's death in 597 the Dalriata king based on Dunadd, Aidan, would have a subject tribe of about three thousand people, and a naval force of twenty-eight boats, each with fourteen oarsmen. As tributary to the Over-king of Ulster he had to pay a hundred and fifty fat oxen and 'one hundred and fifty fat virgin sows', and received as stipend 'three black horses well trained, three women, three full-grown slaves, and three stout ships'. What he owed to the High King of the Picts of Alban is not anywhere stated, and perhaps it was simply military service. At the Convention of Druim Cett, near Londonderry, in 575, Columba helped to straighten out the Dalriata king's relations in Eire, and after that he went, with the Irish Picts Comgell and Kenny, to see High King Bridei I near Inverness.

In the Welsh and Gaelic languages the term *Alban* is still used for Scotland. It is Old Irish *Albu*, Greek *Albion*, and originally applied to all Britain, perhaps derived from the word *alp*, meaning that it was a hilly island compared with Eire. *Alban* gradually was restricted to mean only the un-romanized part of Britain, where the true, genuine Britons lived, those whom the Romans and their imitators called *Picti*, 'tattooees', and the Irish called *Cruithni*. They doubtless called themselves something like modern Gaelic *Albannaich*; and in 1138 at the Battle of the Standard the slogan of the Galloway Picts was 'Albani!' In Ireland too there were tribes called *Cruithni*, who provided a fifth of the Over-kings of Ulster up to 1201. It was two of these Ulster Cruithni that Columba took with him to make a diplomatic deal with Bridei I, perhaps in connection with the attempt to colonize the Isle of Man made by Baetan mac Cairill (572–81), King of the Ulaid of Ulster, who was overlord of Aidan of Dalriata for his Antrim lands. If Bridei I was son of Maelgwyn King of Man he would naturally be concerned about the position of that strategic island.

Bridei I was living in a timbered fort on Craig Phadruig, near the Beauly Firth, possibly his summer castle, like Queen Victoria's Balmoral. To get there Columba had to cope with a Loch Ness monster. He set a bait for it by ordering a young monk to swim the Ness to fetch a boat. The monster rushed at the monk, but Columba made the sign of the cross and told it to go away, which it did. So says Adomnan in his biography of Columba. What he does not say is that Columba converted Bridei to Christianity; and indeed Bridei had probably been a Christian from birth. After initial suspicion, Bridei was amiable to Columba and his Irish Picts. Soon afterwards Columba is reported as 'teaching the tribes of Tay', possibly in the southern part of Bridei's dominions, round Dunkeld and Abernethy. St Kenny founded his hermitage at Kinrymont, but how long it survived is unknown. He was an appropriate enough founder for an academic community, being notably absent-minded. He would go to church with one shoe off and one shoe on, and leave his crozier lying about. But his main missionary effort was in Ireland, at Kilkenny and Aghaboe.

For the more substantial development of religion at Kinrymont we have to wait for the Pictish High King Angus I, who brought there relics of St Andrew between 732 and 747, from Hexham in Northumberland. To put this in perspective, it may be recalled that the Angles from Germany and Denmark entered England about the time the Scots from Ireland were settling in Alban, or Pictland, now called Scotland. The acute Angles, as a schoolboy wrote, came north, while the obtuse Angles stayed in the south. The northern Angles formed the Kingdoms of Deira, in Yorkshire, and Bernicia, up to the Forth, which united into Northumbria. During a civil war a prince named Oswald took refuge in Iona, and when he became King (633–41) brought Columban monks from Iona to run a bishopric and monastery for him, based on Lindisfarne. Another refugee Angle prince, Eanfrith, married a Pictish princess, so that their son was eligible for the Pictish High Kingship, and reigned as Talorcen I (653–7). Picts and Angles got on well for a while, and Iona christianized most of the North and Midlands of England.

St Oswald's brother Oswy enlarged Northumbria by marrying Rhieinfellt, heiress of the Welsh Kingdom of Rheged, round the Solway Firth, based on Carlisle. His son Egfrith (670–85) tried to conquer Alban, but was defeated and killed at Dunnichen, near Forfar, in 685, by Bridei III Bile's son, whose mother was a Pictish princess, sister of Talorcen I. His father Bile was the son of Nechtan, or Neithon, King of the Britons or *Brets* of Strathclyde.

At this period there was controversy about bringing the churches in Celtic lands, which had been somewhat isolated, back into agreement with the Papacy at Rome in such matters as the computation of the date of Easter and the precise form of shaving part of the hair off the head. Most of Ireland had fallen into line with the up-to-date Roman ways, but much of northern Ireland and Strathclyde and Pictland were adhering to older papalist fashions. In 663 Northumbria had conformed to the papalist system, established by the Archbishops of Canterbury, at the Synod of Whitby, where King Oswy found convincing the argument of St Wilfred of York, that St Peter held the keys of Heaven and St Columba did not. Many Anglic monks disliked the papalist tonsure, shaving the crown of the head, and kept to the frontal tonsure, called 'of St John' or 'of Simon Magus', where the hair was removed from in front of a line drawn from ear to ear, so that the cleric looked much more of a highbrow. They sailed off to Ireland. Others went to Iona.

In 688 Adomnan, Abbot of Iona, accepted the Roman Easter computus and tonsure, as most of the Irish had by then. The bulk of the Iona community, however, refused to do so. To settle the dispute, the High King Nechtan IV Derile's son (706–24) wrote to the Abbot of Jarrow in Northumbria, Ceolfrid, for expert arguments about Easter. He also asked for architects to build him a stone church, to be dedicated to St Peter. Probably it was at Restenneth, near Forfar, and the lower part of the existing western tower there can be part of it. Jarrow, which had a good library, recently collected by Abbot Benedict Biscop, had itself employed architects from Gaul. Nechtan IV studied the Easter arguments, with his Council, and voted for the Roman system. In 716 Iona conformed, but in 731 the Strathclyde Kingdom was still holding to the older ways.

In 717, however, there is a laconic note that the 'family of Iona' was expelled by King Nechtan 'across the ridge of Britain'; that is, the mountain watershed of Scotland, running north and south, lately fixed by Bridei VI as boundary between

Dalriada and Alban, or Pictland proper. Nechtan IV also established a bishopric at Abernethy. It is possible that the Columban monasteries disliked the idea of this bishop having power over the whole kingdom that would infringe their former jurisdiction. More likely, they objected to Nechtan's putting Alban under the patronage of St Peter, instead of St Columba. Possibly, too, Nechtan—who himself abdicated in 724 to become a monk—may have been censuring the laxity of the Columban houses, as compared with the up-and-coming Culdees, or *Céli Dé*, a puritanical reformist movement of the time. A final probability is that Nechtan had imposed on monasteries some civil taxation or obligatory services, like the building of roads, bridges, and royal castles, such as kings in England imposed on monks there at the same period.

On the abdication of Nechtan IV there was a bout of civil warfare between rival claimants to the High Kingship, any man being eligible if he were no further than three generations from a former High King, even by a female line. The man who won out was Onuist son of Wurguist, in Irish Oengus mac Forguso, usually called Angus I Fergus's son (731–61). A monk writing a continuation of Bede's history remarked that Angus was a murderous tyrant whose entire reign was a series of bloody crimes. Yet he must be reckoned one of the pious founders of the cathedrals and the university, if not also of the R. and A. It was often the most ill-behaved monarchs who gave the most liberal endowments to monks, in the hope that the prayers of these dedicated men would save their souls from eternal torment.

It happened that St Wilfred of York (*ca* 634–710) had dedicated the Benedictine monastery of Ripon to St Peter and that of Hexham to St Andrew. Then Bishop Acca embellished Hexham with relics of St Andrew. When he was expelled in 732, what did he do with them? Presumably sold them to King Angus. Acca died in 740, and is commemorated by a fine carved cross at Hexham. The likelihood is that they came to Kinrymont between 732 and 740, and that the monastery was in working order by the death of Tuathalan in 747. Angus I, trying to extend his influence south of the Forth, and take advantage of quarrels among the Northumbrian Angles, had been a patron of Lindisfarne. He probably intended his new monastery somehow to rival that eminent place of pilgrimage, with its relics of St Cuthbert. What better than the relics of Andrew, elder brother of St Peter, the rock on whom the Church was founded?

After the Augustinian canons came to St Andrews in the 1120s, discussion arose about the early history of the place, and a Legend of St Andrew developed, in two variant forms, which one may call the Augustinian and the Episcopal. The Augustinian Legend starts with a preamble, in Latin, which means: 'How it came about that the commemoration of St Andrew the Apostle is greater in the region of the Picts, which is now called Scotland, than in other regions; and how it happened that so many abbeys were founded there in old time, which many secular men now possess even today by hereditary right.' The Augustinians were referring to the fact that most monasteries in Scotland had got into the hands of lay abbots, heads of the clans whose ancestors had given the original endowment. A similar development had occurred among the Irish since the eighth century.

The Augustinian Legend tells how the King of the Picts, Ungus son of Urguist, was camped in the Merse, the plain of Berwickshire by the Tweed, with a hostile army about to attack him. Walking with his seven companions, or earls (*comitibus*), he saw a blinding light and heard the voice of St Andrew bidding him advance with the cross of Christ and dedicate a tenth of his inheritance to God and St Andrew. Ungus won the battle. Meantime an angel was guiding from Constantinople one of the guards of the corpse of St Andrew, and he had just arrived at the summit of the king's hill, 'that is *Rigmund*'. He was a monk named Regulus. He met King Ungus at the gate called *Matha, id est Mordurus*, Gaelic for 'great door'. They set up tents by the spot where now is the king's hall, probably the site of the castle. Ungus then gave that place and city to God and St Andrew, with the privilege of being head and mother church of all the churches in Pictland. The Legend then continues about the importance of the place as a centre of international pilgrimage, with many miracles performed. It reads like a tourist brochure for a Latinate public.

13

The Episcopal Legend is a more elaborate formulation, making Regulus a bishop, and bringing him from Patras, where St Andrew was crucified on a saltire. Because the Emperor Constantine, grandson of Constantine son of Helena, wished to take the corpse to Constantinople, the holy Bishop Regulus was ordered by an angel to extract three fingers of the right hand, one upper arm-bone, one kneecap, and one tooth, and hide them. Meantime Angus son of Ferlon—an error for Fergus—was camped at the mouth of the Tyne, to fight Athelstan, King of the Saxons. St Andrew appeared in a dream, and Angus duly won. The angel then sent off St Regulus, who founded an oratory to St Andrew at every place he reached, and finally, after eighteen months of stormy voyaging, came to the land of the Picts, at a place called Muckross, now called *Kylrimont*, 'the cell *or* church of the king's hill'. Wrecked there, St Regulus and his companions got ashore, and erected a cross to keep away demons. Leaving two companions to guard it, they went to Forteviot, and found King Angus's sons; then to Monikie, where Queen Finchem was bearing a daughter named Mouren; then to Kindrochit in Braemar, where King Angus met them as he returned in triumph from Argyll.

The monastery owned lands at Forteviot, Monikie, and Kindrochit. But the Episcopal Legend's main elaboration is about the area given to Regulus by Angus at *Chilrymont* (another spelling). Twelve stone crosses were set up round the dedicated precinct. Angus gave to the basilica of St Andrew 'all the land that is between the sea that was called Ishundenema as far as the sea that was named Sletheuma'—a description baffling today. In the adjacent province, Fife, he gave all East Fife to a line drawn from Largo through Ceres to Naughton, west of the Tay bridges. He gave Chilrymont with its waters, pasture, moors, and so on, exempt from military service and forced labour on forts and bridges, and from all secular exactions. Bishop Regulus then sang *Alleluia*. King Angus presented, in symbolization of his grant, a turf on the altar of St Andrew, in presence of noble witnesses of the blood royal. A dozen names are appended, with the fathers' names. The holy men then built seven churches at Chilrymont: to St Regulus; to St Aneglas the Deacon; to St Michael the

Archangel; to the Blessed Virgin Mary; a fifth for St Damian; a sixth for St Bridget of Kildare; a seventh for the Virgin Muren (presumably Queen Finchem's daughter, who had become a nun). In her church were fifty nuns of the blood royal.

The Episcopal Legend then lists the holy men who came with Regulus and the relics, deacons, priests, hermits from the Tiber island, and virgins from Collossia, later buried in the church of St Anaglas (another spelling). The document was attested by Thana son of Dudabrach, who wrote it for King Pherath son of Bergeth in the town of Meigle (*Migdele*). Ferath, or Vurad, son of Bargot, is sixty-fifth King of the Picts in H. M. Chadwick's numeration, and reigned about 839–42. Meigle in east Perthshire has a splendid collection of Pictish symbol stones. The composer of the Episcopal Legend clearly had access to a copy, attested by a Pictish notary public, of a charter pertaining to Angus I's original grant. The names of the royal witnesses are all found in the Pictish king-lists, and could be genuine names of witnesses. If Irish analogies up till 1600 are relevant, it would seem that kings of the Pictish royal family held land only in virtue of their office, and alienation of a portion of the royal family's land would need consent of relatives within a certain degree, as it were directors of the family's real-estate firm.

The Episcopal Legend goes on: 'These statements we have copied as we found them written in old books of the Picts.' Few today will believe that documentary evidence proved the arrival of seven hermits from the Tiber island. The setting of the arrival in the mid-fourth century is probably aimed at establishing St Andrews as earlier than Canterbury or Iona or Whithorn. The writer next tells how the possessions of the church grew or diminished according to the devotion kings and chiefs showed towards St Andrew. It says that King Angus gave the royal city of *Rymond* called *Regius Mons*, 'Mount Royal'. On the death of the holy men who brought the relics and their pupils, the religious cult perished; but there always remained a body of thirteen Culdees, *quos Keledeos appellant*, 'through carnal succession', which means by sons succeeding their fathers. These Culdees continued to occupy the church of St Andrew, living according to their own judgment and men's traditions, rather than by the statutes of the Holy Fathers. They held in common certain inferior properties, but owned individually much better possessions, acquired from friends and relatives, or from pupils to whom they had acted as 'soul-friends', *animae charae*, the modern psychiatric consultants. After becoming Culdees, they were no longer allowed to have wives in their domiciles, nor other women from whom evil suspicion might arise.

Furthermore, there were seven persons dividing the altar offerings among themselves: the bishop got one-seventh, the hospital, or hospice, another. The remaining five-sevenths went to five individuals who rendered no service at the altar or else-where, but, whenever more than six visitors arrived, gave them hospitality, drawing lots who should receive whom. Now, thanks be to God, since the Augustinian canons had arrived, the hospice welcomed all visitors, and looked after all invalids till they either recovered or died. These mysterious five persons must be monks of the old Celtic foundation, who had become laymen with certain rights and minor obligations of hospitality. The Episcopal Legend says that they had revenues and posses-sions of their own, which after their deaths were divided among their wives, whom they owned publicly, and their children and relatives. The mischief could not be cured till King Alexander I (1107–24) intervened. He enriched the monastery, both otherwise and by restoring the Boar's Raik, originally given by Angus I. The rest of the Episcopal Legend may be left for con-sideration in regard to the study of the virtual refoundation in the twelfth century.

The Boar's Raik runs from Boarhills west along the sea and the south side of the Eden to within two miles of Cupar. Its southern boundary follows roughly the watershed of the 'Riggin o' Fife'. It includes the parishes of Dunino and Cameron and Kemback, and all the area drained by the Kenly Burn. When Alexander regranted the Boar's Raik he presented a couple of boar's tusks, sixteen inches long, which were fixed by silver chains to the altar of St Andrew. But it may be doubted if there was an actual boar chased along to trace the boundary in the eighth century. The boar was probably the old totem boar of the *Orc* tribe, with their fort at Dunork. The Pictish royal family owned that estate, perhaps by inheritance through some heiress, as part of the scattered series of 'discrete estates' that were regular in Celtic lands, apparently even in the Bronze Age.

The clergy put in to run the precinct with its variety of churches were Culdees, a ginger group within the eighth-century church in Celtic lands. The term means 'Companions or Servants of God'. It could include hermits, living alone or in small groups, and monks, practising a stricter observance in community, and probably also canons, that is groups of priests living in community at a church, often a bishop's cathedral church. At Armagh in 921 the invading Danes spared the *Céli Dé* who were tending invalids in the hospital there; and in 936 the cathedral of St Peter at York had *Colidei* as regular clergy, who conducted services and tended poor people.

Who was St Regulus? Possibly the first Bishop of Senlis in France, who was born in the fourth century in Greece. The French call him St Rieul, which sounds like St Rule. If architects from Gaul built Jarrow, and architects from Jarrow came to Pictland to build Restenneth before 724, they might have had a cult of St Regulus that somehow reached St Andrews. Alternatively, if the Legend was furbished up in the reign of David I (1124–53), some cleric might have known about St Regulus of Senlis through King David's wife, the widow of Earl Simon of Senlis. Moreover, in a church council at Paris in about 557 St Kentigern, Bishop of Strathclyde at Glasgow, was present, and signed as Bishop of Senlis: so there could even be some now obscure connection between that see and Alban in the century of St Kenny. The word *Regulus* might connect with *regula*, 'rule': so that a saint named Regulus might appeal to some body of masons as a suitable patron, to whom they would erect a little church in the precinct. The present tower called St Regulus's, or St Rule's, was not so called till about 1500. It was built about 1080, for the first cathedral of St Andrew.

What sort of buildings had King Angus's monastery of St Andrew, and what went on there?

The buildings of the sixth and eighth centuries would be, at St Andrews, mostly of timber, or of wattle and daub. But Angus I might have built an oblong stone church with a stone roof. If so, it is likely to have been the west part of the church later called St Mary's of the Rock, on the cliff edge outside the precinct wall of the medieval cathedral priory. Possibly St Mary's was originally inside a precinct wall of its own, partly on the line of the present one. Most of the churches would be small chapels. The cells for the monks would be small round huts at first, for individual occupancy. But there would be a communal cookhouse—only seventeen feet long at Armagh—and a dining-hall (refectory), and a guest-house, hospitality being a duty for monks, as for laymen. Drying-kilns, store-houses, mills, and workshops would be needed, and sometimes there would be special rooms for reading and writing. The marvellous Books of Kells and Durrow, with their intricate illustrations, could not have been done in dim cells. Irish monasteries usually had round towers, most of them from the eighth or ninth century, but some maybe from the sixth. Due west of St Mary's on the Rock there is a semi-circular tower in the precinct wall, which may stand on the site of an original round tower of the eighth century.

Monk originally came from Greek *monachos*, solitary, and referred to people who withdrew from society to desert places to commune with God in solitude, living on natural herbage and water. They might sometimes be Christians on the run from the police in the persecutions intermittently conducted during the pagan Roman Empire; or they might be like the modern 'beatniks' and 'hippies', amateur enthusiasts rejecting the values of society. In Western Europe monasticism began in the fourth century, in imitation of Egyptian usages, and St Martin, Bishop of Tours from 382, took a lead that was followed by St Nynia, and later by the Irish. The first wide-spread and firmly organized order of monks under a strict rule was that founded in Italy by St Benedict, before 547. Later it developed several specialist branches, running monasteries more or less as prayer-factories on a shift system, endowed by kings with guilty consciences. In the Irish system of St Kenny probably there was a daily routine of seven services, consisting mainly of psalms and short prayers and sets of versicles and responses, that is, fixed formulas of praise and prayer, with set replies. These services were: Nocturns, at midnight; Matins;

Prime, at dawn; Tierce; Sext, at midday; None; and Vespers. The intervals between them varied with the length of the days. The office of Compline, developed from informal prayers on retiring for the night, seems not to have been used in the sixth century in Celtic lands; but could have been developed by the eighth.

Monks normally wore a linen shirt or tunic, covered by a coarse woollen robe with a hood, in the natural colour, tied by a rope or strap round the waist. They slept in their robes on straw mattresses, with hides or woollen rugs. Earnest monks were much given to prolonged immersion in cold running water, to subdue the flesh and withstand the Devil. Another form of mortifying the flesh was to lie prone with outstretched arms, or to stand with arms spread in the shape of the cross, and repeat the Lord's Prayer a given number of times, or the Psalms. Such ordeals were sometimes appointed as penances by the ruling abbot. White robes were worn to church on Sundays, and on those annual feast days when the Eucharist was celebrated. The summons to church was by a bell, of iron coated with bronze, like the bells tied round the necks of camels and other domestic animals in Mediterranean lands. Saints' bells, and their jewelled shrines, often became relics of the clans of the saints.

Though monks were basically other-worldly, more concerned with eternity than time, the Iona community sometimes had a socially useful activity, most notably the promulgation of St Adomnan's Law, in 697, protecting women and children, and clerics and church property, from violence. Before then women had regularly been enlisted to fight in battles, and Adomnan's mother had been horrified to see one woman dragging off another with a hook through her breast. Monasteries often ran schools in early times, and major Irish monasteries became like university towns, sometimes with three thousand monks. Columba's Iona probably had a hundred and fifty monks as an average complement; but one must think of the Kinrymont establishment as much smaller in St Kenny's day, and probably not as much as a hundred and fifty in Angus I's new foundation.

Even if, to a modern idea, the monastic city of St Andrew,

on its headland above the North Sea, might present the general appearance of a shanty-town, or one of those villages set up by the Mediterranean for holiday-makers, it had one thing about it very grand for its period, which still survives, namely the mysterious sarcophagus now in the cathedral museum. The long panel shows the figure of David rescuing a lamb, of which the hindquarters are visible, from the jaws of a lion, illustrating Psalm XXII, 21: 'He shall save me from the lion's mouth.' There is also a hunt in progress amid trees, with various uncertain symbolizations. If a sarcophagus, it could be that of Angus I, the royal founder; but others think it a tomb-shrine of St Regulus, or a relic-altar for relics of St Andrew. How much of the work is 'Pictish' or Mercian is also debated. The date could be around 775.

2

THE BISHOPRIC OF THE SCOTS

'The region of the Picts, which is now called Scotland,' says the Augustinian Legend. How did the name *Scot*, previously meaning 'inhabitant of Ireland', get transferred to mean *Pict*, or 'inhabitant of Alban'? Why also did foreigners stop calling the Irish *Scots*, and renew the older use of *Hiberni*? Why do the Welsh call England *Lloegr*, which possibly means 'Liguria'? These are puzzles not wholly explicable. Similarly, that nation who call themselves *Deutsche* are variously called *Germans*, *Allemands*, *Tedeschi*, *Nyemetsi* and so forth by outsiders. There is little doubt that the Picts went on calling themselves 'men of Alban' for long after foreigners had been writing about their country as Scotia and themselves as Scotti. The Episcopal Legend comments that the bishops of St Andrews had, from of old, been called 'supreme archbishops' or 'supreme bishops of the Scots', but in the vulgar tongue, which was then still Gaelic, '*Escop Alban id est Episcopi Albaniae*'.

The development has to do with the national resistance to the long-sustained invasions by Scandinavian Vikings, which began with an attack on Iona in 795, and with the need to develop a more continuously effective central High Kingship of Alban to co-ordinate resistance. In 842 this High Kingship was assumed jointly by Kenneth I mac Alpin, the Dalriata sub-king in Argyll, whose ancestors had come from Ireland, and were thus *Scotti* in the older sense. In 848 he became sole High King, and in 858 was succeeded by his brother, Donald Alpin's son, who was followed in 862 by Constantine Kenneth's son, to whom succeeded in 877 his brother Aed Kenneth's son. We get next, from 878 to 889, a Strathclyde Briton or *Bret* succeeding as Pictish High King, namely Eochaid son of Run, King of Strathclyde, by a daughter of Kenneth mac Alpin. Foreign reporters of this period pass no comment on the succession to the Pictish High Kingship first of a Dalriata Irishman and then of a Strathclyde Briton; and call them both simply High Kings of the Cruithni or Picts of Alban. Eochaid's accession in 878 cannot be called a conquest of the Picts by the Strathclyders any more than James VI's accession to England in 1603 was a conquest of the English by the Scots, or George I's accession in 1714 a conquest by the Hanoverians. Gaelic had been the literary language of Pictland for generations before the Dalriata succession in 842, thanks to the Irish churchmen like Columba and Kenny, just as the printed English Bible from 1560 made English the language of worship and public discourse in Scotland.

Concerning bishops, medieval Catholics took it for granted that there could not be a church without bishops. Nynia was a bishop. Columba was only a priest, but he kept a bishop on hand at Iona to confirm and ordain and do all that bishops are needed for. Some abbots were themselves also bishops; others, including the Columbans, followed Columba's practice. This meant that the territorial jurisdiction belonged to the abbot, and the bishop was merely a monastic ordaining-machine. However, as more abbacies fell into the hands of hereditary lay abbots, the spiritual functions of the bishop would tend to be extended to cover more and more juris-dictional matters. About 820 Constantine Fergus's son brought relics of Columba from Iona to Dunkeld, and its abbot seems to have been also the chief bishop of Alban. Then in the early tenth century St Andrews was made the chief seat of the national bishop, by King Constantine II (900–43). Early in his reign he had held at Scone, the inauguration place of the Pictish High Kings, a gathering with Bishop Cellach, where an assimilation was effected between Dalriata and the rest of the High Kingdom regarding 'the laws and teachings of the Faith, and the rights of the churches and the Gospels', broadly in theology and canon law. This is a parallel to the assimilation of civil law made under Donald I (858–62), when all Pictland accepted the Dalriata laws of Aed Find (748–78). Somewhat similar was the codification of the laws of several Welsh king-doms by Hywel Dda (904–50). His dynasty is an example of the way in which Celtic kingdoms could be agglomerated by marriage. Guriad of the Isle of Man acquired Gwynedd by marrying its heiress Ethellt; their son, Mervyn the Freckled, married Nest, sister of the King of Powys, and got that kingdom; their son Rhodri Mawr, the Great, married Angharad, heiress of Seissyllwg. Their grandson, Hywel the Good, got Dyfed by marrying its heiress, Elen.

One factor making for codification in church and state was the need of a co-ordinated resistance with allies abroad against the Vikings. Already soon after 800 the Emperor Charlemagne was negotiating with *Scotti*, which could include Dalriata people, about coping with the Vikings. This is the shadowy beginnings of the later 'auld alliance' of Scotland and France. Then it became of interest to the Christian English to ally with the Christian men of Alban against the pagan Danes and Norse in the Kingdom of York, which existed from 875 to 954. Sometimes the alliance turned into an attempt by an English King to make Britain into his empire, as when Athelstan of Wessex came in 934 with an amphibious expedition almost to Aberdeen. But there were other schemes open. In 945, for instance, Edmund of Wessex handed over the Kingdom of Cumbria and Strathclyde to Malcolm I of Alban on lease, on condition that he should be Edmund's ally by sea and land. Then Edgar, first King of all England (957–75), ceded Lothian from Tweed to Forth to Malcolm I's son, Kenneth II (971–95), in return for some sort of homage, or acknowledgement of English overlordship, in respect of that area alone.

At this time, towards 975, the diocese of St Andrews received a great extension of territory from Forth to Tweed, though certain areas belonged to the diocese of Dunkeld. Benorth the Tay, there is a curious jigsaw of areas forming the diocese of Brechin, mixed with northward bits of St Andrews. This must have resulted from the St Andrews bishop, as chief bishop of the Scots, exercising a residual jurisdiction in places where the monastic jurisdictions did not operate.

The fact that the Bishop of St Andrews was styled *primepscop* or *ardepscop Alban*, 'First *or* High Bishop of Alban', suggests that the bishops of Dunkeld, Glasgow, and whatever others there may have been were somehow his suffragans; but that is not quite so. He was simply *primus* among equals. There was no archbishop in the regular sense till 1472. Moreover, King Constantine II, on abdicating in 843, became a monk at St Andrews, and died as Abbot of the Culdees, 'in the house of the Apostle on the brink of the waves', perhaps the west part of St Mary's of the Rock. It is not impossible that he had earlier made St Andrews his administrative capital, for it was not unsuitable for amphibious operations down the east coast, which was a good part of his military business.

Across the tip of Fife Ness, nine miles east of St Andrews, is a structure called the Danes' Dyke, some ten feet wide and four high, walling off the promontory. It is thought that Viking fleets lay on the beaches behind it, at a sort of naval junction, able to switch attacks up the Forth or Tay as it suited them. At the north end of the Danes' Dyke is a cave called Constantine's Cave, where the veteran monarch may have spent some time as an anchorite before settling in more comfortably at St Andrews as abbot. Not that it is by any means an uncomfortable cave. There were fragments of Roman jars found in it, and a place for smelting ironstone. The Prophecy of Berchan says that Constantine II's reign abounded with ale, music, and good cheer. Maybe he used the cave for bottle-parties.

3

ST MARGARET AND THE NORMANS

The Norman Conquest of England in 1066 is a notion familiar from schooldays. But conquests can be made otherwise than by fighting. They can occur in mental attitudes, and even in fashions. Already sixty years before William the Conqueror brought in his army, England had largely succumbed to Norman influences in certain spheres; and in Scotland too one may see something like a Norman conquest, nowhere more apparent than in St Andrews.

The lands under the Bishop of St Andrews had been greatly enlarged by Malcolm II (1005–34) after he secured his frontier on the Tweed by defeating the Danes of Northumbria at Carham in 1018, a victory which he celebrated by large donations to clergy and churches. This Malcolm II was the son of Kenneth II and an Irish princess from Leinster, and is described as 'powerful in resources and arms, and (what was most efficacious) very Christian in faith and deed'. His ally at Carham was Owen the Bald, King of Strathclyde, who died in the same year. Strathclyde was then taken over by Malcolm, nobody now knows by what right or title, and he installed his son Duncan as its King. For the lands he possessed in 'Lothian', the tract from the Forth to the Tweed, Malcolm II himself had to admit the overlordship of King Cnut (Canute), a man half-Danish and half-Polish, who had a vague empire roughly from Moscow to Massachusetts, including England, Denmark and Norway. Cnut stood as godfather to a son of Malcolm's, and was overlord too of the mighty Earl Thorfinn, who held Shetland and Orkney and the northern Scottish mainland, and of the King at Dublin, with his hybrid Norse-Irish subjects. When Malcolm II made recognition of Cnut's overlordship he was joined in the proceedings by two sub-kings from Fife. The High Kingdom of Alban (or *Scotia*, formerly *Cruithentuath* or Pictland) was commonly divided into seven provinces or sub-kingdoms, the rulers of which are sometimes called *ri*, king, sometimes, comically enough, *satrap* (by writers conscious of ancient history from Greek and Roman sources), and, more usually at this period, *mormaer*, a Celtic word meaning 'sea steward', i.e. Commander-in-Chief, Coastal Forces. The Norse called them *jarl*, whence the term *earl*. Angus with Mearns was, in the eighth century, considered the chief sub-kingdom; then came Atholl with Gowrie; then Strathearn and Menteith; fourth was Fife with Fothreve. (Fife proper seems to have been the peninsula between the firths of Tay and Forth as far west as the River Leven. Fothreve lay west of that, and its name was retained for a deanery in the diocese of St Andrews.) The fifth sub-kingdom was Mar and Buchan, the sixth Moray and Ross. The seventh had been Caithness, including what we call Sutherland, and doubtless Orkney and Shetland; but by the eleventh century this whole region had been lost to the Norse. The seventh sub-kingdom was Argyll, roughly the old Dalriata Kingdom. Whether the local *mormaers* were all branches of the Pictish royal family, or merely related to it by marriage, is now obscure. Whether the seven *mormaers* were the electors of the High King, as the seven German Electors had the right to choose the Holy Roman Emperor, is equally problematical. But some of the *mormaers* could rival the High King in military resources, like the Douglases in the high Middle Ages.

On Malcolm II's death in 1034 he was succeeded by Duncan I, his grandson, being son of the Princess Bethoc and Crinan, lay Abbot of Dunkeld. Duncan now gave Strathclyde to his brother Maldred. There seems to have been a feeling in Celtic societies that in the selection of a King weight should be given to nearness to the original ancestor of the royal family. On that score Duncan I's claim was perhaps inferior to that of Macbethan (usually known as Macbeth), *mormaer* of Moray, whose mother may have been sister, not daughter, of Malcolm II. Moreover, Macbeth's wife Gruoch could convey a claim, as grand-daughter of Kenneth III. Further, Duncan I proved incompetent in military affairs. In 1040 Macbeth killed him and became High King himself.

Though he has had a bad press through Shakespeare's dramatic use of the story, Macbeth seems to have been rather a good king. Interestingly, he was the only Scots king who ever went to Rome. On his visit there in 1050 he distributed money to the poor 'like sown grain'. He also promoted Latin studies by bringing home books. He was the first Scots king to employ Normans, enlisting a bodyguard of them.

Norman simply means 'Northman'; but it refers specifically to the frenchified Scandinavians settled in north-west France since 911, when their chief Rollo (who had a Scottish wife) became a vassal of the French King, Charles the Simple. They quickly adopted the mixed Celtic–Latin heritage of early medieval France, and became the leading efficiency experts of Europe, in running armies and fleets, monasteries and bishoprics, and every form of government. Norman ladies were often as competent as the men: for example, Queen Emma of England, daughter of Richard I, Duke of Normandy. She married first Ethelred II, the 'Unready', by whom she had the future King Edward the Confessor; and then King Cnut. For a long generation she used her influence to set Norman-French fashions at the English Court and in the English church, which were intensified by her son Edward the Confessor as King (1042–66).

This was the England into which the future Scots King Malcolm III had gone, as a refugee boy of nine, when his father Duncan I was killed in 1040. He went first to his mother's brother-in-law Siward, a Dane who became Earl of Northumbria, and then south to stay with Edward the Confessor, at whose court he learnt French as well as English. In 1045 his grandfather Crinan made an attempt to restore him, but Macbeth crushed it. Probably at this time Macduff, the *mormaer* of Fife, fled to England to join him. It may be from this act of loyalty that the Earls of Fife descended from Macduff had the right to lead the Scots vanguard in battle and to place the Kings of Scots on their throne. Earl Duncan of Fife was the first to speak in the first recorded Scots *parlement* (1173). But perhaps the right was in recognition of the previous importance of Fife as a naval base for operations against the Angles and Danes south of the Forth.

In 1054 Earl Siward took an army into Scotland, which defeated Macbeth at Dunsinnan near Dunkeld, his Norman bodyguard perishing to a man in his defence. Malcolm was then installed as King in Strathclyde and South Scotland, with acknowledgement to Edward the Confessor as overlord for

Lothian. In 1057 Malcolm advanced north and killed Macbeth in a battle at Lumphanan in Aberdeenshire. Macbeth was then succeeded as King in the north by his stepson Lulach the Fatuous, son of Queen Gruoch, and eligible as great-grandson of Kenneth III. Lulach's son Maelsnechtai secured recognition as King or *mormaer* in Moray till his death in 1085. The claim transmitted from Lulach was renewed by Angus, Earl of Moray, son of Lulach's daughter, in 1130, when he got five thousand men to back him, but fell in a fight at Stracathro, in the Mearns. Since parts of the northern lands of the diocese of St Andrews were in the region dominated by these *mormaers* of Moray, the bishops must often have had tricky political problems in securing their temporal interests.

Contemporary with Malcolm II, Duncan I, and Macbeth was Bishop Malduin, Gilla-Odrain's son, who held the bishopric of the Scots from 1028 to 1055, and is called by an Irishman 'the glory of the Gaels'. He gave the church and lands of Markinch in central Fife to St Serf and the Culdees of the island of Lochleven. Macbeth and Queen Gruoch also gave lands to the same Culdee monastery. Macbeth's own name, Macbethan, means 'the son of life', meaning that he was one of the Elect, a soul predestined to salvation; but his murder of Duncan I needed some compensating act of piety. The next bishop, Tuthald, gave Scoonie, at the mouth of the Fife Leven, to the same Culdees. This brings us to Bishop Fothad II, who enjoyed the see from 1059 to 1093, and saw many changes in affairs. In 1069 or 1070 he married Malcolm III to the Princess Margaret, three of whose sons became kings. Her and their influence went far to recast both church and state after the current French and Anglo-Norman fashions.

Margaret had spent the first eleven years of her life in Hungary, being daughter of the refugee Anglo-Saxon Prince Edward, son of King Edmund Ironside, who reigned in Wessex for some months in 1016, ceding most of England to the Polono-Dane Cnut. Cnut took Edmund Ironside's baby sons, Edmund and Edward, to Scandinavia, whence somehow they reached Hungary. Edmund there married a daughter of the King, St Stephen, who had christianized the barbarous, semi-nomadic Magyars. There were no children. Prince Edward

married Agatha, sister of St Stephen's wife, and daughter of
Bruno, Bishop of Augsburg, son of the Duke of Bavaria and
brother of the Emperor Henry II. (Bavarians were at that time
active in promoting religious foundations in western Hungary.)
As a child the future St Margaret was accustomed to an
atmosphere of religious propaganda and radical reform for a
barbarian kingdom on the fringe of Europe. She was also accustomed to the finest products of the arts and crafts of the age.
In 1057 her father brought his family to the court of Edward
the Confessor, and soon died. Here Margaret found a pious
and frenchified atmosphere. Her grand-uncle King Edward,
though nominally married to Edith, daughter of Earl Godwin,
was a childless bachelor with the tastes of a monk. Son of a
Norman mother, he had spent half his time in Normandy. He
brought up Margaret, her sister Christina, and her brother
Edgar, in the internationally leading Norman-French fashion.

On Edward the Confessor's death his throne was taken by his
brother-in-law, Harold Godwinson, who was liquidated inside
the year by William the Bastard, son of Robert the Devil, Duke
of Normandy, and Arlette, daughter of a tanner at Falaise. The
true heir of the Old English royal family was, of course,
Margaret's brother, Edgar the Aetheling, who was chosen King
by the people of London after Duke William's victory at
Hastings, but never crowned. He lived on for nearly sixty
years, without strenuously trying to assert himself as a Pretender, whether young or old.

Two years after the Normans conquered England some people
in Yorkshire and round about conspired to make Edgar
Aetheling King. He went up north with his mother and sisters,
but William the Conqueror followed in force, and the rebellious
move collapsed. Edgar wintered in Scotland. William I then
made Malcolm III's cousin Gospatric son of Maldred Earl of
Northumbria. Malcolm resented it, and some fighting took
place, ending in a compromise, whereby Malcolm gave
Gospatric lands and made him Earl of Dunbar, a key fortress
site in East Lothian. During this period the eventful marriage
was made between Malcolm and Margaret, who had earlier
thought of becoming a nun, as her sister Christina became in
1086. (Malcolm's earlier wife was Ingibiorg, daughter of Earl

Thorfinn, by whom he had a surviving son, Duncan, later King.) William the Conqueror disliked this turn of affairs, and in 1072 entered Scotland with a fleet and a powerful army, largely of cavalry and archers, the formidable Norman combination. The Kings met at Abernethy, and Malcolm III did homage, a gesture of which the precise legal significance was left vague. Probably he acknowledged the overlordship of William I in respect of Lothian, and for estates he held in England by gift of Edward the Confessor. 'Scotia', north of Forth, would be considered to belong to Malcolm by hereditary right, free from any grant or confirmation by any outside monarch. Malcolm also handed over his brother-in-law, Edgar Aetheling, and his son Duncan, who remained a hostage for fifteen years, and became frenchified.

William the Conqueror died in 1087, being succeeded in England by his second son, William II Rufus. Malcolm's homage thus lapsed. Rufus later expelled Edgar Aetheling from estates given him in Normandy, and Edgar went back to Scotland. Malcolm then organized a raid into Northumbria, perhaps to see what support there might be from English nationalists for a move to put the heir of the old Wessex Kings on the throne. So late as 1137, according to Ordericus Vitalis, the native English were detected in a conspiracy to murder all the Normans and put on the throne David I of Scotland, who was the true heir through his mother, St Margaret. Rufus reacted forcefully, coming up in the autumn of 1091 with his brothers Duke Robert of Normandy and Henry, later King Henry I. They went only to the Forth this time, not to the Tay; and Malcolm III did homage to Rufus, perhaps on terms more rigorous than those imposed by William I in 1072.

In 1092 Rufus built a castle at Carlisle, and colonized the area with southern English peasants, 'a multitude of churlish folk'. In 1080 William I had built a New Castle upon Tyne, at the east end of the old Hadrian's Wall frontier. From old Pictish tradition the Kings of Alban may have imagined it was their rightful southern frontier; but it had not in fact been a frontier for several centuries. Rufus's seizure of Carlisle, however, clearly violated the settlement whereby the Scots King's frontier on the west ran down to the Rere Cross on Stainmore. Malcolm protested, and Rufus invited him to confer at Gloucester. On the way Malcolm laid one of the three foundation-stones of Durham cathedral, he being the principal land-owner in 'St Cuthbert's Land'. On reaching Gloucester, he was refused audience by Rufus, and went home very angry. With his son Edward he made a raid into Northumberland, and the pair of them were killed in an ambush near Alnwick. Three days later St Margaret too died, on 16 November 1093.

By the old Pictish system the Scots automatically chose Malcolm III's brother, Donald III, called Donald Bane (or *Bán*, 'White'), as King. This Donald, as a refugee when Macbeth killed his father in 1040, had gone not to England but to the Western Isles and Ireland. More recently he had been *mormaer* in Gowrie. He drove out all the Englishmen introduced to Scotland by his late brother Malcolm III, and was, perhaps astonishingly, joined by Edmund, eldest surviving son of Malcolm and Margaret. Meantime Duncan, the former hostage, had sworn fealty to William Rufus, who granted him the Kingdom of Scotland as a vassal state, and gave him an army of Normans and Englishmen. In May 1094 they chased out Donald Bane; but before long Donald's supporters rallied, and killed most of King Duncan II's troops. They then made a compromise: they would allow Duncan to stay as King if he would promise to bring in no more Normans or Englishmen. He agreed, but six months later was waylaid and killed at Mondynes by the *mormaer* of Mearns. Donald III then resumed the throne, designating his nephew Edmund as successor, by the Celtic practice of tanistry, and giving him south Scotland to govern.

It would be erroneous to think that there was an explicit confrontation of the old Gaelic and the new Norman cultures. Indeed, Donald and Edmund allied themselves with the Norman Earl of Northumbria, Robert de Montbrai, in 1095. The compromise government did not recommend itself to Edmund's brothers, the three younger sons of St Margaret and Malcolm. The senior among them, Edgar, did homage and fealty to Rufus, as Duncan II had done, and was sent up in 1097 with an army to install him, accompanied by Edgar Aetheling. Donald Bane was taken and blinded; Edmund was imprisoned, and became a Cluniac monk at Montacute in Somerset, where he was buried, at his desire, in chains, in penance for his complicity in the death of his half-brother Duncan.

Edgar's reign (1097–1107) is signalized by nothing except his gift, in 1105, of an elephant, described as 'a beast of marvellous bigness', to Muirchertach Ua-Briain, King of Munster and High King of Ireland. This is a reminder that the Scots King was still a Gaelic-speaker, like most of the people and clergy, and interested in relations with fellow-Celts in Ireland, if only to keep in touch about Scandinavian activities on the fringes of both kingdoms. Edgar recognized the rule of the Norse king Magnus Barelegs in the Isles. It is also an indication of the pious King's interest in the crusading movement that had lately become fashionable in parts of Christendom, especially France, which brought Christians in contact with lands having elephants.

King Edgar on his death bequeathed Scotia proper, the old Pictish Kingdom of Alban, to his brother Alexander I, but conveyed southern Scotland, including Strathclyde and Cumbria and Lothian south of the Lammermuirs, to his youngest brother David. Edgar's motive may have been to mitigate somehow the problem of the homage due by the King of Scotland for areas held from the King of England as overlord.

Alexander I took a contingent in 1114 to help his brother-in-law Henry I of England (1100–35) in securing submissions from some Welsh princes. He also married an ill-looking and ill-mannered illegitimate daughter of Henry's, but had no child by her. Like his brother Edgar, who did not marry, and his grand-nephew Malcolm IV, called 'the Maiden', he may have thought chastity helpful towards the salvation of his soul. His acceptance of Henry's disagreeable bastard daughter as wife is consistent with the view that Alexander was about as much a vassal king of Henry's as Duncan II and Edgar had been of Rufus's. David, youngest son of Malcolm and Margaret, achieved independent sovereignty between his accession in 1124 and his death in 1153, after Henry I's death in 1135 led to civil war in England; but, between 1107 and 1124, when merely 'Prince of Cumbria' and successor designate (tanist) of Scotia, he moved closely in the orbit of Henry I, who had married his sister Matilda (originally Edith).

The foregoing narrative of the political tangles from 1066 to 1153 may help towards understanding of the religious developments at St Andrews during this period of its radical reorganization. The key figures are St Margaret and her sons Alexander I and David I.

Nowadays saints and the concept of sainthood are hardly intelligible to most people reared in the Protestant tradition; but for St Margaret saints were a matter of family tradition by no means remote. Two grand-uncles had been saints, St Stephen of Hungary and St Edward the Confessor. A great-grand-uncle was St Edward the Martyr, whose sister was St Edith, a nun of Wilton Abbey. St Margaret's sister Christina became a nun at Romsey, between Winchester and the New Forest, and to her care Margaret entrusted her daughters Edith (later Matilda) and Mary. In Hungary she must have learnt on what grounds the Magyars had preferred the Roman Catholic to the Greek Orthodox system of organizing Christianity, and she was anxious to secure the best Catholic guidance available. She therefore took for her spiritual director the Lombard Lanfranc, who had been Abbot of Caen in Normandy and in 1070 became Archbishop of Canterbury. Her husband Malcolm III had made Dunfermline, on the Forth, his seat of government, and there she built a church to the Holy Trinity and founded a priory for Benedictine monks from Christ Church, Canterbury. About 1128 her son David I endowed it further, and it was raised to the status of abbey, with a splendid Norman church.

A Latin life of St Margaret was written for her daughter Queen Matilda by Turgot, Prior of Durham, who was Bishop of St Andrews from 1107 to 1115. He mentions the fine crucifix she presented to the church of St Andrew, and her 'great religious greed for holy volumes'. Her husband was a tall and handsome man; he was nicknamed *Cendmor*, or *Canmore*, 'big head', or, in the Norse sagas, 'long-necked'—also, in the *Chronicon Rhythmicum* of the fifteenth century, *Cendremor*, 'fat head'. Queen Margaret saw to it that he was always splendidly and elegantly dressed; but she failed to remedy his illiteracy. There is a touching picture of the magnificent warrior kissing any book that she had shown particular fondness for, and ordering its binding to be adorned with gold and jewels. In the style of the international aristocracy to which she belonged, she insisted on courtly ceremonies and brightly dressed bodyguards; but with the Norman addiction to ostentatious charity, with a view to good public relations and the salvation of the soul, she would make the King help her to serve breakfast to three hundred poor persons during the forty days before Christmas and in Lent. Herself she would wash the feet of six poor persons before going to bed, and feed nine orphan babies on her lap when she rose in the morning. She housed and fed two dozen poor persons in the palace all the year round. She encouraged merchants to bring foreign wares, and her sons, the kings, later founded a series of royal burghs, fortified and privileged trading towns, for the development of industry and commerce. From Hungary and England she had brought artistic treasures, and such relics as the Black Rood, containing a reputed piece of the true cross, later bestowed on the abbey of Holy Rood at Edinburgh (1128). Her silver and gilt plate, her tapestries, purple, fine linen, and furs, set new standards for the Scottish aristocracy.

The Normans in their pride looked down on insular saints. Athelelme, a monk of Jumièges who became Abbot of Abingdon, refused to allow any feast to be held for St Ethelwold and St Edmund, considering all Englishmen to be boors. No such sneering, scornful view was possible in regard to the bones of the Apostle Andrew in the old monastery at Kilrymont, and St Margaret promoted his cult there. She endowed a free ferry across the Firth of Forth, at Queensferry, with hospices for the reception of pilgrims, where now the London Government exacts a toll for the crossing of a bridge.

The organization of the church in England struck the efficient Normans as woefully slack and irregular, even after Edward the Confessor's efforts. Even more anomalous must have appeared the ways of the Scottish church to one bred in the reforming zeal of St Stephen's Hungary. With King Malcolm as interpreter St Margaret held discussions with

Scots clerics on sundry points, and secured conformity with the latest Roman usages. For instance, she insisted that Sunday be rigorously observed as a Jewish Sabbath; she demanded that Lent should begin on Ash Wednesday and not on the following Monday, because Sundays were not to be reckoned in the forty days of fasting. She seems to have been horrified that Gaelic was used instead of Latin in the Mass. She deprecated the reluctance of Scots to partake of the Eucharist on Easter day, from their sense of being unworthy. She condemned, as Lanfranc had condemned, marriage of a man with his widowed step-mother or sister-in-law. In the matter of starting Lent late the Celts had simply been following the general usage of the Church till Columba's time. On this and the other matters they seem to have concurred in the Queen's reforms. She made no complaint about their permission of clerical marriage; nor indeed could she conveniently have done so, for her mother was a bishop's daughter. Not till 1139 was clerical marriage uncanonical at Rome. Perhaps she did not even condemn the possession of old church lands by lay abbots, for her son Ethelred became concurrently Earl of Fife and Abbot of Dunkeld, possibly a lay abbot, as Malcolm's grandfather Crinan had been. She gave endowments to Culdees, and to Iona; and the Gaelic Bishop Fothad went on undisturbed to his death in 1093 as *ardepscop Alban*, 'High Bishop of Scotland'. She went round visiting hermits, solitaries 'living the lives of angels upon earth'.

It does not appear that she found reason to complain of the validity of the Holy Orders held by Scottish clerics, or of the system of church government. In 813 the Council of Châlons had denounced pretended ordinations by wandering bishops, 'certain Scots (or Irish) persons styling themselves bishops'; and in 816 the English provincial council at *Cealchythe* (Chelsea) had ordered that no man of Scottish (or Irish) race should administer baptism or Holy Communion, as it was not certain who had ordained them and where. Neither Scotland nor Ireland then was organized into a province headed by a Metropolitan, that is an archbishop regularly authorized by Rome. Bishop Cellach II of St Andrews (970 to *ca* 995) is said, by the *Scotichronicon*, to have gone to Rome for confirmation as bishop, the first Bishop of the Scots to do so. If so, that would have regularized Scotland's position. The York historian Hugh the Chantor states that Malcolm and Margaret sent Bishop Fothad to make submission to the Archbishop of York, as Metropolitan of all North Britain; but Fothad became bishop ten years before their marriage. If they made him do this, it might well have been for political reasons, in connection with Malcolm's intermittent claims on northern England, or Edgar Aetheling's claims. In the next reigns St Margaret's sons were to resist the pretensions of York regarding Scotland.

Bishop Fothad died in the same year as Malcolm and Margaret, and his see was left vacant for fourteen years, while successive Kings doubtless farmed its revenues. Duncan II gave endowments to Durham, and Edgar bestowed Coldingham on the Benedictine priory there. He also asked Anselm, Archbishop of Canterbury, for more Benedictines to go to Dunfermline, perhaps to replace monks expelled by Donald Bane on grounds of nationality. Alexander, before his accession, attended in 1104 the uncovering of the corpse of St Cuthbert, to test its incorruption, a proof of sainthood; and he too was a benefactor of Durham. It was thus natural enough for him, as king, to secure the election of Turgot, Prior of Durham, as Bishop of St Andrews. A recent reform of Durham served, in part, as a pattern for the reform of St Andrews. Till 1083 the cathedral church of Durham had been served by secular clergy, living 'in the world'; but the Norman bishop William of St Carilef turned them out and substituted monks living in a cloister under a rule. He chose Benedictines. Only one of the seculars agreed to stay as a regular.

Turgot became prior in 1087. He was a man of Danish origin from Lincolnshire, and had taught psalmody to the Norse King Olaf and had been confessor to Queen Margaret. When elected to St Andrews in 1107, he at once ran into trouble about consecration. The Archbishop of York claimed the right to consecrate bishops in all Britain north of the Humber, in terms of an agreement made in 1072 with Canterbury. Alexander I refused to allow York's claim. In June 1109 a new Archbishop of York, Thomas II, was consecrated, and in August he consecrated Bishop Turgot, with the proviso

36

'saving the authority of both churches', and without any profession of obedience by Turgot. Having been confessor to Queen Margaret, Turgot may have expected to have authority with her son Alexander; but the King was not nicknamed *Fiers*, 'high-spirited', for nothing. Obscure and irreconcilable differences arose, and in 1115 Turgot returned to Durham to die. The see of York being then vacant, Alexander applied to the Norman Ralph d'Escures, Archbishop of Canterbury, for a nominee. The new Archbishop of York, Thurstan, was not consecrated till October 1119, but representations were made to Pope Calixtus II on his behalf, and a papal letter to the bishops of Scotland ordered that no man be consecrated a bishop in Scotland except by the Archbishop of York as Metropolitan, or by his permission.

Defying this, Archbishop Ralph of Canterbury sent up to St Andrews a Benedictine monk of Christ Church, Eadmer, biographer of Archbishop St Anselm. He was elected in June 1120, and received by Queen Sibylla and the *pauperes scholares*, pupils of the cathedral school; but he soon fell foul of King Alexander. Eadmer wished the jurisdiction of Canterbury to be acknowledged, while Alexander upheld the autonomy of the Church of Scotland. It is notable that he commissioned a poem on St Columba from a monk named Simeon. Emblematic of the contention was that Eadmer, while being inaugurated, accepted a ring from King Alexander, symbolizing the temporal authority held from the King, and himself lifted his pastoral staff from the high altar, symbolizing his spiritual authority. Relations grew more chilly, till Eadmer announced he must go and seek advice at Canterbury. The King said none of his bishops should obey Canterbury: to which the bishop answered that he would not renounce his loyalty to Canterbury even for the whole Kingdom of Scotland. The King grew fiercer than ever. The Bishop of Glasgow and two Canterbury monks then advised Eadmer that he could be of no further service in Scotland. Eadmer accordingly resigned in 1121, giving his ring back to the King and laying his staff back on the altar. On returning to Canterbury he changed his mind, and wrote to Alexander offering to come back and make no more trouble about jurisdiction. The offer was not accepted, and Eadmer died at Canterbury, on 13 January 1124. Thus two English Benedictines had proved recalcitrant, and it is no wonder that Alexander looked to another order for his next chief bishop, and to another nationality. He chose an Augustinian of French birth.

In the first year of his reign, 1107, Alexander the *Fiers* had been in his castle near Invergowrie, west of Dundee, when the place was surrounded by rebels from Moray, presumably backing some rival claimant to the throne. Thanks to the presence of mind of Sir Alexander de Carron he escaped through a sewer and organized an army to chastise the Moray men. Sir Alexander de Carron distinguished himself by carrying the royal standard across the Spey in face of the enemy, and by his stout scrummaging in the mêlée, so that he was nicknamed 'Scrymgeour', and appointed hereditary bearer of the Scots royal standard and constable of Dundee, positions held today by his descendant the Earl of Dundee. In thankfulness for his rescue and victory King Alexander founded a monastery at Scone, the old Pictish inauguration centre, and colonized it with canons of the Augustinian order.

A 'canon' was in origin a priest on the bishop's official list of diocesan clergy, distinguished from a priest serving in a monastery or a private chapel. Such canons tended to live together in clergy houses termed 'minsters', with a common dining-room and dormitory, drawing their stipends from a common fund. They were not under a vow of poverty, but were celibate. The Lateran Synod of 1059 recommended such celibate clergy to live under a fixed rule of life, without private property, under a superior enforcing a rule: as such they were called 'regular' canons, contrasted with 'secular' canons who lived in the world. St Augustine of Hippo had drawn up a rule for nuns, about the year 423, and this was now revised for the new-style regular canons, so that they were termed 'Augustinians', or 'Austin canons', or 'black canons' because they wore black cloaks when outside the monastery. Compared with the Benedictines, the Augustinians had a less severe rule, with shorter services, less fasting and less silence. But different houses of each order could vary greatly in their ways of living and worshipping, and between many houses of both orders there was little significant difference. Austin canons did not engage much in missionary activity or pastoral care of souls, but often ran hospices for sick and aged persons, and for travellers, like the celebrated hospice at the St Bernard pass. In theory they were clergy under the control of the local bishop, a few exempt houses being supervised only by the Bishop of Rome. England received its first Austin house through the Lombard Lanfranc at Canterbury in 1086, a hospital for paupers. Alexander I probably became interested in them through his sister, Queen Matilda of England, who founded for them Holy Trinity Priory, Aldgate, London, about 1107. This soon became fashionable and rich, and founded half a dozen daughter houses. A major bureaucrat in the employ of Queen Matilda's husband Henry I, a certain Gilbert the Sheriff, founded near London the monastery of Merton, which in turn sent out six colonies; and King Henry himself founded five houses, including one at Carlisle. These were all select bands of men, none more than fifty, some fewer than thirteen. Here and there hermits abandoned their solitudes to become Austin canons, because the rule was loose enough to suit their tastes.

From 1215 there was a General Chapter of the Augustinian order, organized internationally, but its decrees were readily rejected by abbeys and priories that did not fancy them. Each house was to most intents and purposes a law to itself, provided it kept on the right side of the local bishop. One of the Augustinians' strongest suits was their hospitality. They could organize excellent dinners. Perhaps that is why Alexander I established them at Scone, the royal inauguration place of the Picts.

What he did was to refound an abbey previously occupied by Culdees. The Culdees may have become decadent, or even died out as a community; or the King may have allowed them to stay in their old church; or they may have simply become Augustinians and been added to the six Black Canons imported in 1115 from St Oswald's priory at Nostell, near Pontefract in Yorkshire, who set about building a modern church and conventual buildings around a cloister. Their prior was a Norman Frenchman named Robert. In January 1124 he was elected Bishop of St Andrews, and set about founding there an Augustinian priory, of which his brother Robert became a canon. (By a Norman and Breton custom two brothers had been given the same name.) Soon their nephews Raoul, Roger, and John were found witnessing charters. It is an example of the piecemeal penetration of Frenchmen into leading positions among the trend-setting classes in Scotland, rather like the clannish 'jobs-for-the-boys' system operated by later Scots careerists in France under the 'auld alliance', or in seventeenth-century Sweden, or in eighteenth-century America, or in various parts of the nineteenth-century British Empire.

The great promoter of this use of French efficiency experts was David I (1124–53); but even by the end of his reign one cannot reasonably speak of a Norman Conquest of Scotland comparable precisely to the Norman Conquest of England. After 1066 less than one per cent of the English land remained in the hands of native Englishmen: William the Conqueror's foreign adherents got ninety-nine per cent of it. In Scotland no more than ten to twenty per cent of the land passed into Norman, Breton, Flemish, or English ownership. No Norman was made an earl. David I held in right of his wife the English earldoms of Northampton and Huntingdon, from which region he recruited some of his hunting cronies for key positions in Scotland. The Bruces were given Annandale as a kind of marcher lordship near a frontier, with the Lindsays, from Lindsey in Lincolnshire, north of them at Crawford on the upper Clyde, and the Breton FitzAlans in Renfrewshire, on the Clyde estuary. Even when rebellions by royal claimants allowed the descendants of St Margaret to expropriate lands, native Celts participated in the regrants, along with Continental incomers.

The Celtic quasi-feudal system was modernized with a precision modelled on Normandy and England, with titles set down in written documents. Offices were renamed, with *mormaers* becoming earls. The Celtic judge called *maor* was replaced by a sheriff, operating from a royal castle, commanded by a constable. In the inauguration of the Kings Celtic custom persisted, a sennachie reciting the pedigree in Gaelic. Celtic tanistry too stayed in use, David I designating his son Earl Henry as King, much as he himself had been recognized tanist in the reign of Alexander I. But in the ecclesiastical sphere

Celtic tradition seems to have dwindled rapidly, and St Andrews soon became a focus of French and English influence. Even the Celtic Culdees, though they maintained a legal continuity till the Reformation of 1560, became rapidly de-celticized. Characteristic of the indifference of St Andrews to its Celtic heritage is that the twelfth-century builders ruthlessly used fine Celtic sculptures in the foundations of their modern church, and that even today Scotland's senior university has no Department of Celtic.

4

THE BUILDERS OF THE CATHEDRALS AND PRIORY

The French Bishop Robert was elected in January 1124, but his patron King Alexander I did not live to see him consecrated, for he himself died on 23 April. Probably having had a premonition of his approaching death, he made a significant symbolic gesture when endowing the church of St Andrew, and making a regrant of the *Cursus Apri*, the Boar's Raik. In token of the gift he ordered to be led to the altar his Arab warhorse, with its harness and saddle, and the royal shield and a silver spear, and a splendid embroidered horsecloth, and various pieces of Turkish armour. The high-spirited King knew that his fighting days were over. For Bishop Robert, however, there yet remained two ticklish fights: first for consecration by three bishops in the canonically necessary fashion; and then for actual enjoyment of the lands and rights conveyed by Alexander. Here he was greatly aided by St Margaret's youngest son, King David I.

David had been about fifteen when his sister Matilda married Henry I, newly crowned King of England. Henry had come to the throne after conspiring, with the Clare family and others, to have his brother William Rufus shot while hunting. Leaving the royal corpse for peasants to cart off, Henry rode to the old Wessex capital of Winchester, and seized the royal treasury. Three days later he had himself crowned at Westminster. As a public-relations exercise he issued a charter of liberties, addressed to 'French and English', undertaking to restore the laws of King Edward (the Confessor), with emendations made by William the Conqueror with consent of his barons; and announced his intention to marry 'King Edward's niece'. This was Edward the Confessor's great-grand-niece Edith, St Margaret's daughter. On her marriage, on 11 November 1100, she took the name Matilda. Her brother David was thereafter brought up as one of the family in the calculating Norman King's household, witnessing his charters and seeing how he ran his kingdom. Henry was nicknamed 'le Clerc', the clerk or bureaucrat, because he liked things put precisely on record.

Clergymen were useful, among other reasons, because they tended to be capable of writing and reading. The clergy backed Henry against the claim of his elder brother, Duke Robert of Normandy, to the crown of England. In 1106 Henry overcame his brother, kept him in prison till his death twenty-six years later, and ran Normandy with the same efficiency as England. Henry exploited his churchmen as civil servants, and also as sources of cash.

The pious David imitated Henry's general example without his cynicism. One point Henry had firmly secured, against Pope Paschal II: that the King of England was entitled to receive homage from bishops and abbots in respect of the temporal possessions of sees and abbacies, which the King controlled during vacancies and vested new incumbents with on their election. David was equally concerned to secure the autonomy of the Scottish Church. In 1126 he wrote to the Pope asking that St Andrews should be made into a metropolitan archdiocese for Scotland; but the Pope, under English pressure, refused. A year later, however, a formula was found whereby Robert was consecrated Bishop of St Andrews at York, 'saving the dignity of either church and the authority of the Apostolic See', without any profession of obedience, by three fellow Frenchmen, Archbishop Toustain (Thurstan) of York, Bishop Ranalf Flambard of Durham, and Raoul Novel, titular Bishop of Orkney, a see then dependent on the archbishopric of Hamburg. Bishop Robert lost no time in proclaiming that the diocese of St Andrews had subject to it all the churches in Lothian down to the Tweed, except for Durham's rights in Coldingham.

Securing effectively the Boar's Raik round St Andrews proved tedious for the bishop. As the Episcopal Legend puts it: 'Satan opposed him in many matters.' He had to endure many injuries and insults, doubtless in expropriating certain unnamed persons who held possession of lands in the Boar's Raik. These may well be the lay persons who received five-sevenths of the offerings at the altar of St Andrew. These men would probably be descendants of the lay brother 'monks' of the sixth- or the eighth-century monastery, now old Celtic landed gentry in the area. The bishop also had to contend, about the year

1128, with a French knight of Burgundian origin, Robertus Burgonensis, who tried to take a quarter of the lands of Kirkness from the Culdee priory of St Serf's island in Lochleven. The bishop had to mobilize his army, led by men with the Celtic names Budadh and Slogadach; and Constantine, Earl of Fife, raised his army. They all met at Cupar, with two judges, Dufgal and Maldoinneth, assisting the earl in his judicial capacity. The Augustinian canons kept a note of the case, because they had advised the Lochleven Culdees.

This is the first indication that a nucleus of canons had been formed at St Andrews to institute the monastery endowed by King Alexander. It was not till 1144 that they got their lands and rights clearly demarcated and secured by the bishop and the King. A charter of Bishop Robert in 1144 conveys to the priory estates named Barrimund, Struuithin, Kinnines, Castdouenald, Drumckarach, Ledochin, Stradkines, Balhucca, Rodmanand, Pettultin, Kinastare, Chinemonie, Drumsac, Balemacdhunechin, Eglisnamin, Ballothen, Sconin, and the mills of Kilremund, Puthachin, and Nidin, and sundry other sources of revenue. (About half the place-names are still used, in various forms, in the locality.)

This charter was given only after King David's prompting. Previously the bishop had wished to avoid diminishing the possessions of the bishopric, clearly hoping that David would grant extra endowments for the proposed monastery. But David reminded him of his brother King Alexander's specific condition that the Boar's Raik grant should be used for instituting a body of regulars. The King and his son Earl Henry, the king designate, came in person to St Andrews and gave their own charters confirming the bishop's gift. Bishop Robert then gave in addition some part of the lands that had come into his possession by expropriation of persons unnamed. On the same day the bishop's uterine brother Robert became a canon of the house, and gave to it his church of Tyningham in East Lothian, and fifty shillings a year. The King's confirmation names additionally the estate of Balgove, west of Strathtyrum, by the Eden estuary, which had a valuable salt-pan, necessary for a trade in salted fish. Pope Lucius II, also in 1144, issued a bull in favour of the priory.

44

When Bishop Robert reached St Andrews in 1124 he probably found already standing there the magnificent grey sandstone tower now called St Rule's or St Regulus's, with the oblong unicellular structure to the east of it, commonly called a 'choir'. It may well have been built in the time of St Margaret (*ca* 1070–93), as a reliquary church, to house the kneecap and other anatomical items of St Andrew. Her son Ethelred, Abbot of Dunkeld and Earl of Fife, was buried in it. The architect may have been Aelric, who worked for St Margaret at Christ Church, Dunfermline, where there was a similar square tower, with an oblong edifice east of it, to which was later added a square choir with rounded apse. The general type of the high square tower derives from Italian romanesque campaniles (bell-towers), like the tenth-century San Francesco at Ravenna, which is self-standing.

St Rule's tower is over 108 feet high, with internal dimensions of $14\frac{1}{2}$ feet. The foundations were dug out to a depth of 6 feet, and the excavation filled with boulders, the upper 2 feet of them packed with clay. The well-cut ashlar masonry starts with courses of large stones, about 33 by 21 inches, and reduces upwards to stones of about 14 inches high. The belfry windows are round-headed. Originally a spire sat on the wallhead, but in the sixteenth century this was replaced by a parapet set on a corbel-table. The choir internally is 26 feet by 20.

In his charter of 1144 Bishop Robert remarks that the church of St Andrew had been up to his time '*permodica*', very small. The Episcopal Legend tells how, after his consecration, the bishop tried to extend the church, by applying to the work his own seventh share in the offerings at the altar of St Andrew. 'But, because the outlay was moderate, only a moderate amount of construction was done.' Then, as King David favoured it, various lay folk subscribed, and the work began to go a bit faster. A *basilica* was thus begun and largely completed, and certain dwellings made for canons, and a cloister.

At this point the bishop appealed to Aethelwulf, first Bishop of Carlisle (1133–57), to send as first prior of St Andrews a suitable person from Nostell, of which Bishop Aethelwulf had been and remained prior. David, as 'Prince of Cumbria', had been much concerned with Carlisle, and continued his interest as King. He fortified it extensively between 1139 and his death, knighted the future Henry II of England there, and himself died there. The cathedral of Carlisle was run by Augustinian canons, the bishop being *ex officio* their abbot: the working head of the convent was the prior. St Andrews developed the same arrangement.

When Prior Robert came on the scene he no doubt found that the bishop had merely enlarged the square-towered church by adding a sanctuary at the east end of the 'choir', and a nave at the west side of the tower. The traces of the sanctuary foundations do not make clear whether it was square-ended or a rounded apse. The early seal impressions of the priory show the square tower, with spire, in the middle of a church having a nave a little higher than the choir, and a small tower at the south-west corner of the nave. The monastic buildings prepared for the canons were very likely of timber, set on the south side of this square-towered church, with the cloister roof attached to the south side of the choir. Details of the western and eastern arches made to give access to the nave and sanctuary added by Bishop Robert appear to be from designs of the master-mason who built the Yorkshire church of Wharram-le-Street soon after 1100, a church given to Nostell priory by the sons of Nigel Fossard, the land-owner who commissioned it. It formed part of a prebend in the church of St Peter, York, held by Aethelwulf, prior of Nostell, and first Bishop of Carlisle.

The Episcopal Legend states that the Culdees, found in possession of the church of St Andrew by the Augustinians, performed their office in their own fashion in a corner of the church. That was presumably in the unicellular 'choir' east of the tower. They did not, however, serve the chief altar, that of St Andrew, but probably served a side altar, used Gaelic along with Latin, and had no elaborated musical liturgy. Bishop Robert would no doubt be anxious for a more elaborate ceremonial, with more advanced music, than the Culdees had favoured; and when the Black Canons settled in one may imagine that not all was fraternal harmony in the 'auld kirk of Sanct Andro'. It could only be a matter of time till Scotland's richest bishopric got organized to build a really modern cathedral church of imposing dimensions, instead of Bishop Robert's 'make-do-and-mend' construction.

46

The starting and building of the great Romanesque and Gothic cathedral were not accomplished without much strenuous local infighting between the old Culdees and the new Augustinian canons, involving the bishops, Kings, and Popes of several generations. When the Austin Canons came, towards 1144, they found a Culdee community of thirteen, holding by heredity their *prebends*, pieces of land and other revenue-producing subjects. The first plan of the innovators was to liquidate them as Culdees, and absorb them among the Austin Canons. In 1147 Pope Eugenius III issued a bull, giving the election of the Bishop of St Andrews exclusively to the Augustinian canons there, together with the possession of all the properties and rights of the cathedral church of St Andrew. He also ordained that, as Culdees died, their places should be taken by regular canons.

Now in 1139 a canonical prohibition had been made against clergymen marrying: so that for the future no Culdee could lawfully beget a son to inherit his prebend. Even allowing for more than average longevity among Culdees, the ancient corporation must have disappeared by the end of the twelfth century if the bull of 1147 had been implemented. But the bishops and Kings changed their minds, and found it expedient to continue a separate chapter of Culdees in rivalry with the Augustinian canons. The canons were kept running their prayer-factory for the salvation of royal and other souls, while the Culdees ran a bureaucracy for the bishops and the Kings, acting as ambassadors and in other public capacities. The change of policy must be later than David I's reign, for he issued an instruction to the canons to receive the *Kelledei* of *Kilrimont* as canons, with all their possessions and revenues, if they should wish to become canons; but if the Culdees refused they could hold their possessions for their own lifetimes, and then each prebend should be conveyed to a canon, so that all the Culdee properties and revenues should eventually be owned by the Augustinians. Probably the next bishop and King decided to keep the Culdees, and refurbish an old church for them.

This was the church of St Mary of the Rock, on the clifftop north of the great precinct wall of the cathedral. Formerly there was a hollow in between, the Kirk Heuch, now filled in.

The foundations of St Mary's church show that the western end was an oblong edifice like the 'choir' of St Rule's. Its foundations were bedded in clay in the same manner as those of St Rule's tower, and that section may date from about 1080, or earlier. About 1160 or later St Mary's was extended eastward, with Romanesque masonry, and about 1249 it was given transepts to make it cruciform, and had a choir added to the east, all in early Gothic style. Documents illuminate the architectural processes somewhat.

Soon after 1200 the Augustinian prior and chapter of the cathedral had persuaded some papal judges-delegate to excommunicate the Culdees, but Bishop William Malvoisine absolved them. Two Kings, Alexander II and Alexander III, compelled the Augustinians to admit Culdee representatives to vote in the election of bishops. The running fight was ended by the Culdees' being made into a secular collegiate foundation on its own and a chapel royal. In 1248 the Culdees still had places in the cathedral church of St Andrew, but in 1249 occurs the first mention of the church of St Mary. In 1252 the Augustinian convent litigates against the 'Provost and Culdees of the Chapel of St Mary'. Then about 1290 a seal is found styling it 'the chapter of St Mary, chapel of the Lord King of Scots'. The clean severance meant that Culdees no longer performed the divine office in the church of St Andrew, even at a side altar, and abandoned their claim to share in electing bishops. In the legal processes around 1250 the Culdees of St Mary's had a provost, more than six 'Culdees acting as canons', and vicars to perform the divine offices for them in St Mary's kirk. One of the Culdees was ambassador to England in 1258, 'Official' (a high legal functionary) of the bishop in 1259, and in 1263 a chaplain to the Pope. Another was the Queen's Chancellor in 1245. Yet another, William Wishart, became archdeacon and then bishop (1273–9). In its later evolution the 'Lady College Kirk' became something like an aristocratic and intellectual club of higher bureaucrats, a sort of seaside Athenaeum; and because it was so closely identified with the old Papist régime it was specially destroyed in 1559 by the Protestant leaders the Earl of Argyll and Queen Mary's bastard brother James, the future Earl of Moray.

The French bishops of St Andrews were not alone in finding it useful to have a set of secular clergy at hand to counter-balance their local prior and monks. In 1189 the Bishop of Coventry grew so tired of the Benedictine chapter of his cathedral that he drove them out. In Dublin Archbishop John Comyn took over the parish church of St Patrick and installed there a secular collegiate foundation of thirteen prebendaries, in 1191. A generation later Archbishop Henry elevated it into a full cathedral, with dean, precentor, treasurer, chancellor, and other functionaries. All this was to keep in their places the Augustinian canons, of the Arrouaise type, who had been put in by Archbishop St Laurence O'Toole to run the first cathedral church, Holy Trinity, about 1163. Professor Geoffrey Barrow has pointed out how St Andrews came near to a parallel development with Dublin. Perhaps it was a little like the nineteenth-century development of a Free Church in opposition to the Established Church. But in the twelfth century it was not a matter of mass movements and popular partisanship, so much as of bishops and Kings manipulating small groups of key men expert in regard to various purposes the magnates had in mind.

David I was succeeded in 1153 by his grandson Malcolm IV, nicknamed 'the Maiden'. When Bishop Robert died in 1159, the young King offered the see to his grandfather's stepson, St Waldef, Abbot of Melrose. Waldef was a son of David I's wife by her first husband, Earl Simon de Senlis. He had been an Augustinian canon at Nostell, and had later become a Cister-cian to preside over his stepfather's foundation at Melrose. The future saint declined to move to St Andrews, though many magnates, lay and clerical, came and begged him to do so. He died soon afterwards. In November 1160 the St Andrews chapter elected as bishop Arnold, Abbot of Kelso, a house founded, originally at Selkirk, by David I before he became King, from Tiron, mother house of a reformed branch of the Benedictine order. Ernald, Ernout, or Arnold, was chaplain to the young King Malcolm, who refused his advice to take a wife, saying that from boyhood he had vowed his virginity to Christ. (The ideal of the Virgin Knight, Sir Galahad, was in the air then, not least in the Breton society into which the King's sister Margaret entered by marrying in 1160 Conan IV,

Duke of Britanny.) Before he died in 1162 Bishop Arnold had secured the King's help in founding an enormous new cathedral in honour of St Andrew. Its original length made it the longest in Britain after Norwich. Malcolm IV attended the bishop's consecration in St. Andrews on Sunday, 20 November 1160, and the laying of the foundation stone for the muckle new kirk may well have taken place then, in the presence of the Bishop of Moray, legate of the Pope, and sundry bishops, abbots, and earls. The siting of the project had doubtless been already decided by Bishop Robert, who had founded the burgh of St Andrews in David I's reign. The King had given him the former royal castle, no doubt on the site of the medieval bishop's castle, north-east of St Mary's kirk and the cathedral precinct. King David had also given him one Mainard the Fleming to be first provost (*praefectus*). Mainard had been a burgess belonging to the King in the royal burgh of Berwick on Tweed, the major centre of Scottish trade in wool and hides to the Netherlands. Malcolm IV's sister Ada married in 1162 Florent III, Count of Holland, and for centuries the Flemish and Dutch commercial and cultural influences were to be as important as the French or English for St Andrews and Scotland generally.

The twelfth-century boom period saw the basic structural layout of the town, with its three main streets radiating westwards from the west front of the great Norman cathedral. In North Street the eastmost part was known as the Fishergate, the *gate* or road of the fisherfolk. They would have access to the harbour by the free space north of the precinct wall, next to St Mary's on the Rock, with Castle Street leading to the gate of the bishop's palace. South Street was laid out along the top of the southward-sloping ridge falling towards the Kinness Burn, with its houses sheltering the tofts, or 'lang riggs', where each burgess grew his kail and kept his cattle on their return from the common pasture. The abundant springs along South Street fed their wells. This area was for centuries the most favoured by wealthy and noble persons for their homes. Midway between North and South Streets was the Mercat Place, with narrower streets leading east and west from it, roughly parallel to the main exterior streets.

How far the burgh was fortified is unknown, but its defences were probably slight. It belonged to the bishop, and his castle was its protection. The monastic city proper, within its old Irish-type cashel wall from the eighth century, probably had its precinct more handsomely defined at this time by a simple heightening or rebuilding on or near the original foundations of the cashel, a process that was repeated for the last time in the early sixteenth century, most of which work is still standing today. Inside the religious precinct were about thirty acres, the wall length being almost a mile. Thirteen towers survive of the sixteen visible in 1683, but none is likely to be earlier than about 1520. The roofless arched structure called 'the Pends', at the east end of South Street, was the gate-house of the Augustinian priory, datable about 1318, when King Robert I (the Bruce) attended the consecration of the cathedral.

From 1160 to 1318 makes 158 years, not an exceptional time for the completion of a cathedral in the medieval period. From Bishop Robert, who projected, and Bishop Arnold, who founded, to Bishop Lamberton, who consecrated, the work had the support of twelve bishops, some of whom were rather remarkable characters, and a series of priors, about whom less is known. Arnold's successor was another Frenchman, Bishop Richard (1163–78), Malcolm IV's chaplain and nephew of David's confessor, Alwin, Abbot of Holyrood. He installed his sister, Hawise, in a house of her own, and had his brother Robert and nephews Gautier and Roland witnessing his charters. Bishop Arnold's brother Eude (Odo) acted as steward, with an assistant, Geoffroi. The chancellor, marshal, chamberlain, doorward, and butler seem mostly to have been Frenchmen.

French was the main medium of conversation, even perhaps among the canons who used Latin in their liturgy and in official writings on church affairs. No doubt they picked up a smattering of Gaelic to give orders to the local Fife folk, as a businessman in Ghana or Singapore will acquire the local dialect to the needful extent, without making it his chief vehicle for discussion. The contempt of the French high clergy for the past artistic heritage of the place, as shown by the use of Celtic cross-slabs for the foundations of the Norman cathedral, has already been mentioned; but somebody had the good taste to rescue the eighth-century reliquary-altar by burying it. Extensive as the precinct was, the area immediately north and east of St Rule's, the first St Andrew's Cathedral, must have been rather crowded, with at least one graveyard, as well as several small churches, in one of which the reliquary-altar was no doubt housed. It must have been tempting to make a clean sweep of all the old miscellaneous stone or timber churches of antiquated styles, just as today city engineers love to bulldoze picturesque or beautiful architecture of past generations in their zeal to construct flyovers and multi-storey blocks of flats. In the south part of the precinct somebody buried another sacred relic, a sort of dummy shrine, in the form of a solid stone block, 3' 10" long, 1' 9" high, and 10½" wide, now housed in St Leonard's School. Its top is cut to resemble a tiled roof, which seems to have originally had two beasts crouching on the ridge.

However indifferent the French clergy in St Andrews might be to its Pictish past, they showed a decidedly nationalist spirit in championing the Church of Scotland against the claims of English archbishops: that is to say, French arch-bishops in England. They were helped in this by the dislike felt by successive Popes for the masterful policy of Henry II of England, an episode of which was the murder of Thomas à Becket, Archbishop of Canterbury, in 1170. Pope Alexander III consecrated Bishop Engelram of Glasgow personally in 1164, though a strong protest was lodged by the Archbishop of York. In 1165 Richard was consecrated Bishop of St Andrews by some other Scottish bishops with papal authoriza-tion. The Archbishop of York descended so low as to forge a letter, purporting to come from King William I (the Lyon) of Scotland, admitting York's claims to superiority. The Pope was not taken in by this, but his patience must have been tried by certain subsequent proceedings of William the Lyon.

In 1178 Bishop Richard died, and the Augustinian chapter elected as successor the Archdeacon of St Andrews, one 'John the Scot', a native of Cheshire who had graduated at both Oxford and Cambridge. He was nephew of Matthew, Bishop of Aberdeen. Whatever John's nationality, the King had in-tended the vacant job for his chaplain, Hugh. He swore 'by the arm of St James' that, if Hugh did not get the job, nobody else would. The chapter, advised by the Bishop of Glasgow, then elected Hugh. Thereupon John the Scot appealed to Pope Alexander III, who sent a legate to install him. John's uncle Matthew mobilized three other bishops, and consecrated John at Holyrood. The King then banished him, for a second time; the Pope replied by excommunicating Hugh and putting Scotland under an interdict. The King thereupon exiled the clergy who backed John, and the Pope excommunicated the King. (An interdict affected the whole people by forbidding marriage, extreme unction, and holy burial, as well as divine service. Excommunication meant the cutting off from all communication with other Christians.)

Pope Alexander then died, and his successor, Lucius III, bent over backwards to reconcile King William, even giving him the Golden Rose, enamelled red and perfumed, which Popes carry on a Sunday in the middle of Lent. The dispute simmered on till Hugh died, and John the Scot was compensated with the less lucrative see of Dunkeld, in 1183. The St Andrews chapter then elected as bishop the King's cousin Roger de Beaumont, son of the Earl of Leicester. He was not even in Holy Orders at the time, and was not consecrated till 1198. He set about building himself a 'palace' inside the castle. In 1192 Pope Celestine III made the Church of Scotland a 'special daughter' of the Holy See, immediately dependent upon the papacy, with no subjection to any English archbishop. In 1225 Pope Honorius III commanded the Scottish Church to hold provincial councils, and this was done on a peculiar system. No metropolitan archbishop was appointed till 1472, but each council chose a bishop as 'Conservator of the Privileges of the Scottish Church', to act until the next council. Thus parity was maintained among the bishops, always allowing for the great differences in their wealth and power. Previous to that, in 1201, Pope Innocent III sent to Scotland a cardinal legate, John of Salerno, who chaired a council at Perth, which is most memorable for its Sabbatarianism. It ordered Sunday to be kept from noon on Saturday till Monday morning. The idea that the Scottish Sabbath is of Calvinist Genevan origin is great nonsense.

On Bishop Roger's death in 1202, and his burial in the old

cathedral of St Andrew, now called St Rule's, another French-man got the see: William Malvoisine, postulated for translation from the bishopric of Glasgow, which he had held for three years. When he died in 1238 Malvoisine was the first bishop to be buried in the grand new cathedral, in the choir, which must by then have been finished. The custom was to build churches from the east end westwards, so that the choir could be brought into use as soon as possible. At St Andrews they laid out the foundations to the full length, 391 feet, the greatest breadth being 168. They had fourteen bays in the nave arcade, more than any church in Britain except Norwich. With a great effort of building they carried up the walls all round to the point where the arches were to start. Then there was an intermission, and the choir cannot have been properly roofed when Bishop Roger died. A point of interest is that the east processional doorway, giving from the nave beside the west wall of the south transept, is of an exterior type, constructed to throw off rain-water. This suggests that the architects were not then con-templating a roofed cloister walk for the doorway to open into. It could be a mere architect's oversight, not without parallel.

An oversight that did not pass unchastised by Bishop Malvoisine occurred at Dunfermline, where the monks failed to supply him with enough wine at supper. The fiery Frenchman promptly deprived their abbey of two vicarages, Kinglassie and Hailes, which they took rather hard, as they had in fact provided enough wine but the bishop's retinue had absorbed it on its way to the episcopal lips.

Malvoisine attended the Council at Rome in 1215, which dealt with the Albigensian and Waldensian heretics, and he was responsible for bringing to Scotland the first Dominican friars, *Domini canes*, 'the Lord's hounds' who tracked down heresy. But he did not endow a friary for them in his episcopal city, having other uses for his revenues. He busied himself in recovering alienated rents due to the bishopric, protected the Culdees and carried further the demarcation of financial interests between them. In confirming to the Augustinians the parishes of Lathrisk and Scoonie, he stipulated that the income should be used for building the cathedral. French though he was, he took an interest in the history of the country and the

church, and wrote lives of St Ninian and St Kentigern, probably prompted by his visits to churches associated with them
during his Glasgow days. During his episcopate some of the
canons quarrelled with the prior, Thomas of Cupar, who was
rigorous in applying the Augustinian rule, and made his life so
disagreeable that he withdrew to the monastery of Coupar
Angus (1211). His successor, Simon, litigated with various
parties about property, and resigned to take the inferior
position of prior of Lochleven (1225). One of his disputes was
with 'Master Patrick and the poor scholars of St Andrews',
presumably the headmaster of a local school. There had
survived from Pictish times certain *scologs*, or scholars, who
in the twelfth century were looked after by the archdeacon; and
no doubt their lands and revenues needed clarification as
much as those of the Culdees. The next prior, Henry of
Norham, resigned office in 1236, leaving the convent crippled
with debt. Apart from litigation, the costs of building the new
cathedral would be burdensome.

No Bishop of St Andrews can have known his far-flung
diocese better than Malvoisine's successor, David de Bernham
(1239–53), King Alexander II's chamberlain. In the year of his
accession the Papal Legate, Cardinal Otto, was horrified to
find that many churches, including cathedrals, had not been
consecrated with holy oil. He commanded this to be done
within two years. Bernham got briskly to work, and consecrated 140 churches and chapels out of about 234 in the eight
deaneries of his diocese. The handbook is extant in which are
listed his itineraries, with details of the services for dedication
of churches, consecration of altars and cemeteries and crosses,
and the 'reconciliation', by salt, ashes, water, and wine, of
churches in which blood had been shed. Bernham also travelled on
the Continent, where he and his brother bishop of Glasgow were
kidnapped by the Emperor Frederick II to prevent their reaching the Council of Lyons where his deposition was intended.

Bernham also took part in the miraculous translation of the
mortal remains of St Margaret from the nave at Dunfermline
into the choir, after her canonization. The King and nobles
were all witnesses that the saint's body could not be shifted.
As Wyntoun musically expressed it: 'Wyth all their power and

their slycht/Her body to raise they had na mycht.' After prolonged prayers somebody hit on the idea of lifting the corpse of Malcolm Canmore into the choir, whereupon the body of his faithful spouse readily allowed itself to be carried after him. Bernham was deeply involved in the settlement of the long-standing contentions whereby the Culdees were formed into a collegiate foundation at St Mary's on the Rock, and seems not to have wished to await the resurrection in St Andrews, for, to quote Wyntoun, 'He chused his laire intil Kelso/Nocht in the kyrk of Sanct Andro.' During his time the priory's affairs recovered greatly, thanks to Prior John White (1236–58). He built the refectory, the dormitory, and the great guest-hall; he litigated with the prioress of Haddington about the right to take every tenth cabbage and leek from the King's garden at Haddington, and with Duncan, Earl of Mar, about tithes given to the canons by the earl's father in Aberdeenshire.

On Bernham's death there was a disputed succession to the see. The chapter elected Robert de Stuteville, Dean of Dunkeld; but neither King nor Pope would consent. The Pope then provided to the bishopric the Archdeacon of St Andrews, Abel de Golynn, who died nine months later, having lost what good-will he had had. One day he chalked up on the cathedral door, in Latin, the statement: 'I possess three things: civil law, canon law, and science.' Next day an anonymous hand had chalked underneath: 'You owe your elevation to three things: fraud, favouritism, and spoof.' The sight of the comment drove Bishop Abel to his bed, where he died a few days later.

His successor was one Mr Gameline, the King's Chancellor, probably a Frenchman who had come in the train of the Queen Mother, Marie de Coucy, whose own chancellor, Richard Veirément, was a Culdee of St Mary's of the Rock. Gameline was a son of unmarried parents, but the Pope dispensed him from that 'defect of birth'. The young King Alexander III had married a daughter of Henry III of England, and the Scots magnates were divided into a pro-English party, headed by Alan Durward, and a pro-Welsh party, headed by the Comyn family. In 1256, the Chronicle of Melrose relates:

Bishop Gameline was outlawed by the King's counsellors; both because he refused to acquiesce in their abominable plans, and because he scorned to give a certain sum of money, as if for the purchase of his bishopric. And since Scotland cast him out, and England refused him passage, he followed Neptune, and went to France; and boldly approached the Roman court, in opposition to his adversaries. After his departure, the King's councillors pillaged the goods of his bishopric, and consumed it at their pleasure.

He returned from exile a year later, and died in 1271.

The next bishop, William Wishart (1271–9), belonged to a French family (Guiscard) long settled at Conveth in the Mearns. He had graduated from Oxford, and perhaps Paris, and served as Archdeacon of St Andrews and Chancellor of Scotland. An ambitious and greedy pluralist, he was rector or prebendary of twenty-two churches. His private wealth proved useful to the fabric of the cathedral, after a storm threw down its western end. In the rebuilding Wishart reduced the length by two bays, to 357 feet, and used the space gained for a large porch (*narthex*). He also completed the nave. Originally all its windows had the round-arched heads seen in the four eastern bays, but Wishart changed to Gothic the six western ones. Similar incongruities are common in medieval cathedrals, where the patrons and architects at any particular period were apt to pick up the latest fashion regardless of its merit or propriety. The new western porch, two bays deep and three wide, was removed in the next century. Such porches were usual in France, rare in England, otherwise unknown in Scotland. Wishart founded the Dominican friary near the west end of South Street; its late Gothic northern aisle, from about 1525, remains, with the most nearly complete vault surviving in St Andrews.

Prior White's work on the monastic buildings of the Augustinians was carried further by Prior John de Haddington (1263–1304), who built a 'great chamber' on the east side near the canons' cemetery. There was now a massive range of stone buildings south of the south transept of the new cathedral, into which the canons would have moved from their former timber structures south of the old cathedral. Whether it remained in use, for servants, guests, and so forth, does not appear. It is also uncertain at what time the parish church of the burgh, dedicated to the Holy Trinity, was built inside the old monastic precinct. Such a church is first mentioned in 1144, when Bishop Robert grants to St Leonard's Hospital, the pilgrims' hostel, 'one-half of the tithes of our ploughs, cows, sheepfolds, piggeries, and horses in the parish of the Holy Trinity' and other items. Bishop David de Bernham dedicated such a church on 17 June 1243. It stood east of the new cathedral, north of the old cathedral, and west of St Mary's on the Rock, but inside the precinct wall. After the new parish kirk was built in 1412 between Market Street and South Street, the old one was used for the university, the Faculty of Arts meeting there in 1419. Towards 1525 Prior Hepburn used its stones for heightening the precinct wall. Among other churches inside the precinct before 1300 would be an early church of St Leonard, near the hospital, and one dedicated to St Peter.

Not only was the monastic precinct well supplied with churches and clerics, but the bishop's burgh had become a substantial trading port. Bishop Robert had referred to the 'Scots, French, Anglic, and Flemish dwellers' in and about it. The 'Anglic' or English element came mainly from the old Northumbria, between Humber and Forth, and included refugees from the Norman Conquest of England to whom Malcolm Canmore had given citizenship in Scotland. From their tongue, with admixtures of Flemish and Scandinavian elements, was evolved the medieval Scots used in the Scots burghs and monasteries for commercial purposes, and in the King's law courts and the Scottish Parliament. For serious literature it was first employed by a churchman, Archdeacon John Barbour, in his patriotic poem *The Bruce* in the 1370s; and then by the court poets from King James I to James VI; and of course later by such writers as Burns, Scott, Stevenson, and MacDiarmid. At a period when English was prohibited in the courts of England under the Normans, and had become a mere *patois*, the northern Anglic was employed in royal burghs under the Scottish Kings. No doubt by the 1280s this 'Braid Scots', or, as Burns and Stevenson called it, 'Lallans', the Lowland tongue, was as much heard in St Andrews as the old Gaelic, or the upper-class French, or the clerics' Latin, which remained the international language for diplomacy and science for five centuries more.

The significance of St Andrews economically in Scotland may be seen from a valuation of the Scottish bishops' sees dating from about 1270. The actual sums look trivial now, with the enormous and continuing devaluation of the monetary unit: but the relative position is interesting. Omitting shillings and pence, the annual income of the Bishop of St Andrews was estimated at £8,018, that of Glasgow at £4,080, Aberdeen £1,610, Moray £1,418, Dunkeld £1,206, Dunblane £507, Brechin £416, Galloway £358, Ross £351, Caithness £286, Argyll £280. (Galloway was still in the archdiocese of York. Orkney is not in the list, being then under Trondheim, as was Sodor and Man, though about to come in with the Scottish province.) Much of the wealth of the diocese lay south of the Forth, with Edinburgh and Berwick as main trading centres; much of it north of the Tay. But the central position of St Andrews on the east coast, trading to Europe, especially the Netherlands and the Baltic, kept it well in the swim, commercially and intellectually.

On the basis of later data, from 1366, Lord Cooper of Culross estimated the populations of the different dioceses thus: Glasgow 107,000; St Andrews 88,000; Aberdeen 35,000; Dunkeld 34,000; Dunblane 20,000; Argyll 18,000; Moray 18,000; Whithorn (Galloway) 11,000; Brechin 10,000; Ross 5,000; Caithness 4,000; and what he calls 'outlying areas' 50,000, making a total population for Scotland of about 400,000. The population of England was about five times as much, and the income of the Church of England also about five times as much. These proportions held good till the parliamentary Union of 1707, since when Scotland has relatively declined.

The fact that St Andrews diocese had in it about a quarter of the nation's population and revenue made its bishop and his 'family' of supporting clergy crucially important when external aggression threatened the independence of the realm. Such aggression arose at the end of the thirteenth century, when the accidental death of King Alexander III led to a disputed succession, giving an opportunity for the Kings of England to intervene. These Kings—conventionally numbered Edwards I, II, and III, which disregards the three English Edwards before the Norman Conquest of 1066—were in origin French magnates, sprung from the Plantagenet Counts of Anjou, and in theory vassals of the Kings of France for their vast possessions on the Continent. All three of them did some bad things in regard to Scotland, but, by the standards of their times, they were not conspicuously bad men, so that bishops and others in Scotland might from time to time reasonably negotiate with them in the expectation of fair settlements. Successive bishops of St Andrews were naturally often in the lead where such dealings were on hand, and St Andrews was the scene of two important parliaments, held by Edward I and Robert I (Bruce), during the first 'war of independence'. It was a complicated, rather desultory war, with several truces, and spasms of civil war in both Scotland and England, and many unexpected diplomatic and military twists. Moreover, it had hardly been wound up formally, in 1328, before the young King of England, Edward III, set it off again, in a way that merged it into the Hundred Years' War between the Kings of England and France.

5

THE HEADQUARTERS OF MILITANT NATIONALISM

On a stormy night in March 1286, after dining and wining with his council in Edinburgh Castle, King Alexander III sailed across the stormy Firth of Forth to Inverkeithing, and rode off to visit his young second wife, Yolande de Dreux, whom he had married in the previous October. His horse missed its footing on the cliffside road, and in the morning the king was found on the shore, with his neck broken. His heiress was his three-year-old grand-daughter Margaret, daughter of Eric II of Norway. Her mother, Margaret, was Alexander III's daughter by his first wife, Margaret of England, daughter of Henry III and sister of Edward I. Already in 1284 the infant Margaret, 'Maid of Norway', had been recognized as heiress to Scotland; but a complication arose when it became known that Queen Yolande was expecting a child. In April a parliament was held at Scone, and the members all swore fealty to their lady Queen Margaret and elected a cabinet of six members to run the government. These *custodes*, guardians or regents, were Bishop William Fraser of St Andrews, Bishop Robert Wishart of Glasgow, Duncan Earl of Fife, Alexander Comyn Earl of Buchan, John Comyn 'the Black' of Badenoch, and James Stewart, the Steward of Scotland. Their seal had on one side the royal arms, on the other St Andrew on his saltire cross. It was inscribed with the statement, *The seal of Scotland appointed for the government of the kingdom*, and the prayer, *Andrea, Scotis dux esto compatriotis*: 'St Andrew, be leader of the compatriot Scots'. The Scone parliament also sent three envoys to Edward I of England, who was then in his French duchy of Aquitaine, to ask for advice and protection. Edward was grand-uncle of the infant Queen Margaret, and had hitherto shown himself a good enough neighbour to Scotland, though he had behaved villainously to the much-enduring Welsh, conquering their country and subjecting their last native prince, David ap Gruffudd, to hanging, drawing, and quartering, in 1283.

The parliament at Scone had sworn fealty to Margaret, but in March 1309 the parliament at St Andrews, having received a friendly letter from Philip IV of France, issued a declaration 'that Robert Bruce, grandfather of the lord Robert King of Scotland, was the true heir of King Alexander, and that he ought to have succeeded to the realm on his death'. Such was the majority view in 1309, but it was not so clear to people in 1286.

Away back in 1238 Robert Bruce had been designated heir to the throne at a time when Alexander II was childless. This Bruce's mother, Isabel, was second daughter of David I's grandson, David Earl of Huntingdon, whose eldest daughter, Margaret, was grandmother of John Balliol, the nearest rival claimant to old Bruce among the men of royal blood. Bruce argued that he stood a degree nearer to the common ancestor who had been King; Balliol's claim was based on primogeniture, his grandmother having been born earlier than her sister, Bruce's mother. In 1286, without waiting for adjudication of the claim, old Bruce seized the royal castles of Dumfries and Wigtown, and Balliol's castle of Buittle in Galloway, all three of them strategic for running in men from Ireland, where Bruce held lands, as also in England. Moreover, in September 1286, old Bruce made a 'band' or contract with James Stewart (who controlled much of the Clyde estuary), Macdonald of Islay, the Earl of Ulster, and other magnates, for mutual support. Further, old Bruce's son, father of the future King Robert I, had married Marjorie, Countess of Carrick, whose forebears had a feud for generations with those of Balliol's mother, the lady Devorguilla, principal founder of Balliol College, Oxford.

The rival claims of the Bruces and the Balliols, with their close kin the Comyns, led to a split in the otherwise solidly patriotic front presented by the Scottish aristocracy and clergy during most of the confrontations of the next half-century. In 1286, however, old Bruce, known as 'the Competitor', was induced to abandon his attempt to stake his claim by force, and things went on smoothly and constitutionally. Old Bruce, indeed, joined with the Black John Comyn and the Bishops of St Andrews and Glasgow in negotiating the Treaty of Salisbury, in November 1289, providing for the shipping of the young Queen Margaret from Norway to Scotland 'free of any marriage contract'. This was followed up in July 1290 by the Treaty of Birgham, arranging the marriage of Margaret to Edward I's heir, the five-year-old Edward of Caernarvon, a condition being that the Kingdom of Scotland should remain 'separate, apart, and free in itself, without subjection to the English Kingdom'. Edward I ratified this on 28 August 1290. Fortunately or not, the prospective union of the crowns by marriage collapsed in September 1290, when the infant Queen Margaret died. On hearing the rumour, Bishop Fraser of St Andrews feared a civil war between Bruce and Balliol, and wrote to King Edward asking him to intervene.

Bishop Fraser belonged to a family, originally French, that had been settled south of the Forth, around the upper Tweed, for over a century, holding lands and the office of sheriff. His seal described him as 'Bishop of the Scots', and the Church of Scotland was a 'special daughter' of the Holy See. One might therefore have expected him to appeal to the Pope to settle the disputed succession to the kingship. Perhaps his urgent apprehension of civil war caused his appeal to King Edward; but his letter ended, in effect, by asking Edward to choose Sir John Balliol as King. In this probably Balliol's claim by primogeniture may have been the decisive point, for at that time the clergy in most countries were favouring succession by primogeniture, as a more certain method of knowing who would be responsible for paying the Church its dues.

Edward I responded by inviting the Scots parliamentary representatives to meet him in May 1291 at Norham on the Tweed. He there demanded whether they could produce evidence that he was not their rightful suzerain. What was called 'the Community of the Realm of Scotland' included the totality of the Scots King's free subjects, not only bishops, earls, and other major land-owners, but burgesses of the royal burghs and quite small lairds and 'goodmen' holding substantial property. At the end of May 1291 the Scots leaders answered on behalf of the Community of the Realm of Scotland that they knew nothing of such a demand for suzerainty made by King Edward previously or by his ancestors, and that they could not answer in the absence of a King of Scots, who alone could reply to such a demand. Edward's lawyers brushed this aside as irrelevant.

Meantime Edward had assembled an army at Norham, which strengthened his hand in dealing separately with the various magnates having claims to the Scots crown. Bruce, Balliol, and others sealed documents acknowledging King Edward's suzerainty and agreeing to accept his judgment. King Edward, himself a competitor, promised his rivals that, if now entrusted with the royal castles of Scotland, he would restore them inside two months of awarding the crown, and that in future, whenever a King died, no more would be demanded than homage and the incidental rights. The Guardians then resigned their authority, and were reappointed by Edward, with the addition of an Englishman, Brian FitzAlan of Bedale. They all swore fealty to Edward as 'superior and direct lord of the Kingdom of Scotland', and other magnates joined in this act, among them Bruce and Balliol, and swarms of lesser folk, including seventy-eight burgesses of Berwick on Tweed. Edward made a short summer tour through Scotland, as far as Perth, visiting St Andrews.

Consideration of the thirteen claims of competitors to the Scottish kingship lasted from August 1291 to November 1292, with some very curious infighting and backstairs negotiation, and a surprisingly plausible application by Florent V, Count of Holland. On 7 November 1292, old Bruce of Annandale, the Competitor, seeing that he was losing for the moment, resigned his claim to his son and heirs. Two days later his son, the Earl of Carrick, resigned his earldom to his son, then aged eighteen, the future King Robert. As all three were named Robert Bruce, it is convenient to call the middle one 'Father Bruce' to distinguish him from grandfather and son. Father Bruce was heir to rich lands in England and Ireland, as well as to Annandale on the western Border, and he planned to bide his time and apply again for the kingship. On 17 November 1292, the court of claims pronounced for John Balliol, who duly swore fealty to King Edward, and on St Andrew's Day was inaugurated King at Scone, being set by the Earl of Fife on the large carved stone chair which served as a throne, probably modelled on the bishops' chairs of the seventh century, an example of which survives at Hexham Abbey.

On 31 December 1292 Edward double-crossed the Scots by

repudiating promises, concessions, and ratifications that he had made previously, in regard to the taking of appeals from Scots courts to his own court in England. The Treaty of Birgham in 1290 had specifically preserved the independence of the Scottish courts, as well as the freedom of chapter elections to bishoprics, and the separate Scottish Parliament. At this point John Balliol proved himself a 'tuim tabard', or empty herald's jacket, the nickname he was given. In Latin and French documents of 2 January 1293 he freed Edward from all obligations made with the Guardians and responsible men of the Scottish Kingdom, and declared the Treaty of Birgham void. In the eyes of Scottish patriots their King John's reputation must have slumped very badly from that point; but for the moment it looked as if they were stuck with him, just as today political parties get stuck with plausible leaders who turn out to be incompetent in crises. Edward I proceeded to goad Balliol with a series of legalistic pinpricks, taking appeals from Scotland to his own courts; but the serious showdown came in 1294 on a different issue.

Aquitaine was held by King Edward as a vassal of King Philip IV of France. After disputation about the terms of its tenure, Philip IV confiscated the duchy in May 1294. A month later Edward formally renounced his homage as duke, and set about contracting alliances with Flanders, another fief of France, and sundry other states that might be useful, including Aragon, Holland, and the German Empire. He also attempted to impose military conscription, for service against France, on the King of Scots, ten of his earls, and sixteen major barons, including James Stewart and the aged Bruce, now in his eighty-fifth year. Edward conscribed also the newly conquered Welsh, who broke into rebellion under Madog ap Llywelyn, and destroyed some of the costly castles Edward had built to hold them down.

The Scots leaders meantime secured from the Pope absolution from oaths taken by them under duress. By July 1295 they were sufficiently agreed among themselves to resume national independence. In a Parliament at Stirling they elected a council of twelve to run the government, instead of King John, and appointed four commissioners, headed by Bishop Fraser, to negotiate an alliance with Philip IV. This was a renewal of the 'auld alliance', and King Philip brought in Norway as well, mainly to supply galleys, additional to those the French got from Genoa. It is notable that two years earlier Father Bruce, pursuing his royal ambitions, had married his daughter Isabel to Eric II of Norway, so that the young Earl of Carrick's sister was diplomatically now in the French camp against Edward I. Grandfather Bruce had died in spring 1295, and the young Robert had been working himself in as Earl of Carrick, drilling the local army of his earldom and getting to know better the local people of importance round his castle of Turnberry. A crisis came for him personally in spring 1296 when King John issued a mobilization order for the Scottish host to muster on 11 March at Caddonlee, near Selkirk, on the Tweed. The Bruces, father and son, refused this summons, and King John expropriated their lands. There was also a showdown with clerics of English nationality in Scotland. Acting for Bishop Fraser, away in France, his vicars-general William of Kingorn and Peter de Champneys deprived twenty-six English clergymen holding benefices in the diocese. Considering the extent of the diocese, the number does not seem high. Meantime King Edward had been arresting Scotsmen in England. The nationalities were already distinct, even though the dialect of Northumberland hardly differed from that of Berwickshire.

Hostilities began in March 1296, with seven earls of Scotland attacking Carlisle, which was defended by Father Bruce on Edward's behalf, inside fortifications built by his ancestor King David I. At the other end of the Border Berwick had nothing but a wooden palisade and a ditch. Edward's troops took it at the first assault. The thirty Flemings in their Red Hall held out to the last. The garrison of the castle surrendered on terms. But the ordinary folk of the burgh, having taunted Edward 'Langshanks' with his personal abnormalities, were massacred. Edward pushed on towards Dunbar, and was faced at Spottsmuir by King John's feudal host, an army that was without serious military experience for over sixty years. The much-practised Edward had no trouble in defeating it, and capturing a great many magnates in Dunbar Castle. King John surrendered in July, and had the royal arms stripped off his surcoat. Edward seized the Scottish regalia, the Black Rood brought from Hungary by St Margaret, and a mass of records and relics. He demanded the Scots throne too, and was given by the Abbot of Scone the block of building stone that is now electronically guarded in Westminster Abbey. King Edward ordered a fine bronze throne to contain it, but seems to have become suspicious. He sent up a further expedition to ransack the abbey of Scone, and then housed the stone he had been given in a wooden chair. At some time after Dunbar Father Bruce applied for the vacant Scottish kingship, and Edward sarcastically asked him, 'Have we nothing else to do but win kingdoms for you?' This reply rankled with the young Robert Bruce, Earl of Carrick, and in the winter of 1296–7 he threw in his lot with the Scots patriots who were planning a rising for the spring of 1297. But in the meantime Edward seemed to be having everything his own way. He moved north as far as Elgin, visiting all the chief burghs and castles with the eye of a conqueror. On Saturday, 11 August, he was at St Andrews, described by a contemporary Englishman as 'a castell and a good toune'. In his methodical way Edward collected written acknowledgements of his lordship from clergy and men of property, including Englishmen, like Sir John Swinburne, ancestor of the poet, and Italians, like Giacomo de Vicia, parson of Idvies in Angus. Some of the documents are in duplicate, for lands held by a man in more than one sheriffdom.

A notable omission from the so-called 'Ragman Roll' of these homages is that of Sir Malcolm Wallace of Elderslie in Renfrewshire, a chief vassal of James Stewart, and the elder brother of Sir William Wallace, the most inspiring leader of the patriot cause in its next phase. The resumption of warfare that broke out in the spring of 1297 was organized at the highest level by Robert Wishart, Bishop of Glasgow, and James Stewart, the principal lay magnate in his diocese. Young Bruce, with his Carrick army, joined them, as did other magnates, like William Douglas. William Wallace was the general in command of their army, conducting at first guerrilla operations. Wallace personally killed the English sheriff of Lanarkshire. North of the Forth the military leader was Sir Andrew Moray, son of a magnate who held lands both round the Moray Firth and on the Clyde. (His uncle became Bishop of Moray, and founded the Scots College in Paris.) In the summer of 1297, while Edward I was in France, Wallace and Moray joined forces and defeated the English occupying troops at Stirling Brig. They then wrote to the German Hansa cities announcing that the Kingdom was delivered, thanks be to God, and that trade would be welcomed. Moray died of a wound received, and Wallace carried on as sole Guardian, with the authority of the Scottish parliament.

Meantime Bishop Fraser had died, at Auteuil, and was buried in Paris, his heart being later brought to St Andrews in a costly box. The Augustinian chapter then elected, on Wallace's instructions, William Lamberton, without whose aid and counsel Robert Bruce would never have secured the nation's freedom. Lamberton belonged to a family owning land at Linlathen in Angus, and in Aberdeenshire, where an earlier William Lamberton, laird of Bourtie, made benefactions to the priory of St Andrews between 1209 and 1228. In the previous years he had been chancellor of Glasgow, and must have been a key man in Bishop Wishart's planning of the Wallace rising. Immediately on election he went off to Rome, where he was consecrated on 1 June 1298, and busied himself negotiating with Pope Boniface VIII and King Philip IV of France.

Among the Scots magnates captured in 1296 had been John Comyn 'the Red', Lord of Badenoch, and his cousin John Comyn, Earl of Buchan. Before the 1297 insurrection was seen to have reached serious proportions, Edward sent them home, in the hope that they would mobilize their followers to support his campaign against the French. On the contrary, they themselves were absorbed into the general nationalist movement. Next year, 1298, when Edward I marched north in person to subdue the rebellion, Wallace gave the Red John Comyn command of a cavalry contingent and put Bruce in command of the royal castle of Ayr and the western approaches from Ireland. The Scots strategy was to starve Edward out, and it succeeded. Edward's superiority in heavy cavalry and archers won him a battle at Falkirk, a costly holding action by Wallace; but shortly after it he retreated south again, having had St

Andrews and Perth set on fire to appease his anger. Later in 1298 Wallace resigned his guardianship, and Bruce and the Red Comyn became joint Guardians. All this was done in the name of King John (Balliol), still a prisoner in England, so that constitutional continuity might be maintained.

Meantime Pope Boniface VIII had been asserting the rights of the Holy See, of which he proclaimed Scotland to be a fief. He told Edward I to stop attacking Scotland, to release Balliol, and to let the dispute be submitted to the papal court. This was a result of the diplomacy of Lamberton and other Scots churchmen. During 1299 Wallace himself went over to France, doubtless to discuss details of a scheme that Philip IV should send over a strong contingent of French heavy cavalry to reinforce the Scots and restore Balliol.

In this connection there is extant a revealing intelligence report from an English spy, concerning a meeting of the Scottish cabinet on 19 August 1299, in Bishop Wishart's manor at Stobo, near Peebles. Bishop Lamberton had returned from France and was in the chair. A member of the Balliol–Comyn faction complained that Sir William Wallace had gone overseas without leave of the two Guardians, John Comyn and Bruce; and he demanded forfeiture of the lands and goods of Wallace. Promptly Sir Malcolm Wallace replied that his brother William was going abroad for the country's good. A rumpus then got up, in which the Red Comyn gripped Bruce by the throat and John Comyn, Earl of Buchan, seized Lamberton, crying out that treason was being plotted. Having regard to Lamberton's past association with the Wishart–Stewart–Wallace party, and his secret contract with Bruce in 1304, it is likely that Lamberton was a Bruce man, and was in 1299 suspected by the Comyn–Balliol party as being a Bruce man. Their fear therefore must have been that Wallace would advise Philip IV to switch his support from Balliol to Bruce. The quarrel was composed, and Lamberton was chosen as a third Guardian, jointly with Bruce and Comyn. One may see the war of independence as run, on the Scottish side, by a syndicate of magnates, clerical and lay, with considerable continuity of personnel, as well as some inevitable personal disputes and factional splits, such as trouble any democratic cabinet. In this syndicate the bishops of St Andrews and Glasgow are especially powerful.

The intervention by Boniface VIII induced Edward I, whose warfare in France was going badly, to hand over Balliol, in 1299, to a papal commissioner, who restored him to his estate at Bailleul in Picardy, where he died in 1313. For a year or two, up to July 1302, a Balliol restoration looked quite likely. The Prince Edward Balliol had been betrothed to Jeanne de Valois, daughter of the French King's brother Charles, and the Pope was backing France and Scotland against Edward I. Bruce and John Comyn had successively resigned their guardianships, and in 1301 Scotland was being quite competently governed by Sir John de Soules, as sole Guardian in the name of King John 'owre the watter'. It was in this situation that Edward I marched north again, with his son, the Prince of Wales, and overran south Scotland to the Forth–Clyde line. Bruce's castle of Turnberry was captured; but north of the Forth–Clyde the Comyns were in control, with Lamberton, and Edward I had every reason to fear that next year Philip IV would send over enough heavy cavalry to tip the scale against him and restore King John.

Such a prospect was naturally disagreeable to Father Bruce, who had meantime been in England, nursing his hopes of an eventual Bruce accession to the Scottish throne. Moreover, he probably knew himself to be near death, and in fact he died in March 1304. Apart from being an 'Old Pretender' to the throne, he was concerned to secure for his family the wide lands in Durham, Essex, Antrim, and elsewhere that were in Edward's power. Accordingly he arranged, during a truce in the winter of 1301–2, that his son and heir, the Earl of Carrick, should submit to Edward I on terms. The document issued by King Edward has recently turned up in the Duchy of Lancaster archives. It guarantees to young Bruce the lands he might inherit from his father, and permission to pursue his right in regard to the Kingdom of Scotland in any fresh adjudication of it in King Edward's court or elsewhere (meaning the papal court). On these terms young Bruce made his peace with the King of England, and thereafter worked his passage back to favour by going through the routine of supplying troops for

Edward's later small-scale activities against the nationalist forces, led by the Comyns. In July 1302 Philip IV had his splendid cavalry sadly mauled by the Flemish infantry at Courtrai, after which his prospect of restoring John Balliol faded out. Further, Boniface VIII quarrelled with the French King and began to make up his disagreement with the King of England. In these circumstances the Comyns too packed in the war, by a capitulation at Strathord in February 1304. The syndicate of Scots magnates had decided to play for time, waiting till old Langshanks should die, and meantime to occupy positions of influence under his overlordship. The Red Comyn, negotiating as Guardian, stipulated that there should be no reprisals by King Edward against rebels, and no expropriation of their inheritances; and that prisoners on each side should be liberated without ransom. Edward accepted all this, except as applying to Sir William Wallace, who was required to surrender at the King's discretion, unconditionally. Comyn also demanded that the people of Scotland 'should be protected in all their laws, usages, customs and liberties' as in the time of Alexander III, subject to amendments to be made by advice of King Edward and the advice and assent of the responsible men of the land.

To give effect to this provision King Edward held a parliament at St Andrews in March 1304, for which Bishop Lamberton returned from France. Edward restored to him the temporalities of his see. The business of this Parliament was largely detailed settlements with individual land-owners. For instance: 'The King commands the restoration to Hugh of Penicuik, a Scottish rebel who has come to his peace, of his lands and heritage in England.' It was no more extraordinary for a Scotsman owning some property in England to fight for Scottish independence than for a Frenchman having shares in a German company to resist the aggression of Adolf Hitler. As usual when parliaments meet, much of the important business was done in the corridors of power, in consultations between influential personalities. Concurrently with this legalistic negotiation, Edward was pursuing his siege of Stirling Castle, held by Sir William Oliphant. With a trace of the paranoiac ferocity that sometimes distinguished him, the old King refused to accept the small garrison's offer to surrender, even unconditionally, and tried out his new-fangled war-machines on the fortifications. To supply them with ammunition he stripped the lead off the roofs of the cathedral and the monastic buildings at St Andrews, paying for it in cash and with the gift of a jewelled case for the arm-bone of the Apostle—a kind of celestial reinsurance policy.

During this siege of Stirling, lasting till 20 July, an important secret event took place, probably on the initiative of Lamberton. On 11 June, at Cambuskenneth Abbey, across the Forth from Stirling, the bishop met Robert Bruce and entered with him into a bond of friendship and alliance against all men, under a penalty of £10,000 to be paid to the Pope's fund for the Crusade to recover Jerusalem and the other Holy Places. Why did Lamberton, 'Bishop of the Scots', pick Bruce, rather than John Comyn, for such a secret compact? Perhaps because he had recognized in him some quality of leadership that was vital to the national cause; perhaps because he believed in the Bruces' inherited right to the throne, which the Scots clergy and nobles were to assert publicly in 1309, at the next Parliament held in St Andrews. At any rate the secret compact of June 1304 must be kept in mind when evaluating Bruce's bid for power in February 1306, and the lamentable and enigmatic stab which he directed against the Red Comyn in the cloister of the Franciscan friary at Dumfries.

In March 1304 Bruce's father died, and the future King secured possession of his lands in England. In 1305, in Edward's Lenten Parliament at Westminster, Bruce came with Bishop Wishart and John Moubray, a Scots baron, to advise Edward on the settlement of what Edward still called 'the Kingdom of Scotland'. They advised him to have ten representatives elected by the Scottish Parliament to attend the next Parliament of England and draw up a constitution for Scotland. This election was made in May 1305, and the ten went to the Westminster Parliament in September. Neither Bruce nor Wishart went this time. Edward now dropped the term 'Kingdom of Scotland', and ordained that 'the land of Scotland' should be governed by four pairs of justices, each pair to consist of one Englishman and one Scotsman. They were to have jurisdiction in four areas: Lothian, from Tweed to Forth; Galloway, meaning the whole south-west; the country from the Forth to the Mownth; and the region beyond the Mownth. Most of the sheriffs and constables of castles appointed were Scots, except in the crucial south-east. Edward's nephew, John of Britanny, was appointed lieutenant of Scotland, a viceroy, with an advisory council, with twenty-two Scots, including Lamberton and Bruce and the Red Comyn. This council was to convene an assembly of responsible men to review the laws of Scotland.

Meantime, in August 1305, King Edward had carried out the judicial murder of Sir William Wallace, at Smithfield in London, by hanging, drawing, and quartering. An English cleric gave him the last consolations of religion. His head was fixed on London Bridge, his four quarters at Newcastle, Berwick, Stirling, and Perth. At this time, perhaps because of documents captured on Wallace's person, Edward seems to have become suspicious of Bruce. He ordered him to hand over the castle of Kildrummy in Aberdeenshire, which he held as guardian for his nephew, the young Earl of Mar. But Edward's suspicions cannot have gone very far. Yet Bruce may have imagined they did go rather far. That apart, if a blow was to be struck for Scottish independence it had best be done before Edward's new régime was allowed to settle in.

Pending the arrival of the viceroy John of Britanny, Bishop Lamberton was chief of a committee of four, two Scots and two English, who were administering Scotland. During the winter of 1305–6 we need not doubt that Lamberton and Bruce were contemplating a rising, with Bishop Wishart. Just where the Red Comyn stood is doubtful. Wallace had made Bruce and Comyn joint Guardians in 1298, and they had quarrelled at the cabinet meeting of August 1299 in Stobo. Still, they were older now, and both patriotic in their ways. It was to Lamberton's interest, and the nation's, that they should settle their differences and join forces. There was, too, the problem of the conflicting claims to the throne. If King John, exiled in Picardy and discredited, were set aside, the effective choice in Scotland lay between Red John Comyn himself, son of King John's sister, and Robert Bruce, as heir of his grandfather, the recognized heir in 1238, and runner-up to John Balliol in 1292.

Bruce invited Comyn to meet him on 10 February 1306, in the cloister of the Greyfriars at Dumfries, a burgh where both of them had business at the sheriff court. From his castle at Lochmaben Bruce sent two of his brothers to escort Comyn from his castle of Dalswinton. Comyn appeared frank and friendly. Bruce took him away for a talk man to man, and proposed a deal: either Bruce should take Comyn's lands and help to make Comyn King, or Comyn should accept Bruce's lands and back Bruce for the throne. One may suppose that Comyn, on hearing this dangerous proposal, remembered how Bruce had made a separate deal with Edward in the winter of 1301–2, two years before the Comyns had themselves capitulated in 1304. Somehow the latent rivalry and suspicion flared up again. Comyn probably said something that annoyed Bruce, high-spirited young nobleman as he was, and abnormally keyed up for the critical encounter. By some subconscious reaction Bruce drew his dirk and stabbed Comyn, who fell to the floor. Bruce ran out to his companions at the doorway and exclaimed, 'I dout I hae slain the Reid Comyn.' Sir Roger Kirkpatrick cried, 'I'll mak siccar.' Meantime Comyn had staggered to the foot of the high altar in the church, where Kirkpatrick ran him through with his sword. The dead man's uncle, Sir Robert Comyn, pulled out his sword to go to his nephew's assistance, but had his skull split open by a stroke from the sword of Bruce's brother-in-law Sir Christopher Seton —a weapon now in the possession of his descendant, Professor Hugh Seton-Watson. Bruce's unpremeditated blow was a matter of regret to him till his dying day, but he lost no time in taking the consequential steps to promote the national rising. Bishop Wishart promptly absolved him for the wounding and the profanation involved, and exhorted the faithful in the diocese of Glasgow to fight for him, as for a crusade. Bishop Lamberton set about organizing King Robert's coronation at Scone, on Friday, 25 March. The English chronicler Walter of Guisborough, a well-informed observer hostile to Bruce, remarks that it was attended and consented to by four bishops, five earls, and the people of the land. The boy Earl of Fife was in Edward's power, but his sister, the Countess of Buchan, rode up from her husband's manor in Leicestershire to take part.

She arrived too late, but Bruce underwent an additional cere-mony two days later, on Palm Sunday, 27 March, when she discharged the duty of the Clan Macduff to enthrone the King of Scots.

The news of these events kindled the ageing King Edward to fury. He ordered his general in Scotland, Aymer de Valence, the Red Comyn's brother-in-law, to burn and slay and 'raise dragon'—that is, to fly the dragon banner that meant no mercy would be shown. Edward singled out particular patriots with bureaucratic minuteness, for instance the Fife laird Sir Michael Wemyss. 'We command you to burn his manor where we stayed, and all his other manors, to destroy his lands and goods, and to strip his gardens clean so that nothing is left, for an example to others like him.' In many parts of Scotland, where English garrisons could reach, much devastation was per-petrated. In June Bishops Wishart and Lamberton were captured, in the castle at Cupar, and sent in irons to Winchester Castle, where they were kept fettered. Valence defeated Bruce in a fight at Methven, on 19 June, and it was some months before Bruce developed that sagacity in guerrilla warfare which later distinguished him. The winter of 1306–7 he spent in Ulster and on the offshore island of Rathlin, concerting plans, and in 1307 he won a series of small victories. Old King Edward died in July 1307, and his son Edward II turned out to be a much less competent commander, and deeply depraved as well; but the full extent of his incompetence and depravity was not at first apparent.

Regarding the bishopric of St Andrews, old Langshanks had tried to install in it the Earl of Buchan's brother, William Comyn, provost of the Culdees of St Mary of the Rock, and had written to the Pope accordingly, without success. Edward II decided to negotiate with Lamberton, and released him on 1 June 1308, to go to Rome. He travelled frequently hither and thither, negotiating truces from time to time; but did not forget to apply some economic pressure to induce William Comyn to back Bruce, confiscating the rents of his provostry of St Mary's and his church of Ceres till he should do so. Bruce was even rougher with the provost's brother, the earl, harrying Buchan itself, and planting on expropriated estates the families of

Gordon, Fraser, Irvine, and others, who could be relied upon as his own backers.

By March 1309 King Robert's affairs were sufficiently established to allow him to hold a parliament at St Andrews. King Philip IV of France had recognized Bruce as King, and invited his alliance in a crusade. The Scots Parliament answered that first things must be put first, and that, after they had secured their liberty and made good the damage done by the English, they would be very happy to go crusading. That was on 16 March. Next day the clergy attending, headed by bishops, abbots, and priors, issued a manifesto declaring that John Balliol had been made King *de facto* by Edward I in defiance of the universal belief of the people of Scotland that Robert Bruce had a better title. The lay magnates made a parallel declaration. In spite of the split caused by the stabbing of Comyn, Bruce had by 1309 the adherence of the majority of the 'Community of the Realm of Scotland'. His crowning victory at Bannockburn in 1314 was followed by another fourteen years of desultory warfare, with long truces, before Edward III agreed to the Treaty of Edinburgh, made on 17 March 1328, ratified by the English Parliament at Northampton on 4 May. In this the King of England renounced all claims to lordship, suzerainty, or sovereignty in Scotland. A marriage was also contracted for between King Robert's son David and Edward III's sister Joan. The neighbour nations thus got back very much to the position of the Treaty of Birgham of 1290, after a great deal of needless bloodshed and illwill, the blame for which lies at the door of Edward I above all.

Bishop Lamberton died in May 1328, a fortnight after the diplomatic termination to the first war of independence. Presumably he died happy. But already his happiest moment may have been the consecration of the great cathedral, on 5 July 1318, in the presence of King Robert, seven bishops, fifteen abbots, and most of the earls, barons, knights, and other substantial men of the kingdom, all of whom made offerings on the occasion. The fact that the pro-English Pope at Rome had excommunicated Bruce did not worry anybody; Lamberton too was later excommunicated.

Modern St Andrews from the east. In the foreground, the harbour and the Kinness Burn, with St Mary's of the Rock behind, and the square tower of St Regulus and the Norman cathedral within the walls of the priory precinct.

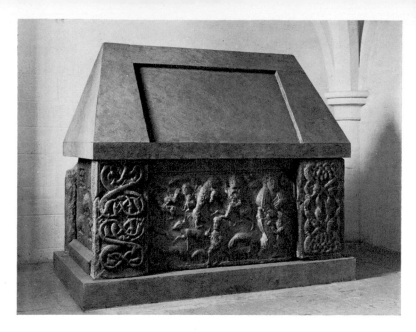

The Pictish sarcophagus. The modern hipped roof is
debatable.

The cathedrals from the sea, engraved by Joseph Swan
from a drawing by James Stewart (1840). The projecting
cliff is probably the original 'headland of the king's hill'.

A graphic interpretation of Renaissance St Andrews by Jurek Pütter.

The murder of Archbishop Sharp on Magus Muir, from his monument in Holy Trinity Church.

In intervals of diplomacy Lamberton bestowed upon the priory a new chapter-house, at his own expense. The original chapter-house was to the south of the south transept of the Norman cathedral, and had four pillars, making it comparatively dark. It was aisled, in the fashion of Cistercian houses. Keeping this as a vestibule, Lamberton built out to the east an unaisled chapter-house, of the Benedictine type, fifty feet long. He gave the canons books for their library, and vessels for the more splendid performance of the divine offices. Contemporary with Lamberton's chapter-house, before 1321, was the richly decorated gatehouse of the priory, 'the Pends', and the similar arcading on the west front of the cathedral, where the thirteenth-century porch was removed. Lamberton did something to repair the castle, where Edward I had stayed in 1304, and built, or rebuilt, episcopal manors at places up and down the diocese from Monymusk on the Don to the Stow in Wedale, near Galashiels.

Within three years of Bruce's death in 1329 the kingdom he had rescued came within an ace of total subjection again. With the death of his nephew Randolph, Earl of Moray, in 1332, the last of the great captains had gone, and the regency for the boy King David II was placed in the hands of Donald, Earl of Mar, another nephew of King Robert, but a most brash and incompetent young man. This gave an opportunity for John Balliol's son Edward to see what he could do. Backed by the young King Edward III of England, he collected some Englishmen and Scotsmen, sons of men who had formerly held lands in Scotland from which Bruce had dispossessed them for their adherence either to John Balliol or to Edward I. With a force of about five hundred cavalry and three thousand archers, he sailed to Kingorn (improperly Kinghorn) in Fife, and made for Scone.

The Regent Mar had a sizeable force of cavalry and spearmen, but was weak in missile weapons. The encounter at Dupplin Moor was an anticipation of the Battle of Crécy, where the Welsh longbowmen wiped out the French knights. On the day when grouse-shooting commences, the Glorious Twelfth of August, Mar's army took the worst beating any

Scots array had yet suffered. The calamity was regarded by some in that age as a 'judgement of God', for the opinion was prevalent that 'the powers that be are ordained of God'. Edward Balliol had himself crowned at Scone, in September; but three months later was chased over the Border from Annan with one boot on and the other off.

Edward III, burning for military glory, came up next year, in 1333, to besiege Berwick. In trying to relieve it the new Regent, Archibald Douglas, came to grief against the Welsh and English longbows at Halidon Hill. Next year, 1334, Balliol held a Parliament of his supporters in Scotland and ceded Berwick to Edward III. Later in the year he sealed a charter granting to the Kingdom of England all the southern counties of Scotland from Haddington to Dumfries. Thus a large slice of the dioceses of St Andrews and Glasgow was cut off.

The bishopric of St Andrews, moreover, was suffering from a want of competence in its incumbent. On Lamberton's death the chapter was divided, some voting for James Bennet (or Bane), Archdeacon of St Andrews, and others for Alexander Kyninmonth, Archdeacon of Lothian. James Bennet was already at the papal court, at Avignon, and John XXII gave him the see. Kyninmonth posted off to Avignon, to find himself forestalled; but the Pope consoled him with the vacant see of Aberdeen. As soon as he heard of the calamity at Dupplin, Bishop Bennet, says Fordun, 'fearing the ferocity and intolerable cruelty of the English, came by night from Lochleven to St Andrews, and, bidding the prior and canons a hasty farewell, embarked for Flanders'. He died a month later, and was buried at Bruges. The see was then left vacant for over nine years. The Augustinian canons, understanding Bennet to have resigned, elected William Bell, Dean of Dunkeld, who went to Avignon, but failed to be confirmed. In addition the poor man went blind, and surrendered what right he had by the canons' election. Edward III proposed different English candidates, but the Pope rejected them.

In this situation it was clearly dangerous for the Scots to leave the castle of St Andrews without a strong garrison, so they destroyed it. In 1336, however, Edward III was in Scotland again in force, and he had it refortified by Henry Beaumont and Henry Ferrers. He also refortified Perth elaborately, meeting the costs by forced levies from the monasteries of St Andrews, Balmerino, Lindores, Dunfermline, Coupar-Angus, and Arbroath, which impoverished them all. In the winter of 1335 the Regent Sir Andrew Moray had won a battle in Aberdeenshire at Kilblain (Culblean) against Balliol's new Earl of Atholl, which led to ferocious reprisals by Henry Beaumont, Balliol's Earl of Buchan. Whatever atrocities had been committed in the first war of independence were as nothing to the miseries caused by the second war, which in one form or other dragged on for generations. What took the pressure off Scotland was the involvement of the vainglorious young Edward III in the Hundred Years' War, begun in 1338, to assert his right to the throne of France. One of its consequences was the foundation of the University of St Andrews.

The reign of Robert Bruce's son, David II, was an unlucky one, made even worse by the occurrence of the Black Death in 1349, 1350, 1361, and 1362. In 1334 he was shipped to France for safety, with his wife Joan, Edward III's sister; and came back in 1341, a young French knight with the fashionable ardour for military glory, so vividly portrayed by the courtly French war-correspondent Froissart. In pursuance of the alliance with France, David II made a raid into England in 1346, and was wounded and captured at the battle of Nevile's Cross, near Durham. His nephew, Robert Stewart, later Regent and King, escaped from the battle, and was thought by David to have fled, whence much bad blood between them. Negotiations for the King's ransom dragged on till 1354; but the arrangement then made was upset by a group of Scots magnates, bribed by the French to renew the hostilities.

In 1356 Edward Balliol, utterly discredited and without supporters by now, surrendered to Edward III the Kingdom of Scotland, which he did not possess. Hoping that David might have influence, Edward released him in the next year to see whether he could persuade the Scots to barter the Kingdom's independence for his own release. Later David sought to bequeath the Kingdom, for he had no child, to Edward III or one of his sons, if Edward III would release him from the unpaid instalments of his ransom; but the Scots Parliament refused to contemplate this. Just as in England the Parliament at this period increases its control over the King's expenditure of taxes for the war with France, so the Scots Parliament steps up its supervision of the King's outlays. But the weakness of the Scots Crown also enabled local magnates to become more powerful, so that, on a smaller scale, later medieval Scotland was bothered with over-mighty vassals, as was France for a long time, and England during the Wars of the Roses. In such a situation the Bishop of St Andrews could not hold his own without a strong military establishment.

In 1342 the Pope appointed as bishop William de Landellis, who ruled till 1385. Wyntoun says he was a young clerk, but 'of lineage a gret gentilman', and had the favour of David II. He was owner of all Lauderdale, and had a taste for foreign travel, making pilgrimages to St James's shrine at Compostella in Spain, and to Rome, as well as twenty-one trips to England in connection with King David's ransom. In 1378 a fire consumed much of the cathedral, which had to be repaired at great expense. All the timberwork of the choir and transepts was renewed. The great central tower over the crossing had to be reinforced. In the nave the nine western pillars on the south side were rebuilt, and embellished with the arms of the lords who subscribed for the work. New lead was put on the roofs of choir and cross-kirk. Landellis also gave to the kirk and the monastery books, jewels, vestments, and furnishings of value. (As in France and England at this time, one is continually astonished at the contrast between the wealth and taste of a few magnates and the state of the mass of the people, living on the subsistence level or in acute poverty.) Landellis did not rebuild the castle of St Andrews, demolished again in 1337, a year after its English refortification. He obtained in 1375 a bull from Pope Gregory XI, allowing the bishops full power to bequeath their personal property, which in the past Kings had been inclined to confiscate; and doubtless the cathedral benefited thereby.

In Landellis's episcopate Prior William de Lothian (1340–54) reroofed the dormitory with polished planks and lead, the eastern guest-hall, the cloister, part of the refectory, and the old church of St Andrew, now St Rule's. He installed a new central-heating apparatus in the cathedral, and one wonders if this caused the great fire. He somehow contrived to get the priory out of debt, and added a hundred books to its library. The next prior was Thomas Bisset, nephew of the Earl of Fife, who was succeeded by Stephen de Pay. On Landellis's death he was elected bishop, but, on sailing to the Pope to be confirmed, he was captured by the English. He refused to burden the monastery with the cost of ransoming him, and died in captivity at Alnwick, in 1386.

The events of the year 1385 must have considerably impoverished the diocese of St Andrews, for there was a major invasion by Richard II of England, in which he burnt the abbeys of Melrose, Dryburgh, Newbattle, and Holyrood, and the town of Edinburgh, and doubtless all the villages on the route. This was in response to an expedition of French knights brought to Scotland by Jean de Vienne, about which Froissart writes amusingly. The general body of the people saw no need for the French allies, and only the Earls of Douglas and Moray seem to have been at all welcoming. The peasantry objected to the French knights riding down their crops, and would not allow them to sail home till they had received compensation in full.

Serfdom had died out early in Scotland, and seems never to have had a wide incidence. The French were astonished at the boldness of the ordinary people. Froissart comments also on their hardiness in war. They would march twenty to twenty-four miles without halting, by night or day. The knights had large bay horses, the common folk Galloway ponies. The camp-followers kept up on foot. They lived on meat parboiled in the hides of the cattle they slew, washed down with burn water. They eked this out with oatcakes baked on metal plates, each man having a bag of oatmeal behind his saddle. Froissart found it no wonder that 'they perform a longer day's march than other soldiers'. The Borderers expressed no great dejection when invaders burned their houses: 'We can rebuild them cheap enough, for we only require three days to do so, provided we have five or six poles and boughs to cover them.' Such was the broad social background of Scotland's first university.

The Anglo-French wars were accompanied by a schism in the church, with a Pope at Avignon recognized by France and Scotland and other states, another Pope at Rome backed by Italy, England, and others. The pro-English Pope at Rome supplied the vacancy at St Andrews by pretending to translate thither Alexander Neville, Archbishop of York. But the pro-Scottish Pope Clement VII at Avignon had already appointed Walter Trail, who had been Official of the diocese of Glasgow, and later its Treasurer, and was ambassador (*referendarius*) at Avignon. He lost no time in rebuilding the castle of St Andrews from its foundations. Some of his work is still visible in the lower part of the projecting tower to the right of the modern entrance.

How necessary a castle was for a bishop was demonstrated in 1390, when King Robert II's son Alexander Stewart, 'the Wolf of Badenoch', having been excommunicated by the Bishop of Moray for seizing episcopal lands, burned down the cathedral of Elgin, and the burgh too, Robert III brought him to book, and the 'Wolf' did penance in the Blackfriars' kirk at Perth, clad in sackcloth. Bishop Trail absolved him on his reimbursing the Bishop of Moray.

Much of Trail's time was spent in embassies. He died in 1401, and was buried under a Latin epitaph calling him 'a flower of the church, an upright column, clear window, odorous thurible, resonant bell'. Such elegant Latinity is a reminder of the importance of Avignon in the early development of the Humanist movement to revive the culture of Rome and Greece. Trail disciplined canons who 'perceptibly' kept mistresses. During Trail's episcopate the prior Robert of Montrose had the misfortune to be assassinated one evening, in 1393, as he was going up from the cloister to the dormitory, by a canon called Thomas Plater, whom he had censured for breaches of discipline. To quote the Rev C. J. Lyon's narrative: 'Two days after the prior's funeral, he [Plater] was brought forth, clad in a long robe; and after a solemn discourse from Walter Trail the bishop, addressed to the clergy and people, he was thrust bound into perpetual imprisonment. There, partaking scantily of the bread of grief and the water of affliction, he soon died, and was buried in a dunghill.' Apparently nobody says that he was immured in the so-called 'bottle dungeon' in the 'sea-tower' of Trail's castle. This is a pit excavated in the sandstone to the depth of twenty-four feet, with sloping sides, widening to sixteen feet at the bottom, which is concave. It has the shape of a bottle, with the neck four and three-quarter feet in diameter. A more sophisticated theory is that Trail built it as a grain-store. When well supplied in advance, a strongly sited castle could hold out for many months in those days, before gunpowder had been fully developed for artillery. In 1337 the Earl of Salisbury had spent five months vainly besieging 'Black Agnes', Countess of Dunbar, in her castle further down the coast; and was moved to the verse: 'Came I early, came I late, I found Agnes at the gate.'

The full extent of Trail's castle cannot now be determined. Part of it on the east has certainly fallen into the sea with the crumbling of the rock. George Martine of Clermont, in his *Reliquiae Divi Andreae*, writing in 1683, states:

> . . . in my time there lived people in St Andrews who remembered to have seen men play at the bowls upon the east and north sides of the castle of St Andrews, which now the sea covers on everie side. . . . And I have heard it crediblie reported, that of old the heritors of Kinkell claimed and pretended to a priviledge of watering all the bestiall on their ground at the Swilcanth burne, which runs at the west end of St Andrews: and for that effect, that they might bring all their goods to that burne, upon the north side of the castle of St Andrews.

It seems that no substantial alteration of the relative level of the sea along this coast need be assumed since earlier than 2000 BC; so the bowling-greens reported by elderly persons in the seventeenth century must have been carried away merely by local erosion, such as is still occurring round the headland on which the castle stands. The strongly fortified part of Trail's castle would enclose about an acre, and there were foreworks to west and south. St Andrews thus became one of the strongpoints of the kingdom, in a military sense.

On Bishop Trail's death in 1401 the chapter elected the archdeacon, Thomas Stewart, a natural son of King Robert II. The Kingdom was now being governed mostly by Robert III's brother Robert, Duke of Albany. The King and the Duke induced their bastard half-brother, 'a man of dovelike simplicity', to resign his claim, so that they might offer the see to one Walter Danielston, a chaplain of the Avignon Pope, claiming to hold hereditarily the important castle of Dumbarton, which he promised to hand over if he were given St Andrews. Danielston's election in July 1402 was much disliked, but led to nothing, as he died in December. Gilbert Greenlaw, Bishop of Aberdeen, was then postulated for St Andrews, but died before confirmation. After these vicissitudes Henry Wardlaw was provided, in September 1403, by the Avignon Pope Benedict XIII, Peter da Luna, and he reigned as bishop till 1440.

Wardlaw was a nephew of Walter Wardlaw, Bishop of Glasgow (1367–87), who had been created a Cardinal by the Avignon Pope Clement VII in 1383. Henry Wardlaw had been a student at Oxford during the controversies aroused by the views of John Wyclif. He may have suffered in the rough treatment meted out to the 'northerners' in the brawls of the time. He also studied at Orleans, Paris, and Avignon. It is clear, however, that he himself had no use for Wyclif's views or the reforming campaign of the Lollards ('Babblers') as they were nicknamed. These forerunners of the Reformation held, among other tenets, the doctrine that 'no man is Pope, or the vicar of Christ, unless he is holy'. The currently orthodox doctrine was that sin did not disqualify a Pope from ruling the Church. John Bower, Abbot of Inchcolm, asserts that, even if a Pope is condemned to Hell, his judgments in the capacity of Pope are sanctioned in Heaven.

Some of the English Lollards took refuge in Scotland from the danger of being burned as heretics in England, but to no purpose. For the Scottish clerical establishment was equally hostile to their subversive opinions. The English priest James Resby was burned at Perth in 1406 for maintaining forty heretical opinions, which were duly refuted by Laurence of Lindores, the 'Inquisitor of Heretical Pravity'. This man became the leading teacher in Wardlaw's university. Moreover, in the charter incorporating the university Wardlaw stressed the need for a learned institution to combat heresies and errors; and the Masters of Arts were required to swear an oath to defend the Church against the assault of Lollards. It is evident that the university was intended not to promote innovation in science or society, but to be a propagandist agency for the existing order, as well as a school for certain professional careers, in the Church, law, and medicine especially.

On Wardlaw's becoming bishop in 1403 the priory had come into a somewhat flourishing state under Prior James Bisset (1393–1416), nephew of Prior Thomas Bisset. He did a lot of reroofing and repaving, and rebuilt the granaries, mills, piggeries, barns, and stables, as well as the *ustrinae*, the central-heating systems or warming-rooms of the monastery. He saw to it that the altars shone with brilliant lights, that the canons behaved themselves in church, that the vestments and vessels were clean, and the priests competent for their duties. He redeemed the lands of the priory that had been mortgaged after the great fire of the cathedral, and left it free from debt, and with a store of iron, lead, planks, timber, coal, salt, and gold, and a full complement of canons.

How many canons there were is not clear, probably fewer than thirty. One of their principal concerns was canon law, or 'decreets', as it was called, and a principal industry of the city must have been the business of the ecclesiastical courts, which dealt with matters of marriage, legitimacy, wills, agreements upon oath, the rights of widows and orphans, the supervision of notaries public, and any cases brought to them by the consent of the disputants. Theology was a secondary interest at this time, and more bishops are found to be graduates in law than in theology. One may be doing them no injustice in suspecting them of more continuous interest in the temporalities of their sees than in their spiritual duties. No doubt many of the clergy had high intellectual gifts, but they applied them to practical affairs and administration rather than to studies that we would consider genuinely academic. Such were the founders of the university and its colleges.

6

THE FOUNDERS OF THE UNIVERSITY

To explain why Bishop Henry Wardlaw founded the university of St Andrews, to the extent that a mere bishop could found such an institution, one has to look far afield and far back in time, to appreciate what was then meant by the term 'university' and what were its values and aims.

Wardlaw's charter of incorporation was dated on 28 February 1412 (1411 by the Old Style), but the intellectual heredity of the idea stretched back centuries before Christ. Without dwelling on the fraternities of learned astronomers and mathematicians and persons of miscellaneous lore who frequented temples in ancient Egypt and the Mesopotamian lands, one may think of Pythagoras and Plato as running universities of sorts. Plato's Academy, founded about 385 BC as a centre for training thinkers and men of affairs, had a strongly mathematical and legal bias, but comprehended all branches of study. From it and similar institutions derived the early medieval university of Constantinople. In the far west of Christendom the great monastic cities of Ireland amounted to universities, and in the seventh century Englishmen resorted thither to be taught, free of charge. Perhaps St Kenny at Kinrymont brought to the site of St Andrews its first tincture of the genuinely academic in the sixth century, but the place did not remain continuously imbued.

While Vikings were inflicting a setback on the Celtic culture of the West, Greek manuscripts were being translated into Arabic by Syrian Christians in the East, giving an impetus to medical and other studies among the Arabs, who then controlled much of the Mediterranean coasts. Partly mediated by Jews, the revived Greek culture resulted in the establishment of the medical school at Salerno, near Naples, in the ninth century. Specializing in medicine, it remained for centuries the leading centre of that branch of science.

The next specialist centre of higher study was Bologna, in central Italy, with its expertise in civil law and the law of the Church, canon law. It took a big step forward about 1140, with the production by Franciscus Gratianus of a handbook of canon law, which became the basis for the enlarged claims of the Popes at Rome to rule the world. Here we see how a single individual in a certain environment and climate of opinion can influence the development of a particular place. By 1200 there were said to be 10,000 students at Bologna, mainly concerned with canon law, and with civil law, the development of old Greco-Roman law. Most of these students were clerics of mature years, often of high rank in the church. Being rackrented by their Bolognese landlords, they received certain privileges and immunities, in 1158, from the Emperor Frederick I Barbarossa. Only about 1200 did Bologna found faculties of medicine and the seven Liberal Arts; and its theology remained for very long a monopoly of the Dominican order of friars.

About the same time as Bologna was booming as a resort of students of canon law, Paris was attracting its thousands for the study of logic as an aid to theology. To grasp the truths of religion it was felt that correct methods of argument were needed. Dialectic was reckoned 'the science of sciences'. Soon after 1100 one William of Champeaux opened at Paris a school for the advanced study of dialectic, just as today one might open a school for advanced motoring, or beauty culture, or judo. It was a private-enterprise venture, but had to secure a licence from the chancellor of the cathedral of Notre Dame, since any private school might compete with the cathedral's own school. One of William of Champeaux's pupils was Abélard, who moved across the river from the Isle of the City to the Left Bank, the Latin Quarter, where the legal control lay with the abbot of Ste Geneviève. A variety of private schools arose both in the episcopal and in the abbatial jurisdiction. Much of their concern was commenting on the theological textbook of Peter the Lombard, Bishop of Paris (died 1160). This was a systematic exposition of the views of the Fathers and Doctors of the Church on such difficult matters as the trinity, predestination, demons, grace, the Last Judgment, hell and heaven. From the swarm of teachers and students there evolved, towards 1170, the University of Paris, recognized by a Pope in 1211. A bull granted by Gregory IX in 1231 recognized three superior Faculties, those of Theology, Canon

Law, and Medicine, and one inferior Faculty, that of Arts. It was the Faculty of Arts that for long predominated in St Andrews.

In the twelfth century Bologna and Paris were by common consent reckoned *studia generalia*, schools to which scholars from everywhere resorted. Their doctors were recognized as entitled to teach anywhere in Christendom. But how were their doctors given their degrees as doctors, which originally meant 'teachers'? Just as there are today colleges of physicians or lawyers, who regulate admission to their professions, so at Bologna in early times the leading lawyers formed colleges (*collegia*, fraternities of colleagues) to confer degrees on those whom they considered qualified. In Paris it was the chancellor of the cathedral who licensed men to teach. The degree of Master of Arts was his licence to begin teaching, to 'incept'. In 1225 the Emperor Frederick II gave a bull to his new school at Naples as a formal recognition. Eight years later Gregory IX gave the masters and doctors of his new university of Toulouse, formed to fight the Albigensian heresy, a bull conveying the right to teach anywhere, *ius ubique docendi*. This right became the hallmark of a university, and even Bologna and Paris secured papal bulls to confirm it to them, in 1292.

Oxford, however, was recognized as a university even without a bull from a Pope, because from about 1168 a great many students had resorted there from different countries. Whatever had been done there earlier, Oxford received a new impetus from the recall of English clerics from Paris as a by-product of Henry II's quarrel with St Thomas à Becket. Its collegiate system developed solidly from 1249, with the foundation of University College. About 1263 John Balliol founded Balliol College, which his widow, the lady Devorguilla, greatly enriched. She also endowed a Franciscan friary at Dundee, where she owned property. Had Devorguilla founded her Franciscan friary at Oxford and given her academic endowment to a university at Dundee, much would have been different in Scottish history, and especially in St Andrews, which, indeed, might never have had a university at all. Dundee might have derived lustre from the poetry of Dunbar and Fergusson, instead of only from that of William McGonagall.

Another Scot who endowed a college abroad was David de Moravia, Bishop of Moray, who gave funds in 1326 for students from his diocese at Paris, where there were in the fourteenth century forty colleges run by different groups. In the same year, 1326, at Bologna the archdeacon founded a college specifically for poor foreign students, regardless of nationality; but it was commoner for patrons to restrict their support. Thus in 1257 a Bishop of Avignon had founded a house at Bologna for eight poor scholars from his diocese, to be supervised by three canons of his cathedral chapter. Bishops of St Andrews might have contented themselves with some such arrangement, supplying funds to keep numbers of students at big international universities like Bologna, Paris, or Oxford, or at the schools of canon and civil law opened in 1303 at Rome for poor foreign students, or the language school founded at Seville in 1254 for the study of Latin and Arabic and other tongues. What moved Bishop Wardlaw to found a university at St Andrews must have been largely the political situation of his time, and the increasing difficulty of getting his aspirants educated at foreign universities.

Apart from that, there was towards 1400 an increasing tendency for rulers to initiate universities for prestige reasons or from a general desire to promote culture locally. Following Italy, France, and Spain, northern rulers began to found universities: Prague (1347), Cracow (1364), Vienna (1365), Heidelberg (1385), Cologne (1388), Erfurt (1392), Leipzig (1409, by migration from Prague of Germans and Poles who resented the dominance of the native Czechs under the inspiration of the reforming Hussite movement). When granting his charter in 1412, Wardlaw was thus early in a movement that took much longer to reach some other fringe areas of Europe. Copenhagen got its papal bull in 1475, Uppsala in 1477. Even Louvain was after St Andrews, in 1426; but soon surpassed it, with its rich municipal patronage, having twenty-eight colleges a century later.

Probably the decisive factor influencing Wardlaw to found his university was the virtual impossibility of sending students to Oxford or Paris at that stage of the Hundred Years' War. Even the young King James I, after a period of schooling in St Andrews Castle, had been kidnapped by the English while voyaging to France, in 1406, to be kept prisoner till 1424. Even if one could sail safely to Paris, the university there, in 1408, had finally abandoned the Avignon Pope, to whom Scotland still gave obedience. For Scots already working in Paris as masters or doctors, the local politics caused trouble, with the brewing-up of the murderous faction fights of Burgundians and Armagnacs. One may suppose that local men of learning in St Andrews had gathered a few young students under their wings, pending the possibility of sending them to French or English or other universities, and that one day, when there were enough students and teachers on the spot, somebody thought they might as well run a university on the premises. Already in May 1410 teachers were reported as having given lectures in the '*studium generale*' of the University in the city of St Andrews'.

A university at that time meant any corporation, and the group of masters and scholars—that is, of teachers and pupils—was not officially a body corporate till Wardlaw issued his charter of incorporation and privileges on 28 February 1412. It is addressed to 'the venerable men, the doctors, masters, bachelors and all scholars dwelling in our city in St Andrews'. It had the consent of the cathedral chapter, and was sealed in the chapter-house built by Lamberton, with its 'curious seats and ceiling'. The aims of the new corporation's studies were 'divine and human law, medicine, and the liberal arts and faculties'. The privileges given include the free power to buy and sell, if the goods sold are not brought specially for trading, everywhere throughout the bishop's regality, without exaction of customs or licences. Beneficed men in the diocese were granted leave of absence to teach or study, provided they supplied vicars for their local functions. The beadles, servants, stationers and parchment-makers of the university, and their wives, children, and maids, were given the same privileges. Exemption was granted from 'all tributes, gifts, exactions, vexations, capitations, watchings, wardings, levies, burdens, and servitudes of carriage'. That is to say, the members of the university were not obliged to guard the castle, pay income taxes or capital levies, or carry teind sheaves to the episcopal mill. The prior and the archdeacon joined the bishop in providing for strict regulation of the prices of bread and ale and other necessities to be supplied by the townsfolk. This is an echo of the old extortionate practices by the Bolognese against their foreign law students.

Application was then made to Pope Benedict XIII, now at the castle of Peñiscola in Aragon, recognized by nobody except Scotland and Aragon. The captive King James and the Scots parliament joined the Church of St Andrews in petitioning for papal authorization. On 28 August 1413 the Pope issued his bull of foundation, his confirmation of Wardlaw's charter, and four minor bulls about details. The foundation was of 'a university of study for the faculties of theology, canon and civil law, arts, medicine, and other lawful faculties'. The six bulls were brought by Henry Ogilvy, MA, on 3 February 1414 amid great bell-ringing, and on the next day, a Sunday, they were promulgated in the refectory of the priory, after which a vast procession went to the high altar of the cathedral, where a 'Te Deum' was sung. Besides the bishop, the prior, and other high ecclesiastics, there were four hundred clerics of one sort or other, also novices and lay brethren, and local spectators. Bonfires and wine-bibbings occupied the rest of the day.

Benedict XIII, in distant Peñiscola, was naïve enough to write thus: '. . . considering also the peace and quietness which flourish in the said city of St Andrews and its neighbourhood, its abundant supply of victuals, the number of its hospices and other conveniences for students, which it is known to possess, we are led to hope that this city, which the divine bounty has enriched with so many gifts, may become the fountain of science, and may produce many men distinguished for knowledge and virtue'. Generations elapsed without these pious hopes being realized in any high degree. But the early struggles of the nascent university make a curious study. Its Chancellor was the bishop, *ex officio*. Its first Rector, or chief executive officer, corresponding to the modern Principal, with functions like those of an English Vice-Chancellor, was the tough-minded Laurence of Lindores, 'Inquisitor of Heretical Pravity', who doubled as Dean of the Faculty of Arts.

This unlovable ecclesiastic was of some international reputation in his day, his commentary on Aristotle's *Physics* being used as far afield as Erfurt, Leipzig, Prague and Cracow. He taught what was called 'the new physics'. He was a champion of Nominalism in the controversy that rent the universities about the nature of *universals*, a problem that still divides the philosophical. A universal is that which every member of a class must have if the same word is to apply to them all. Thus *holiness* is a universal possessed by all things called *holy*. Plato and Aristotle and St Thomas Aquinas held that universals are *real*, though giving different senses to that term. Orthodoxy around 1400 held that universals were real. Against these 'Realists' the Nominalists argued that universals are mere names, not realities, and that the currency of a general word for a series of things does not prove the existence of a general thing named by the word. This controversy became so embittered, and so barren, during the century that Italian universities finally got bored with the whole business, and abandoned logic for rhetoric, the art of public speaking. St Andrews, however, plunged into the conflict. In 1418 a majority in the congregation of the Faculty of Arts decreed that the doctrine of St Albertus Magnus, the Realist commentator on Aristotle, should be prohibited, and only Buridan, the Nominalist textbook-writer, should be studied. The Realist minority had to gnash their teeth for nineteen years, till Laurence of Lindores died, after which they secured a decision from the bishop-chancellor that they might teach the 'way' of Albert or of any other philosopher accepted by the Church.

Securing a monopoly of teaching for Nominalism was only one of the centralizing manœuvres of Laurence of Lindores. His master-mind is detectable at work in the introduction of the Paris statute forbidding students to go from one teacher to another or one 'science' (branch of study) to another, to escape the rod of correction, and prohibiting teachers from touting for pupils. In this prohibition, in 1416, one can have more sympathy for Laurence, whatever his motive. It is obvious that, if clergymen holding benefices could live in St Andrews as teachers, they could lead a comfortable country-club type of life if only they had a pupil or two; and pupils with an eye to ecclesiastical careers would shop around for that teacher who might best advance their prospects, or spare the rod on their persons, or perhaps even teach them. Master-minding the development of the university cannot have been child's play in view of the organizational structure whereby the office of Rector was subject to annual election by all members of the university, including, till 1475, the very youngest students. Since Bologna had started the fashion of having 'nations', and other universities had followed it, St Andrews was divided into four pseudo-nations, each of which chose an *Intrant*, who then voted for the annual Rector. At first these 'nations' were: *Laudonia*, Lothian, from Stirling to the Tweed; *Britannia*, the old Welsh Kingdom of Strathclyde, including Galloway; *Albania*, arbitrarily defined as Fife and a vague area north-west of it up the Tay valley region; and *Angusia*, north of Tay. By 1600 *Fifa* had displaced *Britannia*.

As checks on the Rector's powers the bishop acted as Chancellor and the archdeacon came to act as 'Conservator of Privileges'. There was also a division of powers among the Faculties and their Deans. Here the Faculty of Arts and its Dean came to be the most important and controversial. Very early they voted £5 to have a mace made as symbol of their authority, at a congregation on 17 January 1416. It was apparently made in Paris, but touched up in some way at St Andrews, and first used at a General Council in Perth in October 1418, when the university renounced obedience to its founder, Benedict XIII, and acknowledged Martin V, who tactfully confirmed the validity of his rival's bulls. It is a silver rod, partly gilt, 4' 2½" long, with a hexagonal head like a tabernacle. Six angels carry shields, of the King of Scots, the Duke of Albany (then Regent), the Earl of Mar, the Earl of Douglas (who subscribed for it, with Laurence of Lindores), Bishop Wardlaw, and, nowadays, Archbishop Spottiswoode, whose arms have probably been substituted for those of Pope Benedict XIII. Above the heraldic shields are figures engraved, formerly enamelled also, of St Michael, St Margaret of Antioch, St John the Baptist, the Virgin and Child, St Andrew, and either St Ninian or St Leonard.

Though possessed of this splendid status-symbol, the university owned as yet no property. In 1419 one Robert of Montrose, rector of Cults parish, gave a tenement in South

Street, including part of the present University Library, and some annual rents, to found a 'college of theologians and artists' to be dedicated to St John the Evangelist, with Laurence of Lindores as its head. But nobody else contributed anything.

Then in 1424 King James I was liberated by Henry V, and came home with his English queen, Joan Beaufort. He was a versatile and cultivated prince, and enjoyed coming to the university and listening to lectures and disputations. The more worldly students must have taken him as their social model. He is described as a man of outstanding natural gifts, high-spirited, an excellent wrestler, a champion putter of weights and thrower of hammers, a fast runner, a skilful musician and unsurpassed singer. On the harp he excelled, 'like another Orpheus', the Irish and 'wild Scots, who are distinguished at harping'. In the Scots tongue he was a skilful versifier, and many of his poems and songs were known by heart by Scots people in John Major's day, a century later. His *Kingis Quair* and other works are still highly regarded. Boece says he was an exceedingly light and ready dancer. Here we have already the Renaissance ideal of the all-round man, of which the Admirable Crichton was the great exemplar.

King James had a partiality for Perth, and for the Carthusian monastery which he endowed there in 1429, after negotiations begun before August 1426. Perhaps in that connection he petitioned the Pope in 1426 to have the University of St Andrews removed to Perth, but the Pope proved evasive. The King then decided to improve the existing university. Wardlaw in 1430 gave a tenement to the west of the chapel of St John for building a college for the Faculty of Arts, if that Faculty would subscribe funds. They also decided that year to suppress all the private houses of teachers and concentrate teaching in a single 'pedagogy' under Laurence of Lindores and two colleagues. The King in 1432 confirmed the university's privileges, and later sent his Lord Privy Seal to increase the Dean's powers, restrict the students' freedom, and institute an annual goodwill feast for the Faculty of Arts on 6 May, the day of St John the Evangelist, when he escaped alive from a cauldron of boiling water at the Latin Gate in Rome. The move to abolish private teaching fell through quickly. In 1437 James I was murdered at Perth by some quarrelsome cousins, and Laurence of Lindores died, followed in 1440 by Wardlaw.

It may be noted that in 1433 the founders of the anti-heretical academy had 'bagged' their second heretic, when they secured the burning of a Bohemian physician, Paul Crawar, a disciple of John Hus, who had been burned at Constance in 1415 for maintaining Wyclif's doctrines. Laurence of Lindores, for prosecuting Resby, had received only the rectory of Creich parish, in Fife; but John Fogo, Professor of Theology, who convicted Crawar, was awarded the abbacy of Melrose.

An important man in the early years was James Haldenston, prior from 1419 to 1443. Bower states that 'as Inquisitor he sharply rebuked and confuted the heretics and Lollards'. By early support for Pope Martin V he secured the right to wear the mitre, ring, and pastoral staff, which put a select number of abbots and priors much on the level of bishops. Haldenston also left his mark on the cathedral. In 1409 the gable of the south transept had been blown down in a gale, some stones falling through the chapter-house and dormitory and fatally injuring the sub-prior, Thomas of Cupar. It is possible that the east end of the great church was also damaged. At any rate Haldenston removed the two upper tiers of three round-headed windows and inserted the single Gothic window still surviving above the lowest three of the original nine east windows. As a specimen of the Latinity in favour at St Andrews just before the time of William Dunbar, it is curious to consider Haldenston's epitaph with its elaborate rhymes:

> *Qui docui mores, mundi vitare favores,*
> *Inter doctores sacros sortitus honores,*
> *Vermibus hic donor; et sic ostendere conor*
> *Quod, sicut ponor, ponitur omnis honor.*

Contemporaneous with the founding of the university was the shifting in 1412 of the parish church of Holy Trinity to the centre of the burgh where it now stands. Here land was gifted by Sir William Lindsay of the Byres, a cadet of one of the great families introduced by David I. His main castle was at Struthers near Ceres, and Bishop Trail had made him Heritable Bailie and Seneschal of the regality of St Andrews. Lindsay gave six half-riggs on the north side of South Street, each rigg being ten yards wide. Bishop Wardlaw gave a seventh rigg to the west, in 1430, for enlarging the cemetery, which now forms Church Square. In Market Street the seven riggs are still distinguishable from Kirk Wynd to Logy's Wynd. The graveyard protruded southward to about the middle of the present South Street. The Lindsay charter specified that the new church should be aisled, the purpose of this being to allow ceremonial processions. Lindsay reserved the south-east corner for a chapel of the Holy Trinity, with windows bearing his arms, and the right of burial for his family. He endowed anniversary prayers for his soul. Such 'chantry chapel' arrangements were highly fashionable, and Bishop Kennedy was to make a similar one in his foundation of St Salvator's. Before long the Holy Trinity kirk had a dozen separate altars within it, served by different chaplains for stipends; and some of these helped the emoluments of teachers in the university. The prior of the cathedral priory was rector of Holy Trinity, and appointed a canon as vicar, who in turn appointed as curate a clerk elected by the provost and bailies of the city. Out of seventy-eight known chaplains of Holy Trinity forty-eight are called 'Sir' and thirty have the then higher title of 'Master', so that the parish kirk was better served than most.

On the death of the pious founder Wardlaw the university was fortunate to find him succeeded by Bishop James Kennedy, cousin of King James II. Kennedy was the third son of James Kennedy of Dunure, head of an ancient and powerful family in the south-west, and the Princess Mary Stewart, daughter of Robert III. This lady had four husbands successively, and a dozen or more children, so that many thousands of persons today can trace descent from her. Her first husband was George Douglas, first Earl of Angus, head of the 'Red' Douglases, whom Kennedy used to suppress the 'Black' Douglases of the elder line. Her second husband was the bishop's father; her third Sir William Graham of Kincardine, to whom she bore five sons and a daughter. From them eventually issued the famous Montrose and Claverhouse. Kennedy's successor as bishop, Patrick Graham, was his nephew, grandson of Princess Mary's third marriage. Her fourth husband was Sir William

Edmonstone of Culloden, later of Duntreath, and she lived on till at least 1462. Near the Kennedy home in Carrick lived his maternal aunt, the Princess Margaret Stewart, widow of Archibald, fourth Earl of Douglas and also Duke of Touraine in France, an over-mighty vassal if he should chance to fall out with the King.

The Stewarts had inherited the throne through marrying the daughter of Robert Bruce, and James I's position was, in a wide section of public opinion, somewhat shaken by the belief, erroneous in fact, that his grandmother, Elizabeth Mure, had been improperly married to Robert II, and that the true heir of the throne was Malise, Earl of Strathearn, great-grandson of Robert II's second wife, Euphemia Ross. It was a problem in canon law, the sort of issue that made that branch of study important for churchmen. Archibald, fifth Earl of Douglas, had married the Earl of Strathearn's sister, which increased James I's suspicion of him. King James went so far as to arrest the earl, and his cousin Sir John Kennedy, the future bishop's brother, and gaol them, in 1430. James Kennedy was thus involved in high politics while still very young, and brought up in a quarrelsome cousinhood. The insights gained were useful to him later as churchman and politician.

Born about 1408, James Kennedy came to St Andrews about 1426, at an older age than most entrants, and took his MA in 1429. In 1430, when his brother was arrested, the King stopped a grant to him from the customs of Cupar, and the young student went off to the new University of Louvain, where he graduated as Bachelor of Decreets (canon law). In 1437 James I made him Bishop of Dunkeld. He took his episcopal duties seriously, making the parsons and vicars reside in their parishes and preach and visit the sick. He is said to have visited every kirk in his diocese four times a year. That might have happened at Dunkeld, but the diocese of St Andrews, where he came in 1440, was too big, and he was by that time too busy with politics.

That same year, in November 1440, two careerist politicians, Livingston and Crichton, who were ruling the country for the ten-year-old James II, invited to dinner in Edinburgh castle the young sixth Earl of Douglas and his brother. At the conclusion

of the repast a black bull's head was set on the table, a bad sign.
The young noblemen were then murdered. It was said that the
conspiracy had the goodwill of their grand-uncle, who inherited
their estates as seventh Earl. He was known as Earl James
'the Gross', being so corpulent as to have become incapable
of exertion. The gross earl's son William succeeded in 1443
as eighth Earl of Douglas, and proceeded to make a power-
political deal with the most powerful magnate benorth the
Tay, David Lindsay, third Earl of Crawford. Bishop Kennedy,
supporting his cousin, the boy King James II, then allied
himself with the Crichton faction.

Lord Crawford took umbrage at this, and in January 1445
conspired with his wife's cousin, Alexander Ogilvie of Inverquharitie, to harry the bishop's lands and drive off the episcopal
cattle. Though doubtless short of milk, the bishop was not
without resource. Donning his mitre and clutching his pastoral
staff, he seized bell, book, and candle, and solemnly cursed the
earl and his accomplices, excommunicating them for a twelve-
month. Nor were the prelate's comminations ineffective.
Ogilvie and Crawford shortly fell out. The Tironians of the
wealthy abbey of Arbroath had made Crawford's son Alexander, the Master of Crawford, their bailie or justiciar, to take
charge of their legal matters. He brought in a swarm of roughnecks who ate the monks' victuals and drank their beverages.
The monks therefore deposed the Master, and appointed as his
successor Alexander Ogilvie of Inverquharitie. The Master
and his roughnecks seized the abbey and the town, and recruited more men-at-arms from the Douglases and Hamiltons
in Strathclyde. Ogilvie was lucky to secure reinforcement by a
rising magnate in the person of Sir Alexander Seton, Lord
Gordon and future Earl of Huntly, who had chanced to stay
the night at Inverquharitie, on his way from Edinburgh to
Strathbogie. Bishop Leslie remarks that it was 'ane ancient
custom among the Scottishmen that, wheresoever they happen
to lodge, they defend their hosts from all hurt, even to the
shedding of their blood and losing of their lives for them, if
need be, so long as their meat is undigested in their stomachs'.
On Sunday 13 January 1446 the Ogilvies and the 'gay Gordons'
marched on Arbroath, to deal with the Master of Crawford

and his Lindsays, proverbially 'light and gay'. They found them drawn up ready for battle. Meantime the old Earl of Crawford, having heard what was afoot, galloped out from his palace at Dundee to prevent a conflict. As he approached he was mortally wounded, with a spear-thrust through his mouth and neck, by a man strange to the district. Enraged at this, the Lindsays attacked, and slew five hundred of the Ogilvies and Gordons, for the loss of a hundred men on their own side. The dying Earl of Crawford was carried to his castle of Finhaven, to which was also conveyed the wounded Alexander Ogilvie, his former confederate in pillaging the bishop's possessions. On learning that her husband was fatally injured, the strong-minded Countess Marjory went to the bedroom of her cousin, Alexander Ogilvie, whom the surgeons hoped to cure, and proceeded to smother him with a featherbed. The public then observed the interesting fact that the Battle of Arbroath had occurred just twelve months after the two men now dead had harried the bishop's lands. Earl David's corpse could not be buried till Kennedy sent the prior of St Andrews to take off the excommunication.

Another specimen of the ferocity of the times was seen in 1452, when James II, now aged twenty-one, sent an invitation to the eighth Earl of Douglas to visit him at Stirling. They dined and supped amicably in the castle. After supper the young King tried to persuade the earl to break his 'band' with the fourth Earl of Crawford, known as 'Earl Beardie', or 'the Tiger', who had plotted with Macdonald of the Isles and the Yorkist party in England to dethrone James. Douglas refused, and the young King, 'James of the Fiery Face', as he was called, took out his dirk and plunged it into the earl. The gesture was reminiscent of the stab delivered by his ancestor Robert Bruce upon the Red Comyn in the Dumfries cloister. As there, the King's friends came in and proceeded to 'mak siccar'. Sir Alexander Seton, now Earl of Huntly, soon thereafter got his own back on the Lindsays for their victory at Arbroath by defeating the rebellious Crawford at the Hair Cairn near Brechin.

In dealing with the coalition of magnates plotting against him James II relied much on the sagacity of Kennedy. Posterity relished the tale of the bishop's taking a sheaf of arrows and showing the King that they could not be broken when bound together but were readily frangible when separated. Kennedy used the Red Douglases to ruin the Black Douglases, and elevated a series of new minor lords, including the Homes, to replace the over-mighty earldom of Douglas on the Borders. James II afterwards began to pursue lines of his own without the bishop's support; but, after he had been killed in 1460 by the explosion of a gun at the siege of Roxburgh castle, Kennedy cheerfully looked after his widow, Mary of Guelders, though her indiscreet amours were a vexation to him, and guarded the young King James III, who had indeed been born in the castle of St Andrews.

Kennedy's contribution to the guiding of the realm in troubled times was admirable, and his social and financial reforms merit respect; but our immediate concern is with his service to the university by founding St Salvator's College. (Here let it be noted that *Sanctus Salvator* is the Holy Saviour, Jesus Christ Himself; and that the correct traditional pronunciation in the phrase *St Salvator's College* is with a short *a* in the middle syllable, as in the words *orator* and *senator*. The poet Dunbar, an early alumnus, has a verse scanning that way: *Sanct Salvatour, send silver sorrow.* Some older Scots folk within living memory sounded the *t* as a *d*, saying 'Sant Salvador's'; and possibly Bishop Kennedy said it that way.)

St Salvator's was founded, on 27 August 1450, as a college for students of theology and arts, with a twofold function. It was both a seminary for the training of priests and a collegiate church for the performance of daily worship. One door of the ante-chapel opened on to the public road, on the north side of North Street, and the other into the quadrangle. The fabric of the kirk is substantially as Kennedy made it, but the fretted roof has gone, and the original window tracery. The bishop's tomb, made probably at Tournai, and originally designed to stand between pillars in the cathedral, survives somewhat defaced, with the loss of its gilding and colours, and its symbolization obscured. In 1842 the tomb was opened, and the pious founder's physical remains were studied. It appears that Kennedy stood five feet eight inches, was broad-shouldered and muscular, and right-handed; he suffered from rheumatoid arthritis, poor fellow, and possibly bronchitis. In 1842 St Andrews was a hotbed of phrenology, the science that was as much in vogue then as psychoanalysis is now. The local phrenologists got together around the episcopal skull and pronounced that the perceptive organs were better than the reflective, so that 'in point of high intellect the head was somewhat disappointing. Firmness was very large, and Cautiousness, Destructiveness, Adhesiveness and Benevolence were all of super-average magnitude, pointing to a man of determined character, but generous disposition towards his fellow-creatures.'

As head of his new college Kennedy appointed a Provost, who had to be a Master of Theology, and gave him as prebend the teinds of Cults parish. Second in command was a Licentiate in Theology, with Kemback as his prebend. Third was a Bachelor in the same sublime science, drawing the teinds of Dunino. The foundation provided also for four Masters of Arts, all of whom were to study theology, and two of them concurrently to give tuition in arts; and for six poor scholars or clerks. The total of thirteen foundationers was modelled on Christ and his Twelve Apostles. Kilmany parish teinds were applied for general support of the new institution. On 4 April 1458 Kennedy issued a revised foundation charter because some articles in the first had been obscure and others superfluous, while some matters had not been dealt with at all. The Provost now had to give a theological lecture once a week, the Licentiate thrice, and the Bachelor on every lawful day. The Provost had to preach a sermon to the general public four times a year, the Licentiate six times. They all had to reside in the college. The major business of the college was divine service, and prayer for the welfare of the souls of the bishop's royal and other kin, and his predecessors in the see, benefactors and the faithful departed.

In addition to the bishop's donations of a mace and splendid church furnishings, the college kirk was enriched by other benefactors with altars and chaplainries, for example by Provost John Liston, who in 1500 endowed a chaplainry of St Katharine for a lecturer in canon law. Besides the six poor scholars on the foundation the college attracted considerable numbers of commoners from wealthy families, and became the focus of fashionable student life.

The most impressive feature of the buildings was the entrance tower, rising with its spire some 125 feet. The stone spire is a replacement towards 1560 of a timber and lead spire built about 1530. Kennedy left the tower with a flat top. The present unsightly parapet and clock are Victorian additions. The archway under the great tower led to a quadrangle with the great hall and the Schools, or lecture-rooms, on the west side, and dwelling accommodation on the north and east. There was a small court with a cloister on the north side of the church, and a cemetery to the south. The flattened archway with the Kennedy arms was rebuilt in 1846, when the cemetery was removed and its boundary wall moved northward to form the present enclosure. In 1460 Kennedy put in the belfry a bell $31\frac{1}{2}''$ in diameter and $22''$ high, which he named Katharina. It was recast in 1609 and 1686. This bell was the 'Katharine' that summoned the poor scholars from their beds to perform the divine offices. Possibly from it was evolved the mythical *belle*, the Lady Kate Kennedy, niece of the pious founder, in whose honour the students made and currently make an annual procession.

What studies were pursued in the early university, and with what degree of success? Some light on these matters emerges from the minutes of the Faculty of Arts between 1413 and 1588, edited with loving care by Dr Annie Dunlop, the indefatigable biographer of Bishop Kennedy. It is but a gloomy light for those who expect brilliant innovations in the natural sciences or works of profound humanistic erudition as common products of academic activity. But the light is hardly gloomier than what might be observed in other universities of the age. One has to recall that it was primarily a seminary for priests, many of whom were intending to be bureaucrats, and not a scientific or historical research institute. Moreover, the students mostly arrived very young, at thirteen or so, to commence a four-year curriculum in Arts, boarding with 'regent masters', called Regents, in private houses until college residences were available.

Earlier in the development of universities there had been a Seven Liberal Arts course, consisting of the three-way *Trivium*, namely Grammar, Rhetoric, and Logic, and of the four-way *Quadrivium*, Music, Arithmetic, Geometry, and Astronomy. But by the fifteenth century entrant students were supposed to have been grounded in Latin grammar before they arrived. Substantial land-owners would have about their castles a chaplain-secretary capable of teaching some sort of more or less canine Latin, and merchants in burghs could have their sons taught as much or more at the grammar schools. Usually a boy would come to college in October for incorporation, his parent having made a deal with some master offering board and tuition. Latin was the sole medium of teaching, and in theory also the language of the playground.

The backbone of the curriculum was Aristotle, a series of set books in Latin translation. The regent would dictate from the set book, and then discuss what had been taken down by the pupil. Examination was by organized disputation. In the first year the pupil was called a *bejaunus*, from French *bec jaune*, 'yellowbill', the nestling bird gaping for nutriment. He copied out the elementary rules of disputation contained in the *Summulae* of Peter Hispanus, Pope John XXI. In the second year he took down Aristotle's *Logic* from dictation. The actual written copies had to be submitted for inspection at examinations. After eighteen months, if aged fifteen or over, the student reached the degree of Bachelor, and then took another two and a half years to qualify for the licence to teach, becoming a Licentiate, and could proceed to the masterate. The third year was devoted to Aristotle's *Physics* and *Natural Philosophy* (as the Faculty of Arts regulation of 1471 puts it), and the fourth to writing out at least the first seven books of Aristotle's *Metaphysics*. Great stress was laid on ability to argue a question. After all there were heretics and schismatics to be confuted. The debating of sophisms, *sophismata*, was a public exercise.

Regents were supposed to charge students sixpence every time they absented themselves and had to have a lesson dictated to them afresh. Regents had to visit pupils nightly in their studies, but overfamiliarity was discouraged, as breeding contempt. The Faculty had to censure Regents for conniving at students' irregularities. Masters of Arts who were not Regents were forbidden to take students into the town or 'other suspect places', or to take them by the arms in church or elsewhere. Students found guilty of misdemeanours had to beg pardon on their knees, and were liable to public flogging by the Regent in presence of the Dean and others. Nocturnal perambulations were prohibited, and the wearing of fashionable clothes, and the carrying of dirks and other weapons. But dispensation seems always to have been possible on payment. One has even the notion that regulations were made to be dead-lettered or broken on payment of a dispensing fee. Dispensation from examinations was a way of raising money. In listing candidates on the final merit list examiners took account of nobility of birth. Where the pecking-order was particularly close, the manœuvre was to present a group of candidates together in a bracket, *in circulo*. In the fourth year *magistrands*, or candidates for the mastership, submitted to *responsions* before Christmas and *disputations* in Lent, having paid fees in advance. They had to sit on a black stone from 2 to 4 p.m. and be quizzed on the set books.

The baccalaureate was not so much a degree in itself as a certificate of fitness to proceed further. The *licence* at the end of the fourth year was granted by the Chancellor, or his Vice-chancellor, to the kneeling licentiands, as a permit to lecture and dispute anywhere in the world; but there followed later the more solemn ceremony of graduation as Master of Arts. It derived from the Roman slave-owner's manumission of a slave. The magistrand ascended on to a chair among the masters present, and was given a bonnet (*birettum*, beret) for his head, a ring for his finger, and an open book, symbolizing that he was wedded to the duty of revealing the secrets of the written word. At first only one master was allowed to graduate at a time, for he had to give a dinner, including the provost, bailies, and 'honest citizens' of the burgh, and to present bonnets to the examiners and gloves to the rest. The Faculty minutes lament the propensity of students to waste money on personal extravagances in clothing and other matters, while professing poverty when it came to paying fees. They even had the impudence to offer doctors and masters poor-quality gloves such as servants might wear. The 'mother Faculty' appointed a committee of ten persons, who advised that a bachelor's promotion expenses should be limited to forty shillings and a master's to four pounds, unless he happened to be illustrious and outstandingly provided with benefices, in which case he might be given a dispensation to display his own magnificence and do honour to himself and the Faculty. They even specified that gloves should be of high quality and ornamented with silk round the thumbs.

Once duly made Master of Arts, the new MA was under an obligation to lecture for two years. These were days before the invention of printing, let alone of recording-machines. But, as usual, the obligation to lecture could be dispensed with for cash. A curious functionary of the Faculty was the Quodlibetarius, introduced in 1452 as chairman of the type of disputation called a *Quodlibet*, 'anything you like'. It was a tiresome situation, as disputation tended to descend into defamation, or flyting, like the versified reciprocal vilification of Dunbar and Kennedy. So a salary had to be fixed for the Quodlibetarius, and a public feast in his honour. The Beadle too, a student who carried the mace, received his perquisites.

Our information about the other Faculties is less than about that of Arts. Theology continued to have its stronghold in the priory, as before the founding of the university and the two colleges of St John and St Salvator. The Faculty of Law belatedly came upsides with that of Arts by having a mace made for canon law, some time before 1457. It is of Scottish craftsmanship, based on the Arts mace, but has a larger head. The lower set of six armorial shields has been removed, but the second stage has the original holy persons: St Andrew, St Peter, the Trinity, the Virgin and Child, St Mungo, and St John the Baptist.

In 1461 Kennedy had a mace made for St Salvator's College by Johne Maiel, 'Gouldsmithe and Verlette off Chamber til the Lord the Dalfyne [the Dauphin of France]', at Paris. It is of silver gilt, on an iron core. A figure of the Holy Saviour stands on a globe set in a hexagonal shrine on the head. Three sides of the shrine are open; the other three have castellated projections, each supporting an angel with symbols of the

Passion—pillar, cross, and spear. Below the shrine are the mouths of a dungeon with three chained devils, who hold shields with the arms of the see of St Andrews, Kennedy, and an imperial orb, symbolizing St Salvator's College. Alternating with the devils are a king, a bishop, and a Franciscan friar. In 1458 Kennedy had founded a friary, where now is Greyfriars Gardens, for Observant friars of the Franciscan order. Kennedy's mace is also adorned with three balconies round the rod, set with angels portraying the parable of the talents, monks reading Holy Writ, preachers, and worshippers. The base has a floral ornament with four lions. The rod has a spiral band with James Kennedy's initials, and columbine flowers, symbolizing the bishop's dove-like simplicity, with which the Earls of Crawford and the Black Douglases had become so familiar.

Many students in the episcopal city did not trouble with Arts, but proceeded straight to Law. This presumably led to bad blood, for in 1457 the Artists are found refusing permission to the School of Decreets, the canon lawyers, to open out a window overlooking the grounds of the Pedagogy of St John. The burgh too could be quarrelsome on occasion, and in 1444 Kennedy had to smooth down the ruffled citizens, who had taken the trouble to find out from Cologne what were the legal rights of universities in trading cities. A more elaborate quarrel arose soon after Kennedy's death in 1465, when the man he had appointed as Provost of St Salvator's, the Realist John Athilmer, set off to Rome and secured a bull, in 1469, granting St Salvator's the right to run its own examinations for degrees in arts and theology. In 1470 it came to physical violence. One John Oliphant assaulted the Dean of Arts with a sword and a dirk. Even worse, Masters, chaplains, Bachelors, and students went on the night of 12 March and attacked the Dean and others with bows and arrows and other weapons. The Rector excommunicated Athilmer and nineteen others. A year later a Provincial Council had settled the matter, and St Salvator's submitted. The Faculty then ordained that all wealthy students must board either in the Pedagogy of St John or in the College of St Salvator, thus undermining the economic basis of the private boarding-houses.

Concerning the availability of books, there were no doubt quite a few in the priory, but the university as such had no library till 1456. It was then given a book by Alan Cant, Dean of the Chapel Royal, namely Plutarch's *Magna Moralia*. The edifying tome was borrowed by the Provost of St Salvator's, who lost it. Some more books were given thirty years later, in 1496. Meantime printing from movable types had been invented, a technological innovation that was to promote both reformation of the kirk and the advancement of science.

Both were slow to develop in St Andrews; nor did Kennedy's successor in the see do anything to promote them. He was Kennedy's half-brother's son, Patrick Graham, a St Andrews graduate who had been Bishop of Brechin for two years. He paid the Pope 3,300 gold florins for his translation to the wealthier diocese. Needing money he secured for himself the priory of Pittenweem and the abbacy of Paisley *in commendam*, as it was called. Originally a 'commend' was a means of enabling a bishop to protect a monastery by recovering lands wrongfully occupied by some lay lord, or by tightening up discipline that had become lax. But it was felt offensive by aspirants to benefices that the country's richest bishop should help himself to more revenue-producing positions. Graham's opponents secured an Act of the Scots Parliament, in 1466, prohibiting the holding of such livings *in commendam*. After some further embarrassments, Graham went off to Rome and, without consulting the other Scots bishops, the King, or the Parliament, secured from Sixtus IV a bull, dated 17 August 1472, erecting St Andrews into a metropolitan see, with himself as Archbishop.

Whatever the desirability of such an office, the naïve racketeer had gone the wrong way about getting it. For half a century Kings and Parliaments had been trying to stop the outflow of hard cash to Rome by job-hunters in the kirk, and here was a flagrant breach of their enactments. Moreover, Sixtus IV was toying with the notion of a crusade against the Turks, who had captured Constantinople twenty years before. He made Graham nuncio to collect money, including a tithe of the incomes of the Scots clergy. Preferring to 'keep their ain fish guts for their ain seamaws', the bishops, led by Spens of Aberdeen, set the King's mind against the new Archbishop. Before he landed on his return he was treated as a lawbreaker. James III took into his own hand the temporalities of the see. Meantime Sixtus IV had not been paid his fees for the elevation, and excommunicated the offending prelate. He was put under house arrest in his castle, while letters went to the Pope accusing him of grave crimes. After due inquisition, Sixtus IV deposed him, on 9 January 1478, as a heretic, schismatic, forger, perjurer, blasphemer, and simoniac (that is, one guilty of simony, the buying or selling of benefices). The deposed Archbishop was gaoled successively in the monasteries of Inchcolm, Dunfermline, and Lochleven, went mad, and before long died.

Some aspects of the Italian Renaissance were exemplified by the next Archbishop, William Schevez (1478–97). Of a local family that had provided some minor episcopal officials, he graduated MA in 1456, with Graham, and later studied at Louvain medicine and astrology, 'sciences' then closely allied. In 1471 he became a physician at James III's court, and in 1474 Archdeacon of St Andrews, still doing odd personal jobs for the King, such as paying for 'the sewing of the King's sarks' and looking after the silver horse-trappings of the royal chargers. When Graham fell from royal favour, Schevez was put in as coadjutor bishop and vicar-general, to run the revenues of the see into the King's pockets, one may imagine. After Graham had been deposed, Schevez quickly stepped into his chair. Cannily he got the King and Parliament to ratify to him all the lands and privileges held by his predecessors. The King also granted lands in Fife to the archbishop's nephew. Unfortunately for Schevez, he was grouped by the bulk of the nobility as merely one of the low-born favourites to whom the King showed such marked preference at court, among them an architect, a tailor, and a musician.

The King's younger brothers, the Duke of Albany and the Earl of Mar, were bred in the warrior tradition, and lacked his taste for the fine arts. They conspired with sundry noblemen, or were suspected of doing so, and James arrested them. Mar died in gaol. Albany escaped to France, where Louis XI, that wiliest of monarchs, exploited him to embroil Scotland anew with

England. Albany was sent over to England, where he made a deal with the Yorkist King Edward IV. Albany was acknowledged by Edward as King of Scotland, holding as vassal of the King of England. In return, Albany would hand over to the English Berwick, Lochmaben, Liddesdale, Eskdale, and Annandale. This was much less than Edward Balliol had ceded to Edward III. An English army then marched north, and James III marched south to face it. At Lauder the Scots magnates halted, and put their heads together with Archibald, Earl of Angus, the Red Douglas, thereafter known as 'Bell-the-cat'. The result of their conference was the hanging of the King's favourites over the local bridge. Schevez was perhaps lucky not to be among them, but shortly thereafter he was compelled to resign his archbishopric and content himself with the humbler see of Moray. St Andrews was given to the King's uncle, Andrew Stewart, but the Pope never confirmed him: in the upshot Stewart got Moray, and Schevez returned to St Andrews. His affairs and King James's were somewhat eased when Richard III overthrew Edward IV in England, and Albany ceased to be a trouble. But fresh embarrassment arose in 1485 when the new Pope, Innocent VIII, began dunning the archbishop for moneys due. In prolonged and obscure negotiations Schevez seems to have come out on top, going personally to Rome to deal directly with the Pope. On 27 March 1487 Innocent VIII made St Andrews what was called a primatial church, and created the archbishop a *legatus natus*, with all the rights in Scotland enjoyed by the Archbishops of Canterbury as primates in England.

This piece of one-upmanship by St Andrews aroused the jealousy of Schevez's travelling companion at Rome, Robert Blacader, who had been Bishop of Aberdeen from 1480 to 1483, and thereafter Bishop of Glasgow. While still at Rome Blacader went to the Pope and secured exemption from the archiepiscopal overlordship of St Andrews. On coming home Schevez ran into worse trouble.

In Berwickshire there was an old Benedictine priory of Coldingham, which had for generations been virtually owned and run by the Border family of Home. In 1487 the Pope, Innocent VIII, suppressed the priory and granted half its

revenues for the Chapel Royal at St Andrews. This made Lord
Home very cross. He mobilized his neighbours the Hepburns,
and remoter magnates like the Earls of Angus and Argyll.
Their coalition seized the King's eldest son, aged sixteen,
the future James IV. On the King's side there came together
the Earls of Crawford, Erroll, and Huntly, and Archbishop
Schevez. Among the King's partisans was David Lindsay,
second Lord Lindsay of the Byres, bailie of the archbishop's
regality. He led a thousand cavalry and three thousand foot
from Fife to join the head of the Lindsay clan, Lord Crawford,
who mobilized a comparable force from Angus. Lindsay of the
Byres appeared at the trysting-place, riding 'ane great grey
courser' of remarkable beauty and celerity. The loyal baron
presented the noble quadruped to King James, asserting that it
could beat any horse in Scotland, if the King would but sit
well.

After preliminary parleyings, the rival coalitions faced each
other at Sauchieburn, near Stirling. King James then called for
the great grey horse, and went up to an elevated place to view
the enemy's array. The rebel lords had in their forefront Prince
James, with the royal standard displayed. The sight reminded
the superstitious King of a prophecy made to him long before
by a witch, that he should be destroyed and put down by the
nearest of his kin. It is not known what astrological predictions
Schevez had supplied for the day. The King then withdrew,
while the rival lords started battling. When the Annandale men
advanced, shouting their slogan, the King spurred away. As he
rode through Bannockburn the horse leapt a burn and threw
off the monarch at the door of a mill. Falling in his heavy
armour, he got a concussion. The miller and his wife dragged
him indoors, not knowing who he was. When he revived he
asked for a priest, and told them he had been their King that
morning. The miller's wife fetched in a priest who was passing,
the rebel Lord Gray's secretary, as it chanced. He came in and
asked the King if he would survive, given good medical
attention. The King said he thought he might survive, but
would like a priest to give him his sacrament. The priest
answered, 'That shall I do hastily,' as Pitscottie recounts, 'and
pullit out ane whinger [knife], and gave him four or five straiks

even to the heart, and syne gat him on his back and had him away'.

The ambitious Bishop Blacader of Glasgow promptly sided with the successful rebels who controlled the young King James IV, but nothing was undertaken directly against Schevez, even though he had lost his patron. Blacader lobbied at Rome to have his see made an archbishopric, and James IV backed his petition; but the Dean and Chapter of Glasgow opposed it. So did Schevez. Both prelates began to give away diocesan lands to bribe important nobles, and Schevez made over to the Earl of Argyll the St Andrews lands around Muckhart. On 9 January 1492 Blacader was made archbishop, but without the status of primate and *legatus natus*, so that St Andrews was still a step ahead. Blacader then intrigued to be made a Cardinal, and enlisted Ferdinand and Isabella of Spain on his side, but was disappointed by the Pope.

In these ludicrous squabbles of the princes of the Church nothing was done to advance either true religion or university studies. Glasgow had started a university in 1451, and Aberdeen set up another in 1494, at King's College, Old Aberdeen, both of them, like St Andrews, at that time small and without attractions for foreign scholars, but not quite hopeless or useless. It was a redeeming feature in Schevez that he owned, and apparently loved, some medical and other books.

A scandalous piece of royal jobbery was perpetrated on the death of Schevez. James IV put in his eighteen-year-old brother, James, Duke of Ross, as administrator of the arch-diocese, with an understanding from the Pope, Alexander VI, that he would be consecrated archbishop on reaching the canonical minimum age of thirty. He was called James, like his elder brother, because the senior was a weakly infant, and the parents wished, in the event of his premature death, to have another James handy to maintain the succession. The Duke of Ross was further enriched with the abbeys of Holyrood, Dunfermline, and Arbroath, and the chancellorship of the Kingdom. He seems to have done nothing in his brief life but absorb revenues and order a tomb from Bruges, for £25. He died early in 1504, and had a splendid nocturnal interment at St Andrews in the chancel of the cathedral, amid torches and tapers, and the fluttering of 336 black flags, bearing his coat of arms, issued to the processing mourners.

James IV kept the vacant archbishopric in the family once more, this time by providing to it his bastard son Alexander Stewart, borne to him by Marion Boyd of Bonshaw, about 1493. It may seem curious to some that James IV, a pious Sabbath-observer, who would not ride a horse on Sunday, even to go to Mass, should have fathered several offspring outside the bonds of holy matrimony, and that he should put one of his bastard boys into the chief ecclesiastical office of the Kingdom. But in the prevailing corruption of the Church probably nobody was astonished. The see was kept vacant, while the King drew the revenues. Then in 1502 the young Alexander was made Archdeacon of St Andrews, and in 1504 administrator, with the promise that he would be consecrated archbishop when he reached the age of twenty-six. The venal Borgia Pope Alexander VI seems even to have made the boy a Cardinal, for there is a sealing extant describing him as such. This job too could have been done, for a pecuniary consideration, without immediate publicity, *in petto* as the Italians termed it.

Moderns may find it droll that the royal father styles his well-provided young bastard son 'the most reverend and venerable Father in Christ'; but such were the conventions then.

James IV was a fashionable Renaissance prince, and employed a secretary with a good command of the Latin tongue, Patrick Panter. After teaching by him the future archbishop was sent to Italy to be tutored by the great Erasmus, the leading Humanist of the age. With his bastard half-brother, the Earl of Moray, the boy archbishop (as he was called, though never consecrated), enjoyed the most up-to-date teaching. Erasmus took a liking to the pair of them, and in his *Adagia* recalled their happy studies at Siena, when commenting on the saying *Spartam nactus es. Hanc orna.* He wrote of:

Alexander, Archbishop by the title of St Andrews, . . . endowed with all the gifts of perfect manhood. A graceful figure he had, a rare dignity of mien, and the stature of a hero of myth. His disposition was very quiet; yet he was eagerness itself to learn all the branches of knowledge. I lived with him at one time at Siena, and trained him in the maxims of rhetoric and in Greek letters. What a quick mind he had! How happily endowed! How flexible! How comprehensive! At one and the same time he was studying the lawyers, far from attractive by reason of their barbarisms and the loathsome verbosity of their commentators: he had lessons on rhetoric and would declaim on a prescribed theme, exercising both the pen and the tongue: he was learning Greek and rendered his daily portion at the stated time. In the afternoon he would turn to music, the monochords [*a set of strings used to teach intonation in singing*], the pipe, the lute; sometimes, too, he would sing. Even at meals he would pursue his studies: his chaplain kept reading some instructive book, the Pontifical Decrees, St Jerome, or St Ambrose, and never stopped unless one or other of the doctors at the table pointed out something or Alexander did not follow and asked a question. Again, there might be tales from the company, but short ones, and with a literary flavour. In fact, his whole time was given to study, with the exception of what was devoted to religious services or to sleep.

Any spare time the young student had he bestowed upon history, says Erasmus. 'He loved a jest, the jest of the scholar, not made to wound, flavoured not with the coarse wit of Momus but with the finer sort of Mercury.' Telling how the young man was killed beside his father at Flodden, Erasmus exclaims: 'What hadst thou to do with the war-god, most gross of all the deities the poets sing, thou who wast consecrated to the Muses, nay to Christ himself?'

Enriched with the abbey of Dunfermline and the priory of Coldingham, held *in commendam*, the Archbishop and Cardinal designate came home from Italy in 1509 with plans to do something for the university as its Chancellor. Fresh from Erasmus's influence, he aimed to revive the languishing Faculty of Arts in the Pedagogy of St John. He began by rebuilding the old chapel of St John, and gave it the teinds of Tarvit parish with a view to erecting it into a college. But the scheme was not carried out. Instead, the Archbishop joined with the energetic prior, John Hepburn, to found a new college, later known as St Leonard's. In the north-west part of the priory precinct there was a hospital or hospice of St Leonard, originally designed for

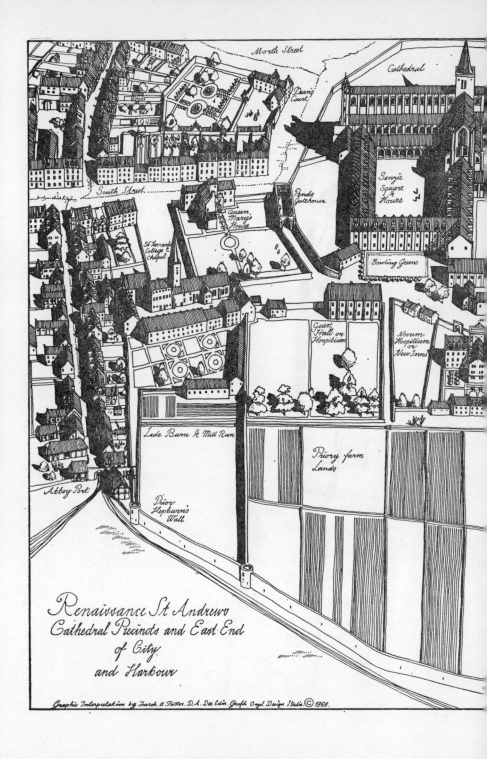

Renaissance St Andrews
Cathedral Precincts and East End
of City
and Harbour

Graphic Interpretation by Frerk. a. Pitter. D.A. Des Edin. Graph. Oxyl Design Studio © 1968.

St Regulus's
tower &
Chapel

St Mary's
of the Rock

Provost's House

Tidal
Harbour

Holy Well
Granary

Sea Yett
or Gate

Sands

Mill

Teindo Barns

Teinda
Yett or
Gate

pilgrims to the shrine of St Andrew. From the Culdees it had passed to the Augustinians. In their joint foundation charter, on 20 August 1512, the Archbishop and prior frankly admit that the relics had been ceasing to work miracles: 'whereas in the course of time the Christian faith had been established in our parts, and miracles and pilgrimages, as we may without impiety believe, had in a measure ceased, so that the Hospital was without pilgrims'. Earlier priors had put into the vacant Hospital 'certain women chosen by reason of old age, who give little or no return in devotion or virtue'. Accordingly they were now resolved to create a college from the Hospital and its endowments, 'with intent to steady the tossing bark of Peter and make better the church of God, so far at least as it is committed to our own jurisdiction and power, now that it is falling away from virtuous exercises'. We feel here a breath of the Reformation. Some people are apt to overlook the fact that the movement for reform arose within the church as well as outside it. One may speak of a Catholic Reformation of an evolutionary type, though overshadowed in its early stages by the revolutionary results of the breakaway Protestant Reformation in several countries.

Prior Hepburn's immediate concern was reform of his own Augustinian order, and especially of the cathedral chapter under his charge. He needed recruits of good quality. Therefore what he instituted was called 'the College of Poor Clerks of the Church of St Andrews'. Its Principal Master had to be a canon of the priory and a graduate in theology. Of the four chaplains two were to work as Regents. Provision was made for twenty poor scholars. Hepburn was a precisian, and prescribed minutely for his collegians, their dress and rations. They slept two to a room, and were sent out once a week, in crocodile formation, to sport on the links, eschewing such 'dishonourable games' as football. At a later date the St Leonard's youths seem to have conflicted with their more fashionable contemporaries from St Salvator's, for in 1612 the Scottish Privy Council decreed that 'quhen the occasioun of their recreatioun and pastyme is presentit, that then the studentis of Sanct Leonardis addresse thameselffis to St Nicolas feildis [*beside the East sands*] and the studentis of the Auld

College [*St Salvator's*] to the commoun linkis [*by the West sands, the modern golf-courses*]'.

Till 1545 St Leonard's College, as it was usually called, was an annexe of the priory, but then it became a college on much the same basis as St Salvator's. And in the meantime, in 1537, Archbishop James Betoun had founded St Mary's. Prior Hepburn appears to have rebuilt the twelfth-century church of St Leonard for his new college, and erected to the west of it a square tower, midway in height between the Holy Trinity's and that of St Salvator's kirk. Later the church was extended eastward. It formed the north side of a quadrangle having a college hall and living-quarters. The south range, rebuilt in the early seventeenth century, survives, somewhat transmogrified, as part of St Leonard's School. The cemetery to the north of St Leonard's kirk was for folk of the parish formed by lands given to the hospital as endowments. The kirk was both a parish kirk and a chapel for the collegians. Besides the twenty 'poor clerks', who were presumably intended as novices of the Augustinian order, there were other students enrolled, some of whom played leading parts in the impending Reformation.

The foundation of St Leonard's College in 1512 completed a century from Bishop Wardlaw's charter of 1412. In that century the university had attained no more than a conventional respectability in the traditional academic subjects of the period, but it had helped to foster the talent of a notable trio of poets in the Scots tongue. The great *Makar* William Dunbar graduated in 1479; Gavin Douglas, later Bishop of Dunkeld and translator of Virgil's *Aeneid* into Scots verse, in 1494; and Sir David Lindsay of the Mount, Lord Lyon King of Arms, in 1508. The vitality of his play, *Ane Pleasant Satyre of the Thrie Estaits*, in which he attacked abuses in Kirk and State, was strikingly manifested when Sir Tyrone Guthrie revived it at the Edinburgh International Festival in 1948. That this important poetry was the most notable product of a century of academic activity is just another proof that the spirit bloweth where it listeth, and the extracurricular studies of students are often the most vital contribution of universities to the advance of culture. Another extracurricular activity, and indeed an

I

activity that was to achieve a worldwide vogue, was the Golf, to the origins of which cult a special chapter must be consecrated.

7

THE ORIGINS OF GOLF

Golf was invented in Scotland soon after the foundation of the University of St Andrews.

This momentous fact has not hitherto been fully appreciated, even by writers on the game with close Andreapolitan connections, like Robert Clark, Sir Walter Simpson, H. S. C. Everard, Andrew Lang, J. B. Salmond, and James K. Robertson. Just as logarithms were the brainwave of a St Andrews student, John Napier of Merchiston, so the invention of golf may plausibly be ascribed to an earlier intellectual connected with the university. His anonymity was preserved for the sufficient reason that the activity was officially discountenanced. Indeed, it is remarkable that this pastime, which has become for many a lucrative profession or an obsessive religion, first appears in documents as an offence against the state, punishable by Act of Parliament.

In 1458, on 6 March, a day which fell into the year 1457 by the Old Style that persisted in Scotland till 1600, in the reign of James II, the Parliament of Scotland was busying itself with the defence of the realm, and decreed, *inter alia*, as follows (Ch. 6):

> Item it is decretyt and ordanyt that wapinschawings [*military exercises*] be haldin be the lords ande baronys spirituale and temporale four tymis in the zeir. And at the fut ball and the golf be utterly cryit doune and nocht usyt. And at the bowe marks be maide at ilk paroch kirk . . .

Every man was to fire at least six bow shots every Sunday at the targets set up near the parish church. Any man who failed to do so was to be fined two pennies, and the fines were to be given to those who performed the required practice, to buy drinks with. The Act of James II was apparently not obeyed properly, for on 6 May 1471 James III's Parliament tries again:

> And that ilk sheriff stewart bailze and uthers officiars mak wapynschawing within the bonds of thar office eftir the tenor of

the act of parliament. Swa that in defaut of the said wapin-schawyng our Souerane lords leiges be nocht destitut of harnes quhen thai haf neid. And at the futbal and golf be abusit [*disused, abandoned*] in tym cummyng and the buts maid up and shuting usit eftir the tenor of the act of parliament.

Twenty years later, James IV's legislature enforced a fresh prohibition, with a collective fine on the parish of forty shillings for every breach.

And attour that in na place of the Realme be usit fut bawis, gouff, or uthir sic unproffitable sportis, bot for comoun gude and defence of the realme be hantit [*practised*] bowis shuting, and marks therefore ordinit in ilke parochoun . . .

Such legislation against ball-games was tardy in Scotland compared with other countries. In 1319 Philip the Tall of France banned all ball-games in favour of archery. In 1397 the magistrates of Paris forbade ball-games on every day except Sunday, because working men were leaving their families for days on end to play at *jeu de paume*, a type of tennis, and other games. Kings of England from 1363 to 1409 tried to suppress football in the interests of archery. The first Scots statute against football dates from 1424, and it must be emphasized that it does not condemn golf also. Golf was condemned first in 1458. From these facts it has been inferred that in 1424 golf was not yet sufficiently widely practised to be a menace to the desired archery. Supposing golf had been invented in St Andrews soon after the promulgation of the papal bulls found-ing the university in 1414, the dominance of St Andrews throughout Scotland as a commercial centre, and as a resort of the trend-setting upper classes and intellectuals, might well have diffused the 'unproffitable sport' widely throughout the realm, though it were still officially frowned upon. The first evidence of legitimation of golf as a permissible recreation is in 1502, in the reign of James IV, when the Lord High Treasurer's accounts record:

Item: the xxi day of September, to the bowar of Sanct Johnes-toun [*the bow-maker of Perth*] for clubbs. xiiij s. [*14 shillings*].

Later entries arouse speculation about costs:

[22 February 1506] Item for xij Golf Ballis to the King . . .
iiij s. Item the xviiij day of Julij [1506] for ij Golf Clubbes to the
King. . . ij s.

Clubs at one shilling each and balls at three for a shilling may
seem disproportionately priced to the modern purchaser, who
pays much more than three times as much for a club as for a
ball. Whatever the relative prices of the appurtenances, the
cost of golfing seems not to have deterred many English people
from taking it up within eleven years of James IV's marriage
to Margaret Tudor, sister of Henry VIII, whose first wife,
Katharine of Aragon, writes to Cardinal Wolsey on 13 August
1513 that, while the King was busy with war, 'all his subjects
be very glad, I thank God, to be busy with the golf, for they
take it for pastime'. The English, however, appear to have gone
off the game quickly, for no more is heard of it in England till
after 1603, when James VI reintroduced it on inheriting the
English throne, through Margaret Tudor.

About the origins of the Scottish invention there has been
much speculation. Games with balls go back at least to Homer's
Nausicaa and her naked handmaidens on the beach at Ermones
in Corfu, where Odysseus had crawled ashore at the mouth of
the Ropa river, in which local Greek women still do their
laundry. Games with balls and some sort of stick must have
been widespread in many cultures. From them descend cricket,
baseball, hockey, croquet, polo, and several other organized
sports still pursued. From what varieties of stick-and-ball game
could golf have been evolved?

The early Gaels played a fierce game called *iomain* with a
curved ash-stick, termed a *caman*, and a leather ball stuffed with
wool. Neighbouring parishes sent forth teams to drive the ball
through a low goal shaped like a bow. From such parochial
battles of the past were developed the modern Irish hurling and
Scottish shinty. The old Celtic heroes played this game, and it
was doubtless to keep his eye in that the legendary Cuchulainn
diverted himself on a journey by taking his *caman* and wallop-
ing a silver ball across the fields *en route*. Ruaraidh Erskine of
Marr thought a kind of primitive golf might be implied in a
Gaelic tale, unfortunately undatable, entitled *Gaisgeach na*

Sgeithe Deirge. In this the Hero of the Red Shield goes out in the morning with his three foster-brothers 'to drive the ball'. He competes against the three of them combined, and it is said that 'he would put a half-shot down and a half-shot in on them'. The interpretation might be that he could beat them all without exerting his full strength; or else that he could beat the best ball of the three after giving them half a stroke. Perhaps the competition was in covering the maximum distance in a given number of strokes. The type of ball the hero drove is not stated. The ancient Romans played with balls of various types, including the *pila paganica*, or 'countrymen's ball', which was of leather stuffed with feathers. But there is no evidence that it was driven by a stick, and some indication that it was struck by the hand or thrown and caught.

At one time golf was played with balls of wood, as appears from an account in 1614 of a siege of Kirkwall Castle in Orkney, where the Earl of Caithness tells about 'cannone billetts [*bullets*] . . . brokkin lyke goulfe balls upoune the castelle'. Clearly the cannonballs split into totally separate pieces, like wooden balls, whereas leather balls would only split at a seam, and lose some stuffing. Balls of wood are employed in two Continental games, *chole* and the *jeu de mail*, pall-mall. The Belgians still play *chole*, striking an egg-shaped ball of beechwood with a club having an iron head faced like a spoon. There are various spellings of the name, including *soule* and *choule*. In documents it first appears in 1147; and there seem to have been different ways of playing it, some of them like football, others like hockey. The Belgian variety, called *crosse*, is a hybrid between hockey and cross-country golf. There is one ball and one goal, which may be several miles away across country. The two opponents, or the two opposing teams, agree on a target, say a church door or cemetery gate, and then bid the number of turns in which they undertake to hit the target. Each turn has three strokes, and after each turn the opponent is entitled to a stroke back, *renvoi*, whereby it may be propelled into some 'bad lie', such as a bunker or pit full of sand surrounded by banks of turf. This process is called *décholer*. The contractors bidding the smaller number of turns to reach the goal are termed *choleurs*; those who are concerned to frustrate them are called *décholeurs*, and their only preoccupation is sabotage within the rules. If there were no special hazards near by, as on stubble fields, they might simply swipe the ball a long way backwards towards the starting-point. They are under no obligation to hit any target themselves. One feels it must be a highly enraging game. *Chole* seems close to the English word *choler*, and the *choleurs* must be liable to become cholerous through the manœuvres of the *décholeurs*. If the putative St Andrews intellectual evolved golf from some game like *chole* or *crosse*, surely it was a humanitarian reform, and a step in the painful march of civilization.

The acumen of Mr Robert Browning, who edited *Golfing* from 1910 to 1955, and wrote an excellent history of the game, detected a strong probability that Scotsmen in France were playing *chole* on Easter Saturday of 1421, just before the battle of Baugé, when they killed the Duke of Clarence and other English commanders, and gave the English invaders of France their first sound beating of the century. Among the seven thousand Scotsmen serving in France there may well have been one who imparted the game of *chole* to a younger brother or a son studying at the University of St Andrews, who then effected the improvement that made it golf.

But one may suspect golf owes something also to the French *jeu de mail*, or *paille-maille*, from Italian *palla*, ball, and *maglio*, hammer or mallet. The English called this pall-mall, and pronounced it *pell-mell*. Indeed, there is a thoroughfare in London named for it since Charles II played there. In one form it was close to croquet, the ball being driven through an iron hoop in an enclosed precinct; but there was a long-driving cross-country form of the game that resembled golf. In 1863 one G. Robb published his *Historical Gossip about Golf and Golfers*, in which he describes the game of *mail* as then recently played in the south of France. The club was hammer-shaped, with a springy handle about as long as a golf-club. The head was about four and a half inches long by two thick, bound with iron, and the ball a solid piece of boxwood, about two inches in diameter. A good player could drive it about two hundred yards. The early courses were side-roads, and each section was about half a mile long, the goal at the end being a touchstone, and the winner was the player who attained it in the smallest number of strokes. Players also had contests at targets, of the size and shape of archery targets, set at a distance of fifty yards. The bullseye was a central hole six inches in diameter. To put the ball through the bullseye was considered a fluke, like holing out in one at golf. But good players frequently struck the target outside the bullseye. Sometimes a large glass bowl was hung in the middle of the target, and he that hit it was obviously a smasher.

It may be noted that Mary Queen of Scots, a few days after her husband, Lord Darnley, had been murdered and had his house blown up, was alleged to have been seen playing golf and pall-mall in the fields beside Seton Palace, east of Edinburgh. It looks as if the two games could be played on the same terrain. Maybe Queen Mary's golf was the propulsion of a ball into a succession of holes, while her pall-mall was the striking, or at least aiming at, of a target. But one or two pieces of information raise doubts here. For instance, in 1613, as we read in a Spalding Club Miscellany volume, a certain John Allan was 'convict for setting ane goiff ball in the kirk yeard, and striking the same against the kirk'. Was this mere irreverence? Or was the kirk door, or some other part, the agreed target? In a Justiciary case on 2 March 1632 William Hangetsyde, of Kelso, and his son Robert were accused of the 'slauchter and death of umquhile Thomas Chatto zounger sone to Thomas Chatto merchand indweller in Kelso committit within the kirkzaird of Kelso upoun the first day of Februar last be geving him ane deidlie straik with ane golf ball struckin out with ane golf club under his left lug upoun the vene organe thairof'. The Hangetsydes were playing 'ane bonspill [*match*] at the golf within the said kirk zaird with certane utheris thair compagniones and associatis', and the unfortunate Thomas Chatto was a mere spectator. It may be noted that the Dutch game of *kolven*, which is somehow related to golf, was in 1456 prohibited in churches and churchyards by the town of Narden. When played inside the church it may have been akin to croquet, or the modern Dutch and Frisian *kolven*; but in churchyards it might have been more like a form of pall-mall.

Using a golf-club to drive a ball at a target, rather than towards and into a hole, is exemplified also in the eighteenth century. The Rev Dr Alexander (nicknamed 'Jupiter') Carlyle, of Inveresk, tells in his autobiography how he was invited in 1758 to dine with the actor David Garrick at Hampton, on the outskirts of London, and play golf on Molesey Hurst across the Thames. Carlyle found the 'golfing ground' very good. But the relevant point is his performance after dinner. There was an archway between the upper and lower gardens of Garrick's house. Dr Carlyle astonished the party by the skill with which he propelled a ball through this archway down a slope into the river. Garrick begged the club as a souvenir of the feat. Of course, even today such an unusual stroke might be attempted off the regular golf-course. A student might take a swipe at the Martyrs' Memorial or the big smoking-room window of the Royal and Ancient Club itself. Whether such an activity could be strictly termed *golf* is another question. But in the early days one need not assume extreme systematization of the game or definition of the term.

The word *golf* itself means, basically, 'club'. It is cognate with the Dutch noun *kolf*, meaning 'club'. Less closely it is related to German *kolbe*, Icelandic *kolfr*. The English *club* is a form derived by metathesis, shifting of the positions of the vowel and the internal consonant. Scots, as a Germanic language, would have the noun *golf*, meaning a stick with one end heavier than the other, even if no Dutchman had ever used his *kolf* to engage in the game known as *het kolven*, 'the clubbing'. And the Scots word *golf* certainly does not derive from the Dutch name, even if the Scots game may owe a little to the Dutch game, *het kolven*, though perhaps less than to the French *jeu de mail* and the Belgian *chole*. In its modern form *het kolven* is played in enclosed, sometimes roofed, courts attached to inns in North Holland and Friesland. Two posts are set up, weighing up to half a hundredweight apiece, and sometimes coated with bell-metal to resound when struck. The distance apart of the posts may be from forty feet to forty yards, depending on the size of the enclosure available. The ball is about the size of a cricket-ball, but elastic, being made of worsted wound round a core and covered with leather. It weighs about two pounds. The club has a heavy head of iron or brass, straight-faced, and a shaft about the length of a golf-club, but thick and stiff, like a garden rake. The object of the game is to hit the further post and then return and hit the starting-post, in the fewest strokes. A skilful *kolver* can sometimes hit the further post so squarely that the ball rebounds a good way towards the starting-post. It is clear that this type of *kolven* is more akin to croquet than to golf. But in the early seventeenth century matters may have been different.

The earliest extant description of *het kolven* is said to be in a poem of Gerbrand Adriaenszoon Bredero (1585–1618). He tells how the *kolver* puts on his ice-spurs or something stiff to enable him to stand on the smooth ice. He then takes a stance with his club of ash wood weighted with lead, or *syne schotse klik*, 'his Scottish club' or *cleek*, of leaded boxwood. The feather-ball, invisible from the drive-off to the fall, is keenly marked by ball-spotters, fore-caddies, as he golfs forward to a post, or strikes out for the furthest distance, stroke against stroke, aiming at a white target or at a flag in a hole. Each player notches a stick to record the number of strokes taken. Any man neglecting to do so is disqualified. We seem to have here two types of game: one consisting of a comparatively short game, aimed at hitting a post; and the other of a long-distance game, involving a great many strokes. How far one could drive a somewhat elastic cricket-ball-sized sphere over ice is a moot point. If it were a modern golf-ball it could easily run half a mile over smooth ice. The poet Bredero also wrote plays, in one of which he makes an old gentleman complain that a lady near by has been hit on the head by a ball struck by a *kolver*, and that the game ought to be prohibited. Indeed, the earliest prohibition from Bredero's native Amsterdam is found in the fourteenth century.

There is also some evidence from drawings and paintings, usually uncertain in interpretation. There is even a stained glass window at Gloucester Cathedral, towards 1350, with a now headless figure addressing a sort of hockey stick at a non-existent but apparently stationary ball. In 1363 the game of hockey, *cambuca*, was forbidden in England; and probably the window showed a hockey-player about to bully off. But it might be the English equivalent of an Irish *hurley* or *caman*, for Layamon, towards 1200, described players driving balls 'wide over the fields' in the sports attending King Alfred's coronation in 872. It might, however, represent some form of the game of *chole*.

A variety of games akin to golf may be seen in a Flemish Book of Hours, done by Simon Bennink and pupils between 1500 and 1520 at Bruges. The illuminated borders illustrate numerous types of ball game, and such things as hoops and tops. Mr Robert Browning discerned that no single border in the book is devoted wholly to any single game. For example, one shows a child on his knees using a baton to putt a large ball into a hoop or can, while beside him is a crossbowman and above the crossbowman an archer with a long-bow. Another border shows a child on his knees, with a longish golf-club, putting a ball into a hole, or possibly at a roundish wooden jack. On the left a standing figure addresses a ball with a golf-club or the like, possibly playing *chole*, and in the middle two men stand, one of them with a club over his shoulder, looking at a ball on the ground. A man in a doorway suggests that the context may be the *kolf-bann* of an inn. At least one of the games represented may be *het kolven*, and another some child's putting game.

A Rembrandt etching of 1654 shows the inside of an inn, with a view through an open doorway of a man playing *het kolven* with the large ball. There are a good many Dutch paintings of figures with clubs, mostly on ice, and usually with the large post at which the ball was propelled by the *kolver*. The most curious is Adriaen van de Velde's painting of 1668, where a man with a kilt addresses a ball, no doubt having in view a post in the ice about forty yards away, while another kilted man holds a club and watches him. Of two other spectators one has knickerbockers and a cloak and the other either knickerbockers and a cloak or a kilt and cloak. Recalling Bredero's reference, half a century earlier, to the *kolver* with his Scottish club, it seems possible that the kilted men are Scots making do on the Dutch ice with *kolven* for lack of the springy green links of Scotland that were the home of the first golf.

Among the Dutch paintings are some of children with apparent golf-clubs and golf-balls resembling the old feather-stuffed leather ones. The first in date of these child-pictures is that now at Holdenby House, traditionally said to be of a Scots prince.

It is very likely Prince Henry, eldest son of James VI, born 19 February 1594. His brother Charles I's daughter Mary married in 1641 the Prince of Orange. But already at his christening, at Stirling, the Dutch connection with Scotland was shown in the gifts brought to him by the ambassadors of Holland and Zeeland. In the two-way traffic between Scots and Dutch it was as easy for the Dutch to borrow as for the Scots. The Dutch borrowed some Scottish type of club, and called it '*schotse klik*'; but it is not certain that the Scots borrowed anything from the game of *kolven*.

For instance, the Dutch *tuitje*, the heap of snow or earth used for propping up a ball for the initial stroke, cannot have given rise to the Scots term *tee*, which does not originally mean that. The term *tee* is used for a mark in the game of quoits, and the mark towards which the stones are propelled in curling. In golf it originally meant simply the spot on the ground where the ball was placed for driving off for a new hole. In the rules adopted in 1775 by the Honourable Company of Edinburgh Golfers it is laid down: 'Your Tee must be upon the ground.' That was a prohibition of perching the ball up on what the Dutch call a *tuitje*. Likewise there is no plausibility in the theory that the golfing term *stymie*, now obsolete, derived from the Dutch phrase *stuit mij*, 'It stops me.' A *stymie* was the situation on the green when an opponent's ball blocked one's way to the hole, being not within six inches. To lay a man a stymie was to put him in an awkward predicament. The term is an application of the Scots word *stymie*, found early in the sixteenth century, meaning a man with defective vision, or a man who behaves awkwardly, like a purblind person, so 'an awkward fellow'. When a golfer saw his opponent's ball blocking the way of his own ball towards the hole he called it a *stymie*, and the Dutch had nothing to do with it. Further, no one has shown that the phrase *stuit mij* formed part of the technical vocabulary of *het kolven*. Golf borrowed no technical terms from Dutch.

Whatever he may have borrowed in the way of hints from *chole*, the *jeu de maille*, or *het kolven*, the anonymous genius from the early days of the university of St Andrews invented a new game when he thought up the *golf*, *gouf*, *gowf*, *gauff*, or *goiff*, as it is variously spelt in early references. Mr Browning puts the point well: '. . . it was the Scots who devised the essential features of golf, the *combination* of hitting for distance with the final nicety of approach to an exiguous mark, and the independent progress of each player with his own ball, free from interference by his adversary.' Very acceptable, too, is the conclusion of Garden G. Smith, in *The Royal and Ancient Game of Golf*, written by him with Harold H. Hilton (1912):

> . . . there seems to be no reason for doubting that, in all its essential particulars, golf is a purely Scottish product. . . . anything more typical of the slow, canny, yet strong and resourceful Scottish character than golf is not to be found in the whole range of Scottish institutions. Golf, in fact, in its conception and essence, is the very epitome of the elements which have given the Scottish character its strength and individuality. It is the game of the patient, self-reliant man, prepared to meet whatever fortune may befall him.

One essential feature of golf is, as Mr Browning phrases it, 'the *combination* of hitting for distance with the final nicety of approach to an exiguous mark'. The small hole, marked from afar by a flag, is clearly the most practical form of 'exiguous mark'. In order to combine the 'hitting for distance' with the 'final nicety' it is necessary that there should be a series of tracts of ground between a series of tees and holes. These successive tracts, of varying lengths, are called *holes* by a transference of meaning. Thus one may speak of a long hole, a short hole, a dog-leg hole, or a Stationmaster's Garden Hole, signifying the tract of turf, whins, sand bunkers, and so forth, from one teeing-ground to one final exiguous cavity.

Because golf was an unofficial activity, officially discountenanced for generations, one cannot expect to find from its inception precise descriptions of the lay-out of courses. The first document mentioning *holes* dates from 28 December 1625, in the Burgh Records of Aberdeen, when the musketeers, pikemen, and two-handed-swordsmen of the good town exercised 'in the principall pairt of the linkes betwixt the first hole and the Quenis hole'. This seems to imply a plurality of holes on links that were described, in 1661, as 'a fair plaine' and were the venue of devotees of the golf, which was already popular at

Aberdeen. That golf could still be played in 1721 on a one-hole course is perhaps implied by James Arbukle, in his poem *Glotta; or, The Clyde.*

> In winter, too, when hoary frosts o'erspread
> The verdant turf and naked lay the mead,
> The vig'rous youth commence the sportive war,
> And, arm'd with lead, their jointed clubs prepare;
> The timber curve to leathern orbs apply,
> Compact, elastic, to pervade the sky:
> These to the distant hole direct they drive;
> They claim the stakes who thither first arrive.

It is suggested by Garden Smith that Glasgow Green was unplayable in summer through the length of the grass, or because it was too much frequented. It has a restricted space, and perhaps did not allow of more than one *hole*, though naturally that could be played in the reverse direction also if it had a suitable orifice at each end, into which to direct the compact elastic leathern orb. In 1744 there were five *holes* at Leith Links, but again they could all have been played in reverse, to make ten holes, or played thrice round, as was the regular custom at Leith. At St Andrews before 1764 there were twelve holes, in the sense of orifices in the turf. Golfers drove off from the Home Hole to the second, being the first to be holed out in, and so on to the twelfth hole, near the Eden, and then back again, filling twice the intervening orifices and then the final (Home) hole, which, though called the first, was the last to be holed out in. Thus they played twenty-two *holes*, in the sense of tracts of land from tee to literal hole, filling ten orifices twice and two once each. Given fifteen *holes*, as at Leith, or twenty-two, as at early St Andrews, the element of 'final nicety of approach to an exiguous mark' thus began to gain importance relative to the 'hitting for distance'.

The earliest surviving document about golf on the St Andrews links dates from 1553 (25 January 1552, Old Style), and is an acknowledgement by John Hamilton, Archbishop of St Andrews, of the permission granted to him by 'our lovittis provest bailleis conseill and communitie off our citie of Sant-andros to plant and planis cuniggis', that is to plenish, or supply, coneys, or rabbits, and 'tak the profitt of the saidis cuniggis and to use thame to our utilitie and plesour'. The primate reserved to the burgh the full ownership of the links, with their hereditary rights to pasture animals or dig up turf, for burning on household fires or covering roofs, and also their rights to 'playing at golf, futball, shuteing, at all gamis, with all uther maner of pastyme as ever thai pleis'. The Archbishop was not allowed to build dykes or other enclosures for his rabbits, and the inhabitants were not allowed to poach them. The Archbishop's *cuniggairs*, or rabbit burrows, were to be in the north part of the links next adjacent to the Water of Eden. The document survives by accident. About 1800 it was handed over to the burgh's lawyers at Edinburgh for a lawsuit, and got lost, till a bookseller bought it for a shilling on its way to be pulped. He sold it to the university for forty-five shillings, and in 1922 the University Court restored it to the Town Council. Doubtless the citizens had been golfing for generations before the parchment was made up.

Other early casual mentions appear in the register of the St Andrews Kirk Session after the Reformation. On 18 December 1583 the clerk noted:

> The quhilk day it is delatit that Alexander Milleris tua sonis
> ar inobedient to him, and that thai, with Nicholl Mane, William
> Bruce and utheris thair complices, playit in the golf feildis
> Sonday last wes, tyme of fast and precheing, aganis the ordin-
> ances of the kirk. The sessioun ordanis thame to be warnit and
> accusit thairfor.

On 29 March 1598 'Dauid Gray pewderar and Thomas Saith tailyour' were accused of 'prophaning of the Saboth day in playing at the gouf eftir nune'. They begged forgiveness, and were told they would be fined forty shillings each if they offended again. On 19 December 1599 a tariff of penalties was fixed for playing 'the goufe and uthir exercise' during times fixed for divine services. For the first offence there would be a fine of ten shillings, raised to twenty for a second offence: then 'for the thrid fault publick repentance, and the fourt fault deprivation fra their offices'.

King James VI, however, came to the rescue in 1618, having

received from the common people many complaints during his journey in Scotland the previous year. He allowed them to take lawful recreation after the end of divine service, 'such as dauncing, either men or women, archerie for men, leaping, vaulting, or any other such harmless recreation'. But he prohibited such recreations to 'any that are not present in the church at the service of God before their going to the said recreations'. Charles I in 1633 renewed the permission, again with the proviso that persons engaging in recreation should have gone to church first. When Charles II came to Scone to be crowned King by the Covenanters, which ceremony took place on 1 January 1651, G. M. Trevelyan writes that: 'He partook of the sober vanity of golf in the company of staid persons.' All his ancestors since James IV had played it.

James VI in 1603 appointed William Mayne, bowmaker in Edinburgh, official 'clubmaker to his Hieness'. He also took steps to cheapen the supply of golf-balls for the people. On 5 August 1618 he granted a patent for twenty-one years giving to James Melvill, William Berwick, and their associates, the monopoly of making or importing golf-balls. This was done because 'thair is no small quantitie of gold and siluer transported zeirlie out of his Hienes Kingdome of Scotland for bying of golf ballis'. It is sometimes said that these golf-balls were imported from Holland, but golf was not played in Holland. France has been proposed as the most abundant supplier of balls for various games, though the French also did did not play golf. Melvill undertook to 'furnische the said kingdome with better golf ballis, and at ane more easie rate than have beine sauld there these manie zeiris past'. No retailer was to be allowed to sell any ball unless it had been either made or imported by Melvill and partners. In fact Melvill's patent was never enforced, and the poor man was fined some years later for employing 'lawless souldiers' to try and enforce his right of search given in the patent.

In 1506 James IV paid four shillings for twelve golf-balls, but in an Edinburgh testament of 1568 we hear about 'Thre dosan of golf bawis, price thairof xxiij s.' Were these much dearer golf-balls of the same kind as the King's? On 23 November 1585 John Dickson, servitor to the Master of Orkney, writes to

Andrew Martin: 'Ye will remember to bring with you ane dossen of commoun golf ballis to me and David Moncreiff.' Perhaps the 'commoun golf ballis' were of wood, and the costlier balls of leather stuffed with hair or feathers. In an Edinburgh testament of 1612 we learn also of an estate including 'fyve scoir tuell flok goiff-ballis', probably a shopkeeper's stock of balls stuffed with tufts of waste wool. Impecunious amateurs might make their own balls of any material that came to hand.

When the fifth Earl (later first Marquis) of Montrose was a student at St Andrews his bear-leader John Lambie kept accounts, during 1628 and 1629, from which it appears that he paid £11. 8s. 'for sax new clubs and dressing some auld anes, and for balls'. He bought two 'goffe balls' once for ten shillings, and paid a caddy three shillings 'who carried my Lord's clubs to the field'. Another item is: 'My Lord taking ane drink in Jhone Garns before he went out and after he came from the golfe, 45 sh. 4d.' Montrose also made bets on his games, and one afternoon had to pay out ten shillings. Values had changed by 1676, when Lord Murray, another St Andrews student, wrote home that he had spent 1s. 6d. for two golf-clubs, and 3d for mending another, 1d. for a golf-ball, and 6d. for a lost bet on a game. He also paid 1s. 10d. for a club and three balls to send to Robertson of Struan, later a notable poet and irreconcilable Jacobite. Already in the early seventeenth century there were specialized types of club: 'play clubis', 'bonker clubis', and an 'irone club'. The earliest surviving set consists of six woods and two irons, found at Hull with a newspaper of 1741. They are all of ash. The heads of the woods are faced with bone and weighted with lead. Only two of the shafts have grips.

As the first named player of golf was James IV, and the first named lady golfer Mary Queen of Scots, it is interesting to find that the first promoter of an international competitive foursome was their descendant James Duke of York, later James VII and II. During the winter of 1681–2 he was in Edinburgh as the King's commissioner to the Parliament, and played a lot of golf on Leith Links. Two English noblemen having disputed with His Grace about the origin of the game, a match was arranged between them and the Duke with any Scotsman he might choose to partner him. He chose one John Patersone, a shoemaker. They won, and the Duke gave him half the substantial sum staked by the English lords. The prudent shoemaker invested this in building a house in the Canongate, with the arms of the Paterson family, the crest of a hand holding a club, the motto *Far and Sure*, and the pronouncement *I hate no person*, which is an anagram of the name John Patersone. Compared with the winnings of modern professionals this may not seem spectacular. But the game was still rudimentary in several ways. For its systematization and refinement we must await the Age of Reason in the eighteenth century, and the founding of the Royal and Ancient Club in 1754.

8

THE LUTHERAN REVOLUTION

St Andrews in the sixteenth century attracted international attention at some crucial moments in the international struggle of parties in the Christian world, the warfare, sometimes hotter and sometimes cooler, between the older traditions of church-government and doctrine and forms of worship, associated with the Papacy at Rome, and the varying systems of Protestant Reformation championed by such men as Martin Luther and John Calvin. The Archbishop of St Andrews in his castle became at times the key personality of the struggle between English Protestants and the Catholic French, and later Andrew Melville, as Principal of St Mary's College, was to make St Andrews a key position of the Calvinist International in its attempts to reform England, and eventually France, in the likeness of Geneva. Compared with the massacre of St Barth-olomew in France, or the executions, by burning and otherwise, of hundreds of English Protestants by Bloody Mary and of English Papists by Bloody Elizabeth, St Andrews saw few sensational disturbances; but it had a handful of spectacular martyrdoms and the dramatic murder of a Cardinal. On the whole, reviewing the course of events, one is struck today by the lack of spontaneous reforming movement inside Scotland and by the strong elements of continuity between the states of religion immediately before and after the critical date of 1560, when the Scots Parliament repudiated the authority of the Pope, forbade the Latin Mass, and adopted a reformed Confession of Faith. Groups of people in Scotland tended merely to react to events and influences from outside rather than to take initiatives of their own, and it was more or less fortuitous that the belated Reformation took place when and as it did.

Archbishop designate Alexander Stewart having been killed at Flodden in 1513, the chapter elected to the vacant see John Hepburn, their prior since 1482, and co-founder of St Leonard's College. He then withdrew in favour of William Elphinstone, Bishop of Aberdeen since 1488, who, however, died in October 1514. Meantime there was a political tangle. James IV's widow, Margaret Tudor, had married in August 1514 Archibald

Douglas, sixth Earl of Angus. On Elphinstone's death they promoted the candidature of the poet Gavin Douglas, the earl's uncle. Nobody seems to have bothered about the fact that already in October of the previous year the Medici Pope Leo X had provided to the archbishopric his nephew, Cardinal Innocenzo Cibo, not yet aged twenty-one. The Douglas faction seized the castle of St Andrews, but had to yield it, after siege, to a stronger coalition formed by Hepburn with the aid of Lord Home.

Matters were still unsettled in May 1515, when there arrived from France to take over the Regency of the Kingdom the Duke of Albany, son of James III's brother. He was heir apparent to the three-year-old King James V. After Albany the next heir was James Hamilton, first Earl of Arran, a son of James II's daughter Mary. The Hamilton proximity to the throne was a curious factor throughout the next half-century. Meantime Andrew Forman, Bishop of Moray, had been fishing in the troubled waters. The French had bribed him with the archbishopric of Bourges to press upon James IV the policy of invading England if Henry VIII attacked France; and this had led to the carnage at Flodden. Trading Bourges to the Pope's nephew Cardinal Cibo, Forman wriggled himself into St Andrews, securing the temporalities in 1516. Gavin Douglas was compensated with Dunkeld, where the local candidate's backers shot at him from the cathedral tower; and Prior Hepburn was gratified by his brother's getting the bishopric of Moray and his nephew's becoming prior of Coldingham. Forman was a smooth type of racketeer, who spent most of his revenues on sumptuous entertainments to make friends and influence people.

Others of the Scots were far from smooth. For example, when the Regent Albany went off to France, he left as his agent the Sieur Antoine d'Arces de la Bastie, commanding French garrisons in the castles of Dumbarton and Dunbar, and on the island of Inchgarvie in the Firth of Forth. His duty was to keep order on the Borders. The Homes lured him to intervene in a sham fight, chased him into a swamp, cut off his head, and gleefully paraded with it, tied by the long curled and scented locks to the saddle-bow of Home of Wedderburn. From such a stock sprang the philosopher David Hume.

After Forman's death in 1521 the next archbishop was James Betoun, who had been Archbishop of Glasgow from 1508 and was well versed in politics. He was sixth son of the laird of Balfour in Fife, and a graduate of St Andrews. One of his brothers became Lord High Treasurer, which helped his career. James Betoun sided with the Hamiltons against the Douglases, and was lucky to escape being killed when the Douglases beat up the Hamiltons in Edinburgh in 1520, at the affair known as 'Cleanse the Causeway'. When Gavin Douglas invited him to intervene to prevent bloodshed, Betoun, believing the Hamiltons would win, struck himself on the chest and said, 'By my conscience I knaw not the matter.' As he struck, the armour-plated waistcoat beneath his archiepiscopal robe gave a clatter, which prompted the poet Douglas to retort: 'I persave, my lord, zour conscience be not good, for I hear thame clatter.' After the Douglases had won, Gavin saved Betoun's life. A little later, in November 1524, the Queen Dowager Margaret Tudor and the pro-English party secured an ascendancy over Albany and the backers of the 'auld alliance', and Betoun found himself thrown into prison, in the castle of Edinburgh, for some months. On his release by the Queen he found a growing agitation by adherents of the novel doctrines of Martin Luther.

Luther was the son of a German iron-smelter, and had a good education by teachers belonging to the Brotherhood of the Common Life. As a student of law he was one day terrified by a stroke of lightning, and joined the order of Hermit Friars of St Augustine (Austin friars, not canons). He became an expert theologian and sub-prior of the friary at Wittenberg. Here he became obsessed with the problem of sin and the means of conciliating God's favour in view of the great Day of Judgement. His meditations led him to stress the doctrine of justification by faith alone, not by human works.

What brought him into public life and conflict was his objection to a campaign launched towards 1517 for the sale of indulgences by Pope Leo X for the rebuilding of St Peter's Church at Rome. Indulgences had grown up over centuries from the earlier practice of the Church regarding penances. Instead of fasting, or standing all night in a river, or enduring some other mortification of the flesh, a penitent sinner was allowed to subscribe money to some worthy object, such as a crusade to rescue the Holy Places from the Infidel. Indulgences had even been given for contributions towards the repair of the cathedral at St Andrews. But the particular indulgence Luther took objection to was widely felt in Germany to be a sham. The money was thought to be needed to pay the great bankers, the Fugger family of Augsburg, for money lent to Albert of Brandenburg, Archbishop of Magdeburg, for bribing the Pope to let him hold additionally the archbishopric of Mainz. Many in Germany felt that too much German bullion was being carted south across the Alps in connection with indulgences. Popes had been claiming to secure from Christ the remission of punishment due for sins, even the sins of souls now in purgatory.

All this seemed to Luther erroneous, the more so since he had visited Rome, in 1510, and observed the racketeering and depravity of the ecclesiastics there. On 31 October 1517 he pinned up on the door of the castle church at Wittenberg his Ninety-Five Theses against the abuses of the system of indulgence. Archbishop Albert of Magdeburg and Mainz had employed a Dominican, John Tetzel, as public relations officer to promote the sale of the indulgences; and the Dominicans were not slow to answer Luther's attack. The Pope cited Luther as a heretic. Luther appealed to a General Council of the Church. One thing led to another. Luther appealed to the German nobility to reform the abuses in the Church. The Pope appealed to the new young Emperor, Charles V, to execute a bull excommunicating Luther and his partisans. The Emperor held an imperial Diet at Worms, in the Rhineland, and Luther was asked to retract his heretical teachings. He refused to do so until he should be convinced by the evidence of Scripture or of manifest reason. He said, 'I am held fast by the Scriptures adduced by me, and my conscience is taken captive by God's word.'

Thanks to the printing-press, the Bible had become much more widely available, in the Vulgate Latin version, and recently in the Greek edited by Erasmus. There was thus a bigger public outside the monasteries with access to the texts on which the controversy was raised. Sheltered by the Elector of Saxony, Luther translated the New Testament from Greek into

German, a work that profoundly affected the future of the German language, literature, and society. German nationalism more or less lined up on Luther's side, and Archbishop Albert found it expedient to stop his attempts to raise funds by peddling indulgences. In 1525 Luther broke his vow of celibacy by marrying Catherine von Bora, an ex-nun, and they had five children. The further development of the Lutheran agitation in Germany, with the peasants' revolt, unsupported by Luther, and the league of Evangelical princes, and the eventual compromise, are not immediately relevant to the Scottish Reformation; but the first stages of Lutheranism did make a major impact.

In 1525 the Scots Parliament legislated against the import of Lutheran books into Scotland, and in 1527 against all persons disseminating Luther's opinions. Leith, Dundee, and other east-coast ports were particular hotbeds of Lutheran ideas. The English translation of the New Testament by John Tyndale was also shipped in, copies being printed in the Low Countries. The English Ambassador at Antwerp reports them as going 'most part to the town of St Andrews'. A Scots version of the Bible had been begun by Matthew Nisbet, an Ayrshireman, but was not completed and printed: so that English became the medium in which most Scots folk came to know the Scriptures.

The first Scot to suffer for the Reformed cause was a young aristocrat, Patrick Hamilton. Born about 1504, he was second son of Sir Patrick Hamilton of Kincavel, a natural brother of the Earl of Arran, and of Catherine Stewart, daughter of Alexander Duke of Albany, son of James II. In 1520 he took the master's degree at the University of Paris, enjoying an income as commendator of the abbey of Fearn. From Paris he went to Louvain, and came to St Andrews in 1523, being incorporated on 9 June, with the venerable historian and theologian John Major. He must have annoyed the Greekless Regents by criticizing the practice of studying Aristotle through commentators, not through the exact text. His main activity seems, however, to have been choral music, of which there had been a great development in the past half century. Perhaps the greatest *tour de force* was the motet 'O bone Jesu', for nineteen solo voices, written by Robert Carver, canon of Scone. Hamilton wrote a mass for nine voices, and conducted it in the cathedral as precentor of the choir.

In 1527 Archbishop Betoun got wind of Patrick Hamilton's Lutheran opinions, and sent for him; but Hamilton went off to Wittenberg. There he found the plague raging, and moved to Marburg, enrolling in the new university founded by the Landgrave of Hesse. Here he published a set of Latin theses, which were printed in English in Foxe's *Book of Martyrs*, and were long known as 'Patrick's Places', containing a digest of basic divinity. Late in 1527 he returned to his home near Linlithgow, and married. He knew well what risk he ran, for the French party was in the ascendant, and not long before a French officer of Albany's, de la Tour, had been burned in Paris for having spread Lutheran opinions in Scotland. Hamilton is said to have felt that the cause of Reform needed martyrs.

When Betoun sent him a further summons, he went to St Andrews. Discussions of his opinions were continued for several days, with courtesy and ready admission that there were abuses needing reform. Betoun was related by marriage to the Hamiltons, and seems to have wished the young man would go away and keep quiet. But some others about the archiepiscopal city were otherwise minded. He was arrested and brought into the cathedral for trial on the charge of maintaining thirteen articles condemned as heretical, in the first place that a man is justified not by works but by faith alone. This was a characteristic Lutheran position. Hamilton admitted holding seven of the opinions, but regarded as disputable the other six, including the theses that there is no purgatory, that the Pope is Anti-Christ and that every priest has as much power as the Pope, that the Confessional is not necessary to salvation, and that it is devilish to teach that remission of sin is purchased by penance. The Council condemned him on all counts, his main accuser being the Dominican prior, Campbell.

Next day, the 29 February 1528, Hamilton was brought again to the cathedral for sentence, and handed over to the civil power for execution. There was a fear that his brother and others would attempt his rescue, so haste was made. The magistrates took him to a stake set up in North Street, in front

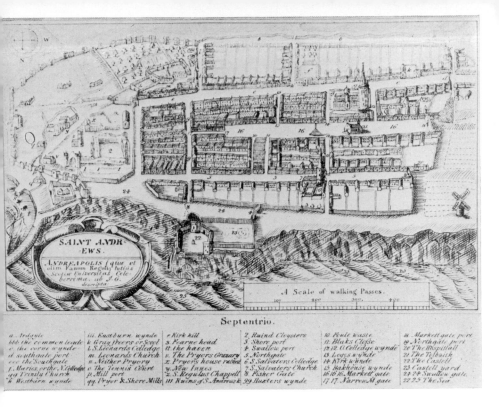

Plan of St Andrews in 1642, from a drawing by James Gordon, Minister of Rothiemay.

A reconstruction drawing by Alan Sorell of the cathedral precinct.

The 'bottle dungeon' in the castle.

'The Brighton of the North'—promenaders and golfers on St Andrews links about 1795, from a drawing by the Rev. John Cook.

The Market Square and Tolbooth (demolished 1862).

Holiday-makers in August 1870, showing bathers in the Step Rock pool and
horse-drawn bathing-cabins along the West Sands.

of the tower of St Salvator's College. Betoun called on him to recant. Hamilton replied, 'I will not deny my beliefs for fear of your flames. I am content that my body should be burned here rather than that my soul should burn in Hell for denying my true faith.' The executioners were inexperienced, and the burning took six hours. Six hours, during which Hamilton's adversaries taunted him with his heretical doctrines. He challenged them to attest the truth of their own opinions by putting their little fingers into the fire. As they could not get the fire going properly, on a showery day with strong wind from the North Sea, a baker named Myrtoun ran to fetch a bundle of straw and flung it on the pile. A sudden gust raised a flare that flew out upon the Dominican prior and burned the front part of his black cowl. The crowd of armoured men stood in silence as the flustered friars and canons ran about with bundles of straw and smeared faggots with gunpowder. As the gallant martyr was slowly roasted and charred, one of the crowd shouted that he ought to give a sign if he still held the doctrincs for which he had been condemned. Hamilton managed to lift three fingers of his scorched and blackened hand, and cried out, 'How long, Lord, shall darkness lie over this Kingdom? How long wilt Thou suffer the tyranny of mcn?... Lord Jesus, receive my spirit.'

The University of Louvain, on hearing the news, sent a congratulatory letter to the Archbishop and the doctors of Scotland. John Major complimented Betoun on his scriptural name Jacobus, James, which means 'supplanter', for having annihilated the Lutheran heresy, and he made what was considered an elegant pun, that the herb *betony* had been applied to the poison-bite. But Archbishop Betoun must have been less pleased when a friend cautioned him against burning any more heretics, remarking: '. . . if ye will burn them, let them be burnt in deep cellars, for the reek of Master Patrick Hamilton has infected as many as it blew upon.' On the south face of St Salvator's tower, half-way between the tops of the niches for statues above the arched entrance, there is a face on the stone, said in old local tradition to have been impressed there by the dying glance of the young martyr. In the cobbles the initials P. H. commemorate the event, and every year on the last day of February a service is held in honour of Patrick Hamilton.

A striking instance of the immediate effect of Hamilton's judicial murder was the conversion of one of his accusers, Alexander Alane, a canon of St Andrews. He began to censure the debaucheries of priests. The prior was at this time Patrick Hepburn, successor to his uncle. Prior Patrick had himself, at a dinner party, admitted to having had carnal relations with a dozen women, seven of them married. He took umbrage at Alane's observations, and imprisoned him in very unpleasant conditions detrimental to his health. Friends among the other canons contrived his escape to Sweden. Later he lectured at Cambridge, and ended up at Leipzig, becoming Rector of its university. Another Lutheran sympathizer was the Principal of St Leonard's, Gavin Logie, senior canon of the priory. Under his tolerant rule 'to drink of St Leonard's well' was a phrase meaning to have Lutheran sympathies.

In this atmosphere some of Betoun's advisers pressed forward the burning of another heretic, Henry Forrest of Linlithgow, probably a former student of St Leonard's. John Knox states that 'after long imprisonment in the Sea Tower of Saint Andrews [*which Professor Croft Dickinson surmised to mean the Bottle Dungeon*] [he] was adjudged to the fire . . . for none other crime but because he had a New Testament in English'. Apparently in confession to a Grey friar, William Laing, he had expressed agreement with Patrick Hamilton's articles of faith, and the Franciscan betrayed the secrets of the confessional to the archbishop. They burned him, in 1532 or 1533, on the highest part of the cliffside between the cathedral and the castle, so that the flames could be seen by the people in Angus.

Betoun did a little also in the intellectual fight against Lutheranism by fetching back from Paris, where he had a great reputation, the ageing John Major, or Mair, who began in 1531 to lecture in theology. In 1534 he was made Provost of St Salvator's, which office he held till his death in 1550 at the age of eighty. He had congratulated Betoun for the burning of Hamilton. He has been called, in philosophy, the last of the Schoolmen; today he is more interesting as a historian, and a theorist of the principle of limited constitutional monarchy, which was the Scottish governmental tradition.

Towards the end of his life James Betoun fell far out of favour with James V, as the young King took over affairs himself. In 1532 James reorganized the supreme law court as a College of Justice, on an Italian model, as some think, though others find rather a French inspiration. To pay for it he applied to the clergy, and Betoun was reluctant to find the money. Further, the King lent an ear to the rumours that Betoun had plotted with the Hamiltons, and had expressed the hope that he would see his niece's son, the new Earl of Arran, King. James even suspected that the Archbishop might be plotting with Henry VIII in England, though historians seem agreed that the prelate, in his days of chief political responsibility, had played a weak hand adroitly and never given way to either English or French blandishments or threats. At any rate, the King placed the Archbishop under house arrest. In drafting a justification to the Pope, James mentioned as one reason the fact that the Archbishop could get from his castle at St Andrews to the frontier at Berwick in six hours. One could hardly go faster today, and it is a reminder of the centrality of St Andrews in relation to the east coast of Scotland when coastal shipping services were abundant. While the Archbishop's house arrest lasted, the man responsible for his surveillance was the Earl of Rothes, chief of the Leslies, and hereditary sheriff of Fife. The Earl's son was later to stab the Archbishop's nephew David Beaton, who was already high in the King's favour and deeply committed to the 'auld alliance' with France. This was strengthened when James V married early in 1537 Madeleine, daughter of Francis I, and after her death took to wife the strong-minded Marie de Guise-Lorraine, widow of Louis d'Orléans, Duke of Longueville. James had seen her when in France a year before. She sailed over with a large fleet sent to fetch her, the Archbishop being carefully kept out of the arrangements. Lindsay of Pitscottie tells of her arrival:

Also, the queine landit verrie pleasant in a pairt of Fyfe, callit Fifenes, besyd Bukony [*Balcomie*], quhair shoe remained quhill horss cam to hir: and the king was in Sanct Androis for the tyme with monie of his nobilitie, awaitting on hir home coming: who, when he hard word that the queine was landit in sick ane pairt, incontinent he rod furth with all his wholl lordis, both

spirituall and temporall, and mett the queine, and ressaved hir
with great joy and mirrines, of fearssis [*farces*] and playes maid
and prepared for hir. And first she was ressaved at the new
abbey yett [*gate*]. At the east syd thairof, thair was maid to hir
ane triumphant fears [*farce*], be Sir David Lindsay of the Mont,
knyght, alias lyon king of armis, who caused ane great cloud
to cum doun out of the heavines abone the yett: Out of the
quhilk cloud came doun ane fair ladie, most lyk ane angell,
having the keyis of Scotland in hir hand, and delyvered tham to
the queines grace, in signe and tokin, that all the heartis of
Scotland war oppin for ressaving of hir grace: with certane
orationes maid be the said Sir David to the queines grace,
desiring hir to fear God, and to reverence and obey hir husband,
and keip hir awin body cleine according to Godis will and
commandementis. This being done, the queine was ressaved in
his lodging, quhilk was called the New Innes.

The Hepburn priors had within the past twenty years
heightened and embellished the precinct wall of the priory.
The new gate was probably that by the harbour, the Sea Yett
or Mill Port, leading up Pends Road, on the south side of which
stands an armorial archway, twice rebuilt in the nineteenth
century, the sole relic of the New Inn, or Hospitium Novum.
At ten the next morning, Mary of Guise . . .

. . . passed to the abbey kirk, quhair shoe saw manie lustie
lordis and barrones, weale arrayed in thair abulyiementis
[*habiliments*] againes hir cuming: also the bischopis, abbotis,
monkis, and channones, maid regular and great solemnitie in
the abbey with mess, songis, and playing on the organes. Eftir
this, the queine was ressaved be the king in the abbey to hir
denner, quhair thair was great mirth of shalmes, trumpettis,
and diverss utheris instrumentis all that day.

Next morning she visited the colleges and kirks of the town . . .

. . . and when shoe came home back to the pallace againe, shoe
confessed to the king that shoe nevir saw in France so many
pleasant fearsis in so little rowme, as shoe did that day in
Scotland: for sheoe said it was showin to hir in France, that
Scotland was bot ane barbarous countrie, desolat of all pleasant
commodities: bot now shoe saw the contrair. Also, shoe said,

shoe never saw more fair personages of men and vomen as shoe had seine that day in so little boundis. At thir wordis, the king was greatlie rejoyced, and said to hir, 'Forsooth, madame, ye sall sie better or ye goe.'

The royal pair spent forty days in St Andrews '. . . with gritt mirrines, sick as justing [*tournaments*] on horss, and running at the listis, archerie, and hunting, and all other princelie games'. The French lady is not stated to have tried her hand at the golf. They went on to Cupar, Falkland, Stirling, Linlithgow, and Edinburgh.

The most conspicuous extant monument in St Andrews of the Franco-Scottish alliance reinforced by Marie de Guise is the façade of St Mary's College, built by French architects soon after her first visit. Archbishop Betoun has the credit of founding it, if credit there be: for one may well wonder if he would not have done better to concentrate such funds and personnel as were available on improving the two existing colleges in the town.

In 1537 he had applied to the papacy for leave to erect a college within the city of diocese, and maybe he planned a college elsewhere, for instance in Edinburgh, which had been growing in importance. The papal bull was issued on 12 February 1538, from Paul III, authorizing a college of theology, canon and civil law, physic, medicine, and other liberal disciplines; a complete university, in fact, with powers to examine and award its own degrees. Its object was to combat heretics by providing well-educated supporters of the established church. Betoun's charter states as an aim 'that the militant Church of God may daily more abound in men endowed with a knowledge of literature'. A well-trained clergy in the parishes was certainly essential if heretics were to be refuted.

In December 1538 the Archbishop's nephew David Beaton, Abbot of Arbroath, was made his coadjutor. He had studied at St Andrews, Glasgow, and Paris, and the French had attached him to the 'auld alliance' by giving him the bishopric of Mirepoix, in 1537. Late in 1538 he became a Cardinal, and on his uncle's death in February 1539 became Archbishop. The only

Scot previously given the red hat was Walter Wardlaw, by the Anti-pope Clement VII. Beaton's promotion was largely motivated by the Pope's anxieties about the activities of Henry VIII of England, who had stumbled into becoming a Protestant champion.

The Welsh family of Tudor had come to the thrones of England and Ireland in 1485, with the Lancastrian faction's final victory in the Wars of the Roses. Henry VIII succeeded his father in 1509, as an athletic young man of eighteen. He proceeded to marry his deceased brother Arthur's widow, Katharine of Aragon, and begot a series of children. Unfortunately they all died but one, the Princess Mary, later the Queen known as 'Bloody' Mary. The trouble appears to have been syphilis, of which a virulent form had invaded Europe after the return of Christopher Columbus's first expedition to America. It played havoc in several royal and noble families, and was a contributory factor in the puritanism of the Protestant Reformation.

About 1525 Henry VIII began to worry intensely about securing a male heir or two for his upstart dynasty, and seems to have felt that he had erred morally in marrying his deceased brother's wife, an excellent woman to whom he was much attached. He therefore began to negotiate with the Pope for a divorce. After some years, the project fell through. Henry then turned nasty about the Pope, and about churchmen in general. Earlier on he had opposed Luther's agitation, and in 1521 the Pope had recognized him by that title of 'Defender of the Faith' which still appears on British coins. Henry decided to set up as his own Pope, so far as England and Ireland were concerned. Enlisting the laity by anti-clerical measures, by 1533 he had secured parliamentary backing. Having divorced Katharine, he married Anne Boleyn, and the result was, disappointingly, another daughter, Elizabeth, later the Protestant champion. In 1536 Anne Boleyn was convicted of adultery and beheaded. Henry then married Jane Seymour, who bore him a sickly princeling, the future Edward VI. He secured further lay support by dissolving the monasteries, and giving their wealth to his partisans. Many a Scots lord and laird reflected on these moves with deep interest.

In matters of theology, Henry rejected Lutheranism, and the doctrines adopted by the league of German Evangelical rulers; but he allowed English translations of the Bible to circulate, some of which reached Scotland. There was a curious reaction from Ireland to these measures, and to Henry's attempts to enforce his own notions of law with the aid of modern artillery. A syndicate of Irish chiefs offered the crown of Ireland to James V of Scotland, son of Henry VIII's sister, Margaret Tudor. Much in the religious and other history of Europe might have been different if James V had formed a United Kingdom of Scotland and Ireland before the Protestants of England had established a satellite government in Scotland. James V refused to play ball with the Irish chiefs, but Henry himself did so. He handed out a series of earldoms and other honours, to secure their partisanship, as he had secured that of the Welsh careerist squires; and before long Gaelic *kernes* were crossing the Irish Sea in an English effort to conquer Scotland.

Shortly before Cardinal Beaton became Archbishop the Pope had ordered execution of his bull of excommunication against Henry VIII. There were also Catholic refugees in Scotland, for Henry had put down with some brutality risings in northern England by partisans of the old unreformed Church. Beaton seems to have lent himself to a sort of crusade against Henry VIII, and he eventually prevailed on James V to collaborate. James had had an unhappy upbringing, with his Welsh mother and Scots stepfather, who were uneasy folk. He turned out a suspicious, capricious man. Though rather popular among the people, sharing their sports, and writing poems of some merit in Scots, he was distrusted by the nobles and the clergy. In his perpetual desire for money for splendid living, he used the law and confiscated property, in ways not invariably thought fair by the aristocracy. He put his own favourites into jobs normally given to magnates. He exploited the Church by putting his own bastards into lucrative abbacies, and alarmed churchmen by attending a performance of *Ane Pleasant Satyre of the Thrie Estaitis*, by his old tutor, Sir David Lindsay.

The disloyalty of the ruling class was seen in 1542, when Henry VIII got tired of trying to persuade his Scots nephew to share his Protestant policies. The first English army sent in was smartly beaten up by the Earl of Huntly, at Haddon Rigg. Henry then dispatched a much stronger host, and James mobilized to meet it. At Lauder the Scots magnates refused to cross into England to fight there. Much annoyed, James excluded them from his council. The clergy told the King the recalcitrant lords had all been reading the Old and New Testaments in English, and were heretics, who ought to be burned and have their lands confiscated. James then planned an attack across the western frontier. He detached part of his army under his favourite Oliver Sinclair, who began to skirmish with a small English contingent. Some of the recalcitrant lords beat a hasty retreat, Sinclair's force got tangled in a boggy area at Solway Moss, and a group of important magnates ended up as prisoners of war. When he heard the news, James was utterly demoralized. He retreated to Falkland and took to his bed. The deaths of his two sons had already caused him to think he was being punished for his sins. When a message came from Linlithgow that his wife had borne him a daughter, he recalled how the crown had come to the Stewarts through Marjorie Bruce, and exclaimed, 'Fairweill, it cam with ane las, and it will pass with ane las.' He turned his face to the wall, and shortly died.

Once again Scotland was faced with the problem of an infant monarch. Indeed, between 1406 and 1587 there were 89 years out of 181 when the sovereign was under age. It is rather remarkable how well, on the whole, the Scots managed the recurrent problem of regency. This time there was a brief struggle for the post of Regent between Cardinal Beaton and the Earl of Arran, who won, with the help of the Douglases. Arran was heir presumptive to the throne if the infant Queen Mary should die, and he had shown Lutheran sympathies. Henry VIII's object was to arrange for his son Edward to marry the baby Mary. He released the Scots lords captured at Solway Moss after they had agreed to work for peace with England, repudiation of the French alliance, and the establishment of Protestant Reformation. In July 1543 treaties were signed at Greenwich, making peace and arranging for Mary to marry Prince Edward when she was ten.

But Henry had still a long way to go, thanks mainly to

Cardinal Beaton. He had been gaoled by Arran, but bribed the Douglases to release him. He then fetched back from France the fourth Earl of Lennox. This magnate was also of royal descent, and would be heir presumptive if Arran could be excluded as illegitimate. Arran was the son of his father's second marriage, to Janet Beaton. Its validity depended on the validity of his divorce from his first wife, Elizabeth Home. He had divorced her in 1504, after fourteen years of marriage, but cohabited with her till 1510, when he had divorced her again. Six years later, in 1516, he had married Janet Beaton. In such matters of canon law the Cardinal was not without cards to play. The Lennox family declared that Arran was illegitimate. With remarkable speed the Earl of Arran changed his whole tune. Hardly was the wax hard on the sealing of the treaties of Greenwich than Arran did penance for his apostasy to the Lutherans, and brought into his council of regency both Beaton and the Queen Mother, Marie de Guise. The Scots Parliament duly met, and by the end of 1543 annulled the treaties with England, renewed the alliance with France, and re-enacted various statutes against heresy.

Henry VIII, not unjustifiably, complained that his 'Assured Lords' had taken his money and done nothing for it. Furious, he sent up an amphibious expedition. Landing at Granton, it burned Edinburgh, Holyrood, and Leith. English forces also devastated the Borders. Next year, 1545, the Scots scored an exceptional victory over an English force at Ancrum Moor, in Teviotdale, slaying several hundred, and capturing others, for the loss of two Scots. Pitscottie narrates: 'Att thir newis king Harie brunt lyk fire, and was boldened with ire, so that a long space no man durst speak to him.' Later in the year the Earl of Hertford came up and burned seven monasteries and over 240 burghs and villages, mostly in the south-east.

These two years of so-called 'Rough Wooings' destroyed a good deal of Church property, but on the whole confirmed the people in adhesion to the French alliance. Hertford had been ordered by King Henry to 'turne upset downe the cardinalles town of St Andrewes . . . sparing no creature alyve within the same'; but Hertford never came near the place. Beaton was the mainspring of the resistance movement, having to rely much

149 L

on bribery. Some disaffected magnates, including clan chiefs in the Western Isles, had taken English money, but were usually willing to come into line if the French would pay them more, or if the Cardinal could arrange for them advantageous leases of Church lands. The Earl of Lennox was particularly bothersome: he intercepted 30,000 crowns sent from France for other purposes, and put himself into the English royal succession by marrying Lady Margaret Douglas, Margaret Tudor's daughter by the Earl of Angus. The son of this marriage, Henry Stewart, Lord Darnley, later married Queen Mary and sired James VI and I. Lennox's rivalry with Arran was one problem; Arran's rivalry with Marie de Guise was another. In November 1544 both Arran and Queen Marie summoned separate Parliaments, to Edinburgh and Stirling respectively, and it took all Beaton's diplomacy to reconcile the parties. Marie de Guise must have been happy when a French garrison came over, but in the country it was not liked.

Henry VIII's strongest card in the poker game was the promotion of Protestant propaganda. Ideologically, the Catholics were embarrassed by the lack of recent authoritative definition of the positions they had to hold; and no amount of argument could excuse the immorality and illiteracy characteristic of so many of their leading churchmen.

One of the chief Reforming propagandists at this time was George Wishart. He was probably of the family holding the barony of Pittarrow, and may have been a student at King's College, Aberdeen. He is said to have studied and taught Greek at Montrose. Because at places the Greek New Testament is at variance with the Latin Vulgate used by the Roman Church, the then Bishop of Brechin, John Hepburn, thought that students of Greek were dangerous heretics, and suitable candidates for public combustion. Wishart is supposed to have been accused of heresy and to have fled to England in 1538, being then aged about twenty-five. Later he studied in Germany and Switzerland, and was a member of Corpus Christi College, Cambridge, in 1543. One of his contemporaries there, Emery Tylney, describes him as 'black-haired, long-bearded, comely of personage, well spoken after his country of Scotland, courteous, lowly, glad to teach, desirous to learn, and well travelled'. He had commonly by his bedside 'a tubbe of water, in the which (his people being in bed, the candle put out, and all quiet) hee used to bathe himself'. Apparently his cleanliness was next to his godliness. One recalls the early Celtic Christians' prolonged immersions in cold water to keep the Devil at bay.

Wishart returned to Scotland in 1543 during the negotiations for the betrothal of Prince Edward Tudor to the infant Queen Mary, and preached in Dundee, Ayrshire, Perth, Leith and Haddington. He had picked up the Lutheran practice of inciting the general public to clean up the churches by destroying images and other liturgical appurtenances. His host in Ayrshire, John Lockhart of Barr, was outlawed later for stealing from churches in the counties of Ayr, Renfrew and Lanark 'sundry eucharistic chalices, altars, and ornaments of the mass: and also for casting down and breaking choral stalls and other stalls and glazed windows, etc. in the years 1545, 1546, 1547, and 1548'. It seems to have become a hobby for Lutheran magnates and their strong-armed tenants to go round looting objects of value, as well as destroying the merely beautiful decorations of the church, such as altarpieces, with their sacred pictures designed to promote a spirit of devotion in worshippers. The Sheriff of Ayr, Sir Hugh Campbell of Loudon, posted a guard at the kirk of Mauchline to preserve a specially beautiful altarpiece from Wishart, who went down to the market-place instead to rouse the rabble.

This process of 'casting doun' was later taken by some to mean that the Reformers had demolished churches, which was usually not done. Walls and roofs were at this stage left intact, and only the images and other objects considered 'idolatrous' were removed. One can imagine how partisanship was embittered as the process of 'casting doun' spread round the country, especially when it was associated with Henry VIII's 'Rough Wooings'. To many Scots of the traditional allegiance Wishart must have appeared like a subversive agent of a foreign power, and not merely an honest Scotsman concerned with purity of religion and a reform of Church-government and worship on the basis of the Bible.

Wishart's powers as a preacher were astonishing. At Mauchline he preached for three hours on a hot day, and converted 'one of the most wicked men that was in that country, named Laurence Rankin, laird of Shiel. . . . The tears ran from his eyes in such abundance that all men wondered. His conversion was without hypocrisy, for his life and conversation witnessed it in all time to come.' So writes John Knox.

Some time earlier Wishart had been prohibited from preaching further in Dundee, and had foretold 'trouble unlooked for'. While in Ayrshire he heard that plague had broken out in Dundee. He hastened back to that city, and preached at the east gateway, in the Seagate, with the healthy citizens inside and the plague-stricken and suspects outside. He also visited and comforted the sick. Cardinal Beaton sent to assassinate him one John Wigton, who had been curate of Ballumby in Angus, and for three years had been a prisoner of the Cardinal's. Beaton had bribed him, says Knox. As Wishart came down from the pulpit after a sermon he saw the priest standing with his hand inside his gown. Wishart seized his hand, which was gripping a dagger. Wigton fell down and confessed. The plague-stricken worshippers wished to lynch the intending assassin, but Wishart embraced and protected him. Later he went into Lothian, where John Knox joined him, carrying a two-handed sword, which he continued to parade with. The Earl of Bothwell forbade people to attend Wishart's sermons, so that in the great kirk at Haddington he preached to a small congregation where three thousand people had sometimes gathered to see miracle plays put on by the clergy. Wishart prophesied the destruction of the place, which ensued three years afterwards at the hands of the English. He was captured and sent to the Cardinal, who gaoled him in the sea-tower at St Andrews, at the end of January 1546. Beaton then summoned all the bishops and eminent clergy to meet on the second last day of February for the trial. The Archbishop of Glasgow, Gavin Dunbar, had not long before had bitter bickerings with Beaton about precedence, their cross-bearers and retinues coming to blows in the choir of Glasgow Cathedral; but for this errand his lordship of Glasgow came genially enough to endorse the prosecution.

Wishart's trial took place on 28 February 1546, in the cathedral. Cardinal Beaton had mobilized a strong force of men-at-arms to escort the clergy to the church, and another contingent of a hundred soldiers to fetch Wishart. As he passed through the door he gave his purse to a beggar. The dean and sub-prior, John Winram, preached on the parable of the good seed and the evil seed. 'The cause of heresy,' he declared, 'is the ignorance of them which have the cure of men's souls.' He went on to quote St Paul, that: 'A bishop must be faultless . . . not stubborn, not angry, no drunkard, no fighter, not given to filthy lucre.' Some of the clergy must have found this awkward.

After Winram's sermon, Wishart was put up into the pulpit, to hear the charges against him read by the clerk to the court of the Official of the archdiocese, John Lauder, 'his face being sweitting, and froathing at the mouth lyk ane bair'. There were eighteen articles in the indictment. When Lauder had finished, Wishart knelt in the pulpit to pray, and then stood to deliver an oration. He said that he had done nothing but teach the Ten Commandments of God, the Twelve Articles of the Faith, and the Prayer of the Lord, in the mother tongue. At Dundee he had also taught the Epistle of St Paul to the Romans. Lauder then interrupted to say, 'Thou heretic, runagate, traitor, and thief, it was not lawful for thee to preach. Thou hast taken the power at thine own hand, without any authority of the Church.' The bishops then said, 'If we give him licence to preach, he is so crafty, and in Holy Scriptures so exercised, that he will persuade the people to his opinion, and raise them against us.' Wishart then appealed from the jurisdiction of the Cardinal to that of the Regent, the Earl of Arran. This is reminiscent of Luther's appeal to the German princes. Lauder then recited the titles of Beaton, as Cardinal, Chancellor of Scotland, Archbishop of St Andrews, Bishop of Mirepoix, Commendator of Arbroath, *Legatus Natus, Legatus a Latere*. Wishart said he would not refuse to have the Cardinal among his judges, provided the court contained other prelates and some laymen, and that he were judged in terms of the Bible. At this some of the prelates cried out that Arran and other nobles were heretics. They would have proceeded to sentence, had not some advisers persuaded Beaton to have the accusations read again and answered, so that people might not complain of Wishart's wrongful condemnation.

The eighteen articles of the indictment were read out again, and each of Wishart's answers interrupted with a fresh article. One charge was: 'Thou, false Heretic, did say that a priest standing at the altar saying Mass was like a fox wagging his tail in July.' Wishart denied this, but admitted saying that: 'The moving of the body outward, without the inward moving of the heart, is nothing else but the playing of an ape, and not the true serving of God.' Another article ran: 'Thou, false Heretic, traitor, and thief, thou saidst that the Sacrament of the Altar was but a piece of bread, baked upon the ashes, and no other thing else; and all that is there done is but a superstitious rite against the commandment of God.' Wishart then told an anecdote about a talk he had had with a Jew while sailing on the Rhine. The Jew had said, 'It is forbidden by the Law to feign any kind of imagery . . . but your sanctuaries and churches are full of idols. . . . A piece of bread baked upon the ashes, ye adore and worship, and say it is your God.' On hearing this the bishops shook their heads and spat on the floor, presumably to avert the evil omen. Wishart was further accused of saying that Holy Water is 'not so good as wash', and that the invocations of saints and veneration of relics were despicable, and that excommunication by the Church was ineffective; also that 'every layman is a priest'. This too was a Lutheran position, 'the priesthood of all believers'. When accused of asserting that it was lawful to eat flesh on a Friday, he replied with the text: 'They who are clean, unto them all things are clean.' The bishops thought this blasphemous. He was accused of saying that there is no Purgatory. Wishart asked Lauder to refer him to a place in Scripture where Purgatory is mentioned. Thereupon, writes Knox, 'that dolt had not a word to say for himself, but was as dumb as a beetle [*a mallet for beating cloth*] in that matter'.

The clerical court having convicted Wishart, and condemned him to be burned as a heretic, he was taken back to the captain's room in the sea-tower, where he prayed all night. Next morning two Franciscans came for him to make his confession, but he refused to have them, and asked for the sub-prior, John Winram. This good man later joined the Reform movement, and became first Superintendent of Fife in the Knoxian system. After an affecting conversation, Winram reported to the Cardinal and the bishops that he thought Wishart innocent. They refused him leave to give the sacrament to the heretic. At noon the captain invited Wishart to dinner, and he turned the meal into a final communion service. When the Cardinal and bishops had finished dining they went up on to the wallheads of the castle and lay down on cushions and green cloths, while guns were trained on the scaffold, for fear of an attempt at rescue. Wishart meantime was dressed in a buckram coat, and had bags of gunpowder hung round him. Knox says a fire was made ready, and a gallows, in front of the castle, near the priory. Wishart was led out, with his hands tied behind his back, a rope round his neck, and an iron chain round his waist. He addressed the people gathered round, begging them to learn the word of God.

> . . . for the word's sake, and true Evangel, which was given to me by the grace of God, I suffer this day by men, not sorrowfully, but with a glad heart and mind. For this cause was I sent, that I should suffer this fire for Christ's sake. Consider and behold my visage, ye shall not see me change my colour. This grim fire I fear not. . . . I know surely, and my faith is such, that my soul shall sup with my Saviour this night, or it be six hours, for whom I suffer this.

He asked for forgiveness of those who had condemned him ignorantly, and exhorted the people to exhort the Prelates to learn the word of God, 'that they at the last may be ashamed to do evil and learn to do good; and if they will not convert themselves from their wicked error, there shall hastily come upon them the wrath of God, which they shall not eschew.'

The executioner knelt to beg forgiveness, and Wishart kissed him on the cheek, saying, 'Lo! Here is a token that I forgive thee. My heart, do thine office.'

John Knox, following Foxe's *Book of Martyrs*, continues: 'And then, by and by, he was put upon the gibbet, and hanged, and then burnt to powder.' But Lindsay of Pitscottie, who lived near by, and could have eye-witness accounts when he wrote a generation later, suggests that he was partially burned and then strangled. After he had finished praying 'they laid the fire to him, and gave him the first blast of pouder, quhilk was verrie terrible and odious to sie'. There came 'ane thud of wind out of the sea' so strong that it blew down stone walls. Two hundred men sitting on walls near the draw-well in the castle courtyard were blown down, and two of them drowned in the well. Pitscottie goes on:

> And than the captane of the castle exhorted Maister George Wischart to remember of God, and ask forgiveness of his sines; he answered stoutlie, howbeit the fire had perturbed him, and said, 'Captane, God forgive yon man that lyis so glorious on yon wall head; but within few dayis he sall ly as shamfull as he lyis glorious now'. With that they pulled the tow [rope], and latt him speik no more, bot boldenit the gryt fyre about him, and when he was brunt all from the waist doun they bad him remember on God, and make ane signe thairof: to that tokin he lap up ane fute of hight in the fire, quhilk was ane great re-joycing to thame that favoured Godis word.

Among local Lutheran sympathizers who swore to revenge Wishart was John Leslie, brother to the Earl of Rothes. Meantime the Cardinal was engaged in domesticities as well as politics. He had long lived connubially with a lady of rank, Marion Ogilvie, and now, in April, he married off their daughter Margaret to the Master of Crawford, future tenth Earl, who later supported Queen Mary. The young lady's dowry was 4,000 merks, almost royal in scale. (Henry VIII's dowry for his niece, on her marrying the Earl of Lennox, was 6,800 merks.) The Cardinal went to Finhaven in Angus to give the bride away himself, and in the marriage settlements she is called his daughter. On returning to Fife he summoned some of the leading land-owners to concert action against a threatened English invasion by sea. He also made a plan to arrest some Fife lairds whom he suspected of being potential collaborators of the English.

But his local enemies struck first. On Saturday, 29 May 1546, they gathered at dawn in the abbey cemetery, headed by John Leslie and Norman Leslie, his nephew and heir to the earldom, with William Kirkcaldy, younger, of Grange, Peter Carmichael of Balmedie, James Melville, of the Carnbee family, and about a dozen others. Beaton had been adding to the fortifications, and the castle gate was opened early to allow in carts with stones and lime. Kirkcaldy walked in with six others, and asked if the Cardinal was awake. He was asleep. For, writes Knox, 'he had been busy at his accounts with Mistress Marion Ogilvy that night, who was espied to depart from him by the privy postern that morning; and therefore quietness, after the rules of physic, and a morning sleep was requisite for my Lord.' Norman Leslie then came along, with some more. Finally came John Leslie and others. The porter became suspicious, so they broke his head, took his keys, and threw him into the moat. The workmen, a hundred or more, ran away. The invaders went to the bedrooms of the Cardinal's gentlemen and put them all out of the castle, more than fifty men in all, without resistance.

Alarmed by the noise, the Cardinal ran to a postern door, but found it guarded against him. Returning to his bedroom he took a two-handed sword, while his valet heaped chests against the door. Beaton was aged about fifty-two now, and it was natural for him to take up a sword. John Leslie came to the door and told him to open it. Beaton ran to hide a box of gold under a heap of coal in a corner. He then asked, 'Will ye save my life?' John Leslie answered, 'It may be that we will.' The Cardinal asked him to swear it by God's wounds. Leslie replied, 'It that was said, is unsaid,' and called for a brazier of burning coals. The Cardinal or his valet then opened the door, seeing it could be burned out. Sitting down in a chair he cried out, 'I am a priest. I am a priest. Ye will not slay me.' John Leslie struck him first, followed by Carmichael. Melville then, 'a man of nature most gentle and most modest,' says Knox, drew them aside because he saw they were angry, and remarked, 'This work and judgement of God, although it be secret, ought to be done with greater gravity.' He then pointed a sword at Beaton and said, 'Repent thee of thy former wicked life, but especially of the shedding of the blood of that notable instrument of God, Master George Wishart.' He told the Cardinal that he was not moved by hatred of his person, love of his riches, or fear of what trouble he might have caused him. He was striking him only because he had been 'an obstinate enemy against Christ Jesus and his holy Evangel'. Thereupon he ran him through twice or thrice. Beaton's last words were, 'I am a priest, I am a priest. Fye, fye, all is gone.'

Meantime an alarm had gone about the burgh, and the Provost, Sir James Learmonth of Dairsie, came running to the moat, crying, 'What have ye done with my Lord Cardinal?' The conspirators then slung the corpse over the wallhead, by two sheets, attached to an arm and a leg, so that he hung like a St Andrew's Cross. Knox comments, 'How miserably lay David Beaton, careful Cardinal!' Pitscottie adds, 'And when he was lying over the wall, ane called Guthrie pisched in his mouth.' Zeal for the purity of religion could hardly go further. Because it was late May, and the funeral could not quickly be prepared, says Knox, 'it was thought best, to keep him from stinking, to give him great salt enough, a cope of lead, and a nook in the bottom of the Sea-Tower, a place where many of God's children had been imprisoned before, to await what exequies his brethren the Bishops would prepare for him'.

The Leslies and their friends brought in supplies, and were joined by a number of Lutheran sympathizers who felt themselves deeply compromised with the government. They sent to England for aid. The Regent Arran and Queen Marie de Guise started negotiating with the plotters in the castle, the 'Castilians' as they were called. They then besieged them from the beginning of September till late December 1546, bringing up two big guns, named 'Cruik Mow' and 'Deafe Meg'. The Castilians made a passage through the east wall down to the sea, guarded by an iron gate, and got supplies from English ships. Beaton had held as hostage the Earl of Arran's eight-year-old son and heir, and the Castilians had kept a grip of him, much to the gratification of Henry VIII. The siege was rather a sham. The besiegers did some mining, and the Castilians some counter-mining; then a plague outbreak gave Arran an excuse to call it off, on terms. Arran promised to get them a papal absolution for the Cardinal's murder. Pitscottie tells how, when the siege was raised, some of the Castilians would ride round Fife committing arson and rape, for which some godly men in the castle reproved them. At Easter of 1547 came Sir John Knox and joined the garrison, hoping to get from the castle to Germany to study at the Lutheran universities.

Sir John Knox had been born near Haddington about 1514, and may have studied at the university of St Andrews, without taking a degree. By 1540 he had been ordained priest, and in 1543 was working at Haddington as an apostolic notary, that is, a legal official with papal authorization. In 1546 he had carried a two-handed sword in front of George Wishart on his propagandist tour of Lothian. Finally Wishart had taken it from him, anticipating his martyrdom, and told him, 'One is sufficient for a sacrifice.' Knox returned to tutor the sons of two Lothian lairds, Douglas of Langniddry and Cockburn of Ormiston. He brought them to St Andrews in April 1547, and began to preach to the garrison and to the townsfolk, in the parish kirk of the Holy Trinity. His plain and radical utterances were impressive, and folk said he would be burned too. Knox did not preach till he was publicly called to do so, when a group of men, including Sir David Lindsay of the Mount, publicized the doctrine that any congregation beyond the number of two or three had the right to call as preacher any man in whom they supposed the gifts of God to be. Previously Knox had merely acted as a back-room boy, supplying notes for sermons for John Rough to preach. Among the hearers of Knox's first sermon were John Mair, Provost of St Salvator's, the veteran schoolman and historian, and the sub-prior John Winram. Knox challenged anyone to disprove any of his assertions from the Bible. Winram then arranged a debate in St Leonard's College garden between Knox and Rough, for the Lutherans, and certain Black and Grey Friars. They discussed such propositions as that 'Praying for the dead is vain, and to the dead is idolatry', and that 'There is no Purgatory . . . but heaven rests to the faithful, and hell to the reprobate and unthankful', also that 'The Pope is an Antichrist, and so is no member of Christ's mystical body'. The best proof Friar Arbuckle could offer of Purgatory was a passage in Virgil's *Aeneid*, Book VI. Knox also conducted a Communion service in the Protestant manner: that is, with all the faithful participating in both the bread and the wine.

These religious proceedings were rudely disturbed on 29 June 1547, when twenty-one French galleys rowed into the bay. The garrison refusing to surrender, the French fired from the sea, and knocked some slates off houses. The Castilians fired back, killing some rowers chained in the galleys, and some soldiers on land. Arran came up again on 23 July to renew the siege by land. The Italian Leone Strozzi, commanding the French, was expert, and mounted artillery on the walls of the cathedral and on the tower of St Salvator's, to bombard the block-houses, the sea-tower head, and the west wall of the castle. From high on the cathedral they could even fire into the courtyard. John Knox went round telling the Castilians 'that their corrupt life could not escape punishment of God'. At dawn on 30 July Strozzi started a bombardment with fourteen guns, and made a big breach between the fore-tower, which still stands, and the east blockhouse, which has fallen into the sea. A heavy downpour then ensued. The guns stopped firing, and William Kirkcaldy, as commander, capitulated to Strozzi, the terms being that their lives should be spared, English as well as Scots; that they should be transported to France; and that they would be conveyed to any other country but Scotland if the King of France's terms for them should be unacceptable. The galleys a few days later sailed off for France, with 120 prisoners, and spoils worth about £100,000. Knox writes:

> Then was the joy of the Papists both of Scotland and France even in full perfection; for this was their song of triumph:
>> *Preasts, content you now; Preasts, content you now;*
>> *For Normond and his company has filled the galleys fow.*

The castle of St Andrews was immediately razed to the ground. Knox did not know whether this was to fulfil the law which commands places where Cardinals are slain so to be used, or else for fear that England should have taken it.

In September 1547 the Earl of Hertford, now Duke of Somerset, came up in force, and defeated the Regent Arran at Pinkie Cleuch, near Musselburgh. An English force, with Spanish and Greek mercenaries, seized Broughty Castle below Dundee, betrayed to them by the Protestant partisan Lord Gray, and wrought much havoc, burning Dundee and plundering the abbey of Balmerino and nunnery of Elcho. They landed a force at Pertincraig, now Tayport, to burn the Leuchars area, but were ambushed by the Earl of Rothes, Lord Lindsay of the Byres, and Queen Mary's bastard brother, the Lord James

Stewart, Commendator of St Andrews, later Earl of Moray and Regent. They slew 160 of the English force's best men-at-arms and sailors; and, says Pitscottie, 'fra that tyme forth they desired not to land in Fyfe'. While the English controlled the Lothians from Haddington, and held such other useful strongholds as Broughty on the Tay, the French party fought back resolutely. The dowager Marie de Guise showed for a decade the courage and practicality that had enabled her family to build up a power rivalling that of the King of France. Her chief supporter was now John Hamilton, a bastard half-brother of the Regent Arran, who had been Bishop of Dunkeld from 1544 and was now translated to St Andrews. He secured the temporalities of the archdiocese two days after Beaton's death, and the fully official position in July 1549. A worldly prelate, much concerned with the power of the Hamilton family and its presumptive claim to the throne, he was willing to go some way in the Lutheran direction, but remained fairly solid for the French and Papist causes. There came to be a rivalry between him and the Commendator of the priory of St Andrews, Queen Mary's bastard half-brother Lord James Stewart, more conveniently called by the title of Earl of Moray, given him in 1562. Moray was born in 1531, and studied at St Andrews. Another key figure was the sub-prior John Winram, who kept a foot in each camp throughout two most intriguing decades. It is a pity he did not leave memoirs.

Marie de Guise's immediate task in 1548 was to keep her daughter, the five-year-old Queen Mary, safe. She bribed the Regent Arran with the French duchy of Châtelherault, worth 12,000 livres a year, to fall in with her plans. From this time the Regent is called Châtelherault, and his son became third Earl of Arran. Neither was an able man personally, but their political importance continued great. Châtelherault persuaded the Scots Parliament to send the girl Queen to France, to agree to her marrying the Dauphin in due course, and to give the French some fortresses in Scotland. With her four playmates named Mary, the young Queen was shipped from Dumbarton round the west of Ireland to Britanny, and brought up in France by her puritanical grandmother Antoinette de Bourbon. Marie de Guise then collected about a dozen Scots magnates and influential men known to be pro-English and pro-Lutheran, and took them to France for what would now be termed the VIP treatment. They included Moray and Winram, Huntly and Marischal from the north-east, Glencairn, Cassillis, and Maxwell from the south-west. One and all they swallowed the bribes the French King, Henri II, gave them; but they did not stay bribed his way. Marie de Guise secured the release of the gentlemen among the Castilians captured in 1546, but poor Sir John Knox had to serve nineteen months as a galley-slave, till February 1549. His companion in misfortune was James Balfour, who afterwards double-crossed the Reformers and became notorious as the most corrupt man in Scotland. But Knox was friendly with him at that time. Knox records:

The said Master James [*Balfour*] and John Knox being in one galley, and being wondrous familiar with him, would often times ask his judgement, 'If he thought that ever they should be delivered?' Whose answer ever was, from the day that they entered in the galleys, 'That God would deliver them from that bondage, to his glory, even in this life.' And lying betwix Dundee and Saint Andrews, the second time that the galleys returned to Scotland, the said John being so extremely sick that few hoped his life, the said James willed him to look to the land, and asked if he knew it? Who answered, 'Yes: I know it well; for I see the steeple of that place, where God first in public opened my mouth to his glory, and I am fully persuaded, however weak that ever I now appear, that I shall not depart this life, till that my tongue shall glorify his godly name in the same place.' This reported the said Master James in presence of many famous witnesses, many years before that ever the said John set his foot in Scotland this last time to preach.

French garrisons were installed at Dunbar, Inchkeith, Blackness, and Broughty. They did not bother with St Andrews, as the siege had shown its inadequacy in contemporary war with artillery. In an account of campaigning during 1548 and 1549, the Sire Jean de Beaugué wrote:

St Andrews is situated on the sea-shore, and used to be one of the best towns in Scotland. It has the disadvantage of two drawbacks, however; neither its harbour nor its roads [roadsteads for ships] are safe, and it cannot be fortified because it is nearly as large as Turin. Moreover, there is no suitable place for a citadel that would not risk much damage to the abbey, the seat of the archbishop of all the province of Fife [*sic*], and a very large and beautiful structure. So true is this, that the castle, which formerly stood there, and was in great part destroyed by the late Prior of Capua [Strozzi], was commanded not only by the said abbey, but even by the whole town.

None the less Archbishop Hamilton did considerable repair to the castle, simply as his palace, and because he needed a degree of defence against unamiable visitors, even if he could not hope to stand an attack with modern guns. The present fore-tower is largely his work, and shows the cinquefoils from the Hamilton arms.

Some rearmament was also undertaken on the religious front. Provincial Councils were convened by Hamilton in 1549, 1552, and 1559, with John Winram as the chief drafter of documents. They frankly asserted that the chief causes of heresy were two: the moral corruption of churchmen, and their gross ignorance of literature and all the liberal arts. As partial remedy, the Catholic Reformers pressed ahead the development of St Mary's College. In Cardinal Beaton's time its Provost Archibald Hay hoped to make it a trilingual college on the model of the Collège de France, with thorough study of Greek, Latin, and Hebrew, the basic languages of theology and Church history and current controversy. But the plan was shelved. In the same decade a petition to the Regent Arran referred to the university as 'sa desolate and destitute bayth of rederris [Readers], techarris, and auditouris yat it is neir perist and merctis nocht to be callit ane universitie'.

In 1554 Archbishop Hamilton got things going again, his corporation consisting of a Provost or Principal, who must be or become a Doctor of Theology, a Licentiate in Theology, a Bachelor in Theology, and a specialist in canon law. These four were to rule the place. Beneath them were eight priests, all students in theology; and five Regents in Arts, three of them specialists in the three branches of philosophy (physics, meta-physics, and ethics), and the other two specialists in grammar and oratory. There were to be sixteen poor students in arts. Five parishes had their teinds assigned to support the college, with a provisor (steward), cook, and janitor. Hamilton laid down rules for the order of sitting at college services, so that he must have planned a chapel, or else allocated to them the chapel of St John, formerly attached to the Pedagogy. Of Hamilton's buildings, much survives, especially the stair-tower with his arms. The common hall stood on the south, where now white pigeons strut on the lawn.

One feature of the vernacular Catechism issued by Archbishop Hamilton is that it omits reference to the Pope. One may take it that Winram and others around 1552 were close to the position of the Church of England before the death of Edward VI in July 1553, that is a hybrid between the Lutheran and traditional Catholic positions theologically, but with effective rejection of any authority claimed for the Bishop of Rome. A different aspect of affairs was seen after 'Bloody' Mary Tudor came to power in England, and began the burning of heretics to the number of three hundred.

Some Lutherans in Scotland may have feared similar extensive combustions when Marie de Guise became Regent in April 1554, but that princess was a less devoted heresy-hunter, and had a weaker hand to play. She allowed Protestant preachers to go round preaching. What really made her unpopular was a proposal to raise an annual tax on a new assessment of people's properties. Whatever their views about Luther or the Pope, the lords were remarkably unanimous against this notion. In April 1557 Queen Mary married the Dauphin, having in advance signed secret documents by which she bequeathed Scotland to the King of France in the event of her not having issue of her marriage, and meantime pawned it to him for the money spent on her education and upkeep. By this shameless betrayal of her hereditary responsibility she made over Scotland in theory as completely as the Duchy of Britanny had been annexed to the Crown of France, and more completely than Orkney and Shetland had been annexed to the Crown of Scotland. Something of the secret deal may have become known to the eight Scots commissioners sent to attend the marriage, for four of them died mysteriously before leaving France; and there was talk of poison. The Scots Parliament, however, agreed to an exchange of citizen rights between

Scotland and France, and to the Dauphin's being given the 'crown matrimonial' while the marriage lasted. A minority of Scots magnates then began plotting a 'band', or syndicate, in favour of the Reformed religion, and in several burghs congregations were formed to conduct worship in the fashion of the congregations of English exiles on the Continent.

As a warning to Lutheran priests, Archbishop Hamilton—that 'poxy priest', as Queen Mary termed him—tried and burned the priest of Lunan in Angus, Walter Myln, a man aged eighty-two. The prosecutor, Sir Andrew Oliphant, asked him what he thought of the marriage of priests, to which Myln answered, 'I esteem it a blessed bond, ordained by God, approved by Christ, and made free to all sorts of men. But you abhor it, and in the meantime take other men's wives and daughters.' He was also charged with speaking against pilgrimages, and replied, 'I say that pilgrimage is not commanded in the Scriptures, and that there is no greater wantonness in any place than at your pilgrimages, except it be in the common brothels.' This observation makes one wonder about the motives of some of those who journeyed to venerate the kneecap of St Andrew.

After Oliphant had sentenced Myln, and ordered his delivery to the temporal power, there was a delay. No temporal magistrate could be found to do the dirty work. The provost, Patrick Learmonth, had gone out of town. Moreover, the burghers refused to sell or lend a rope to tie Myln to the stake. The burning was put off for a day, till 28 April 1558. The poxy Archbishop then made one of his servants a temporal judge for the occasion, and curtain ropes from the Archbishop's travelling-tent were used to bind him to the stake. His pyre was built close to where Forrest had been martyred, on the clifftop between the priory and the castle. Townsfolk came and threw stones on the site to make a cairn to keep Myln's memory fresh. Knox tells how 'priests and Papists did steal away by night the stones to bigg [build] their walls', but still the cairn was renewed. It must have been a kind of Gallup poll of religious tendencies in the archiepiscopal city.

The next turn of affairs was the death of Mary Tudor in November 1558, and the accession of Queen Elizabeth, her

M

half-sister. By canon law she was undoubtedly illegitimate, and it was natural for Mary Queen of Scots, as heiress of England through Margaret Tudor, to claim the English throne. She and her husband, now Francis II of France, styled themselves additionally Queen and King of England, and used the English royal arms appropriately quartered. This made Elizabeth and her advisers eminently well disposed to the Protestant party in Scotland. It became vital for the English ruling group to establish the Reform across the Border. William Cecil, Elizabeth's chief adviser, contemplated organizing the deposition of Queen Mary, but Elizabeth disliked the notion of any crowned head's being deposed. Meantime tempers were rising in Scotland, and a sharper edge was entering into the controversies. On 1 January 1559 there appeared on the doors of friaries all over Scotland the so-called 'Beggars' Summons', bidding the friars 'flit' on Friday, 12 May, and make over their buildings to paupers and invalids. It is astonishing how much the animosity of the Lutherans was directed against the friars: partly because they did what preaching there was among the people against Lutheran ideas, and partly because they were by their constitutions mendicant orders, begging from the public, and having their convents located in towns, whereas most monasteries were out in the country. As the Lutherans prepared for a showdown, so did Marie de Guise. She summoned all the preachers to meet her at Stirling on 10 May, two days before the 'Flitting Friday' when demagogic assaults were planned against friaries. Meantime John Knox had returned to Scotland, on 2 May, at Leith, after service as Minister to English refugee congregations at Frankfurt and Geneva, and a previous visit to Scotland in 1555–6. He had married an Englishwoman, Marjory Bowes, and would probably have preferred to work in England, but Elizabeth refused him entrance because of his pamphlet, 'The first blast of the trumpet against the monstrous regiment of [i.e., government by] women'.

Dundee and district were already strongholds of the Reform. Accompanied by many lairds from Angus and round about, Knox made for Perth, and on Thursday 11 May preached in St John's Kirk. His denunciations of 'idolatry' caused the congregation to 'cast doun' the images in the approved Lutheran fashion. They also looted the Franciscan and Dominican friaries, and the wealthy Charterhouse founded by James I. Six weeks later Knox wrote to Mrs Anna Locke that 'the brethren . . . put their hands to reformation in Saint Johnston, where the places of idolatry of Grey and Black Friars, and of Charterhouse monks were made equal with the ground.' But when he came to write his History he changed his tune, and blamed the vandalism on the 'rascal multitude'. Calvin was opposed to such destruction, and Knox had come under the influence of Calvin: therefore, on second thoughts, for a public relations exercise, he dissociated 'the brethren' from the excessive activities.

The Protestant cause was at this time directed by the 'Lords of the Congregation', headed by the Earls of Glencairn, Morton, and Argyll, with Argyll's son, Lord Lorne, and an Angus laird, John Erskine of Dun. They armed to defend the burghers of Perth against the righteous indignation of the Queen Regent Marie de Guise, who advanced with a smallish army against them, within ten miles of Perth. There were then some days of coming and going, before the Regent and her French backers were allowed in. Many of the magnates had been dissimulating, and the French Ambassador, d'Oysel, was shortly to complain, 'You cannot tell friend from enemy, and he who is with us in the morning is against us after dinner.' What must truly have shaken Marie de Guise was the open defection of Argyll and Moray, who sent round a summons to the local Protestant backers to muster at St Andrews on 4 June, 'for reformation to be made there'. Archbishop Hamilton hurried into his castle, with a hundred men at arms; this was more than Argyll and Moray had with them at the time, so there was some hesitation whether the reformation should be begun or postponed.

On 9 June Knox preached at Crail, and on the 10th at Anstruther, each sermon being followed by zealous destruction of images. He reached St Andrews on the Saturday evening, 10 June. Though the town council and the lords still swithered, Knox was resolute to preach the next day, even though the Archbishop had threatened to have twelve culverins firing at his nose. On Sunday the 11th he mounted the pulpit of the parish kirk, allegedly the pulpit to be seen since 1930 in the collegiate church of St Salvator, and expounded the text narrating how Christ ejected the money-changers from the temple. The result was that 'as well the magistrates, the Provost and Bailies, as the commonalty for the most part, within the town, did agree to remove all monuments of idolatry, which they did with expedition'. The numerous altars and images of the Holy Trinity were first 'cast doun'. The worshippers then went to the Dominican and Franciscan friaries, and 'before the sunn was downe, there was never inch standing but bare walls'. In the next days the abbey too was invaded, and all the combustible idolatrous material, including mass-books, carried out and burnt on a bonfire where Walter Myln had been burnt. Then or later somebody flung into the latrine of the priory the beautiful head of Christ now in the cathedral museum, and a head of St Andrew, and a royal head, probably that of Malcolm IV. The fabrics of the cathedral and the monastic buildings were not damaged; the canons went on residing there, and about half of them, including the sub-prior Winram, sooner or later adhered to the Reform.

Archbishop Hamilton had been powerless to resist the prior James Stewart (Moray) and his confederates, with the majority of the townsfolk: so he went off to join Marie de Guise at Falkland. They then advanced with their army towards St Andrews. The Protestants marched out and took Cupar, being joined by the Earl of Rothes, the Lindsays of the Byres, the Ruthvens from Perth, and various Lothian lairds, as well as the burghers of Dundee and St Andrews. The armies had a confrontation at Cupar Muir. Rather than shed blood, they parleyed. The Queen Regent and the French then retreated to Edinburgh, and later to Dunbar. Knox received a call to become Minister of the reformed congregation at Edinburgh. The Grey friars of St Andrews, judging that the game was up, made over their property to the town council. But in fact the game was by no means up. The Lutherans were a minority who had won a battle, but not yet the war. By a truce at the end of July, the Queen Regent granted a kind of 'local option' in regard to the choice of religion, but the Reformers completely refused to allow a plebiscite in Edinburgh. The burgh records state the reasons: they could not agree that 'oure religion . . . sall be subject to the voiting of men . . . the maist pairt of men hes ever bene aganis God and his treuthe'. What the Reformers had was a majority of the small idealist intelligentsia, and a growing number of the land-hungry lairds, and a fluctuating support from disaffected elements in the towns. The majority of the general public would be critical or lackadaisical about the old Church, but they might not be prepared to vote for an ill-understood new one. Moreover, there was the awkward fact of French power.

Queen Mary became Queen of France on 10 July 1559, with her husband King as Francis II. They lost no time in shipping in to Leith, newly fortified, a garrison of over three thousand professional soldiers with excellent fire-power. The amateur levies of the Scots magnates were incapable of evicting them without English help. Realizing the precariousness of his own position, the canny Knox handed over his ministry in Edinburgh to the intrepid ex-Dominican John Willock. Intrigues went on with Cecil at Elizabeth's court. He showed willingness again to have Mary deposed, and arranged for the third Earl of Arran, Châtelherault's son, to be smuggled out of France to England. There was a scheme to marry him to Elizabeth, an idea that she rejected when it was later put to her.

Châtelherault himself now turned Protestant, to the annoyance of his half-brother the Archbishop. A further vexation was that Gavin Hamilton of Raploch, who had been made coadjutor bishop of St Andrews in 1551, sided at this juncture with his clan chief, Châtelherault, against his ecclesiastical superior, the Archbishop, another Hamilton. Reinforced by Châtelherault the Lutherans seized Edinburgh in October, and a gathering of lords voted to suspend Marie de Guise from the regency; but they could not hold the town, and withdrew to Stirling early in November. Archbishop Hamilton went in and reconsecrated St Giles' high kirk. The French then captured Stirling, and the Protestant lords split up, some making for Glasgow, others for St Andrews. The French were on their way to recover St Andrews when an English fleet sailed into the Forth. A stalemate ensued, broken by the death of Marie de Guise in Edinburgh Castle on 11 June 1560. Within a month the English and French had both signed an agreement to withdraw. There is little doubt that, whatever its utility in the past, the 'auld alliance' with France had become unpopular in the last generation, and an increasing number of Scots were not unfriendly towards the idea of a new alliance with the auld enemy of England, as now Reformed.

The Protestant party made haste to secure their revolution by summoning the three Estates of Parliament. This they were authorized to do by the Anglo-French treaty just signed, the French commissioners being plenipotentiaries of Mary and Francis II. The Estates were to deliberate on religion, and send representations on the subject to the joint sovereigns, who would then decide. The 'Reformation Parliament' met in Edinburgh, with over a hundred minor barons (lairds) among its membership, claiming to sit there as tenants in chief of the Crown, in terms of an Act of 1426, which had hitherto been dead-lettered. Queen Mary never ratified the proceedings of this Parliament, but had no power to undo them. On 17 August it accepted a Confession of Faith drawn up by a group of Reformers, and on 24 August it abrogated the authority of the papacy and prohibited the celebration of Mass on pain of death.

What the Parliament failed to do was organize and endow a new reformed Church; in effect it left the existing Church organization substantially intact in a legal sense, with all its benefice-holders in possession of what they held, and entitled to receive whatever incomes they had been receiving. Four of the bishops joined the Reform, and three of them went on administering their dioceses as before, in Galloway, Caithness, and Orkney. It is paradoxical to find that in February 1561 Adam Bothwell, Bishop of Orkney, had to shut the doors of Kirkwall Cathedral against the local inhabitants who wished to celebrate Mass, and they fetched a priest to come and celebrate it in a chapel right outside the door of the bedroom where the bishop was lying ill. Even the heretic-burning Archbishop Hamilton came and sat in the 'Reformation Parliament' as Primate of Scotland, and concurred in the repudiation of the Pope and the Mass. The Lutheran revolution turned out to be, from Knox's viewpoint, only half a revolution. The other half was very long in coming, and indeed never has come fully yet.

9

THE PRESBYTERIAN REFORMATION

From the Lutheran semi-revolution of 1560 dates the decline of St Andrews as an important centre of Scottish culture and politics, both absolutely and, still more, relatively to other cities. Archbishops of a sort continued intermittently till William of Orange established the Presbyterian system as the official government of the Church of Scotland, in 1690. But their wealth and power were much less than those of their papalist predecessors before 1560.

A growing fault in the papalist establishment had been its top-heaviness, the diversion of funds and the more capable clergymen from the parishes to the great cathedral churches and major abbeys. One of the first aims of the reformers was to revive Christianity at the grass-roots by having regular services held in every parish kirk, by qualified ministers, aided by educated elders, with competent deacons to manage the local social services of the Church in respect of poor relief and the like. After generations of effort, Scotland did indeed have the services of many hundreds of gifted and able parish ministers and elders, so that, for example, such a critic as the English reformer William Cobbett, who toured Scotland in 1832, was moved to write of the 'exemplary parochial ministers' who administered the distribution of alms to the destitute. To achieve this result a sustained effort of education and agitation and local voluntary organization was required. In these activities St Andrews at times played a leading part, notably in the heyday of Andrew Melville as Principal at St Mary's. Melville, rather than Knox, may be reckoned the chief founder of Scottish Presbyterianism, with its offshoots in the English-speaking lands elsewhere.

By the end of August 1560, after the 'Reformation Parliament' had abolished the Mass and rejected the authority of the Pope, there was a kind of power vacuum in the system of government of the Church in Scotland. The Archbishop of Glasgow, James Beaton, the murdered Cardinal's brother, fled to Paris, taking the archives of his see. He served as ambassador for Queen Mary and James VI, living till 1603. The other bishops either conformed with goodwill, or trimmed, waiting to see how the cat would finally land after its jump. In several burghs groups of Reformers pressed ahead with services much like those then current in England. With local congregations as the effective organizers, one might call this stage of the Scottish Church 'congregationalist'. At the highest political level a scheme was mooted to marry the third Earl of Arran to Queen Elizabeth; but before it could get very far Francis II died, and Queen Mary was a widow. Thinking that she was a reasonable woman, and would go along with the Reform, Knox and the Duke of Châtelherault put their heads together to marry Arran to her. There was no notion of a republic. What the Reformers desired was a godly monarch.

Meantime a committee of representatives from some reformed congregations had evolved a 'First Book of Discipline', which they put forward to govern the Church. In January 1561 it received the backing of many magnates and lairds, on condition that existing benefice-holders of the Kirk should retain their livings for life, subject to making a contribution for parish ministers. About half the canons of the priory of St Andrews went out as parish ministers. Only three local adherents of the papalist kirk emigrated to escape the Lutheran régime. The rest stayed around the disused cathedral, enjoying two-thirds of their revenues, able to enjoy long lies in bed, with no obligation to perform seven services daily. One imagines them saying, 'Thank God for John Knox!'

As 'a thing most expedient for this tyme' the First Book of Discipline in 1561 proposed that 'from the whole nomber of godlie and learned men, now presentlie in this Realme, be selected twelf or ten, for in sa monie Provincis have we divideit the hoill, to whome charge and commandiment shalbe gevin to plant and erect churches, to set ordour and appoint ministeris'. These 'superintendents' were in some sense bishops, and their provinces were dioceses. The sub-prior of the Augustinians, John Winram, became Superintendent of Fife, 'Fotheryk' (West Fife and beyond), and Strathearn, by election on 13 April 1561, 'wythin the parochie kyrk of the citie of Sanctandrois . . . be the common consent of lordis, barronis, ministeris, eldaris, of the saidis bowndis, and otheris common pepill present for the tym, according to the ordor provydit in the Buk of Reforma-cion'. Winram had helped to draw up the First Book of Dis-cipline. The notice of his election was signed by the Minister of St Andrews, eight elders, and three deacons.

A couple of weeks later provision was made for the examina-tion at St Andrews of candidates for the offices of Minister, Exhorter, and Reader. St Mary's of the Rock, 'the Lady College Kyrk upon the hewch', was suspended and declared 'ane prophane hows', that is to say, secularized. Only five of the contemplated superintendents were introduced up and down Scotland. They were inaugurated by a special rite, but not one which purist Episcopalians would consider to constitute 'apostolic succession'. They were at best pseudo-bishops, but they were superior to ordinary parish ministers in emoluments and authority.

In the 'congregationalist' phase of the Reformation elders and deacons were elected annually, not for life. Ministers were elected by congregations, subject to approval by the local Superintendent after examination. The elders of the kirk session could depose the minister, again with the approval of the superintendent. In the sphere of worship, the main difference was the disuse of Latin and the substitution of the vernacular, presumably Court Scots, with an increasing infusion of standard southern English as printed Bibles were perused and digested. Long sermons by black-gowned Ministers were the backbone of services. Metrical psalms, with four-part harmonies, replaced, in general, the sophisticated singing of the vicars choral where there had been such. Holy Communion was normally held only once annually, with all the faithful participating in both kinds, the papalist reservation of the wine for the clergy being a point much resented by Reformers. In regard to law, the monasteries remained corporations owning property, and able to lease farms to local lairds and the like. As monks died off they were not replaced.

Exactly what happened to abbey churches and other buildings is only partially known. Many of them were located remote from populations that could use them, and the local lairds simply stripped them of lead, brass, timber, and anything valuable they could find, and then treated them as quarries. It is not known when the cathedral of St Andrews became a ruin, but it can hardly have stayed intact much after 1600. Like many medieval churches, it was too daring architecturally. In particular, the central tower had given a good deal of trouble long before 1560. If the roof lead were stripped, or merely if it were not thoroughly maintained, winds would blow gaps in the roof. The choir had a heavy stone-vaulted roof, which would set up a stress against the tower, not fully countered by the timbered roof of the nave; and a collapse some day was immensely probable. The notion that Knox led a mob to ding the building down is a myth. It perished because it had ceased to fulfil a desired function, and from mere lack of maintenance. The priory buildings survived as residential quarters much longer.

A notable feature of the Scottish Reformation is the scarcity of martyrs on either side. At most two Scots priests suffered death for celebrating the prohibited Mass, which is about one per cent of the number of Recusants put to death under Elizabeth Tudor, ruling a population only about five times as numerous as the Scots. Most papalist clergy quickly resigned themselves to the new order, and many became ministers; but the Reformation certainly generated an anti-clericalist feeling. The minister was reckoned merely 'the teaching elder'. Cardinal Bellarmine noted that Protestantism had abolished the old distinction of clergy and laity. By enlisting 'lay' enthusiasm in running the parish kirks the Reformation undoubtedly promoted bouts of puritanical inquisition by a moral police force, the elders of the Kirk Session, whom Burns was to call 'the holy beagles, the houghmagandie pack'. In reading the St Andrews Kirk Session Minutes one sees how the elders dealt with juvenile delinquency, petty theft, and malicious gossip, as well as sexual intromissions unsolemnized in advance by holy wedlock. The kirk of the Holy Trinity yet retains, in a side apartment, a piece of furniture, built for two, with the word REPENTANCE inscribed prominently across it. The occupants of the 'stool of repentance' afforded much improving diversion to the more godly, or the less incautious, as the Minister rebuked their errors.

Witch-hunting is the most repugnant feature of the new era

brought in by the Protestants. It grew in part from the new emphasis on the Old Testament text, 'Thou shalt not suffer a witch to live.' In 1569 a former Lyon King of Arms, William Stewart, was hanged at St Andrews for 'witchcraft, nigromancye [necromancy] and utheris crymes'. On 28 April 1572, a female witch was burned, 'against the quhilk Mr Knox delt from pulpit, sche being set upe at a pillar befor him', says James Melville. Witches had, to be sure, been burned in Catholic countries now and then, notably Joan of Arc by the English in France. The worst attacks of the witch-hunting mania in Scotland occurred in the seventeenth century: though equalled or surpassed in parts of the Continent, they are deeply discreditable episodes in the national history. The men who reformed the university after 1560 seem to have been pious believers in witches, just as they were deeply convinced of the incessant activity of the Devil. The name of 'the Witches' Pool' became attached to a rock-rimmed area of sea below the cliffs west of the castle, a little east of the Step Rock bathing-pool. The early Victorian 'Martyrs' Memorial' is a memorial to four Protestant martyrs of the sixteenth century. How many witches perished in the Witches' Pool by drowning, or elsewhere by burning, or by being strangled at the stake and then burned, has not been calculated. Rather droll is that John Knox himself was accused of having used witchcraft to secure the consent to marriage of his second wife, Margaret Stewart, daughter of Lord Ochiltree, 'ane damosil of nobil blude, and he ane auld decrepit creatur of maist bais degree of onie that could be found in the countrey'.

A bewitching face was seen a few times in St Andrews in the 1560s, that of the perennially controversial Mary Queen of Scots. She returned from France in 1561, reaching Leith in a sea-fog on 19 August, and being serenaded at Holyrood with psalm-tunes accompanied by three-stringed fiddles. As a great and controversial concession the Reformers allowed her to hear Mass in her private chapel. Well-schooled by the Guises, she aimed to recover Scotland and England for the papalist Church, but she had to play a waiting game, with almost no reliable helpers. At first she was disposed to trust her half-brother Moray, the Commendator of the priory at St Andrews, and she may have sometimes stayed in his house, the New Inns, as her mother had in 1538.

It was at St Andrews in February 1563 that a young French courtier, Chastelard, was beheaded for over-familiarity with the Queen. Knox tells how he danced with her a dance called 'the Purpose', 'in the which man and woman talk secretly—wise men would judge such fashions more like to the bordell [*brothel*] than to the comeliness of honest women'. When noblemen sought audience of Mary, they would find Chastelard installed, 'and sometimes she would steal a kiss of his neck'. The young gentleman felt emboldened to ensconce himself under the royal bed. Mary commanded him away. Gossip developed. Mary told her half-brother Moray to dirk the man. He promised, and then renegued. The crazy Frenchman attempted once more at Burntisland to enter the royal bed-chamber. He was tried at St Andrews and beheaded on 22 February, just where is not known. On the scaffold he recited a poem of Ronsard, and Knox says 'he made a godly confession'. The Frenchman Brantôme gave his last words as 'Adieu, the most beautiful and the most cruel Princess of the world.'

It is a grave error to think that Queen Mary was prone to sexual promiscuity. Knox, who suspected and disliked her, specifically says, 'We call her not a whore . . . but she was brought up in the company of the wildest whoremongers, yea, of such as no more regarded incest than honest men regard the company of their lawful wives.' This admission seems more plausible than his later accusation that she was indeed a whore. Her nature is perhaps best revealed by a report of the English Ambassador Randolph, who called to see her in January 1565 while she was staying in a merchant's house at St Andrews with a small retinue. She told him, 'I sent for you, to be merry, and to see how like a bourgeois wife I live, with my little troop; and you will interrupt our pastime with your great and grave matters. You see neither cloth of estate, nor such appearance that you may think that there is a Queen here.' She was an excellent and tireless rider, fond of hawking and archery, willing to try her hand at the golf, and played music 'reasonably well for a Queen'.

From St Andrews she rode to Wemyss Castle, and met her

176

papist cousin Lord Darnley, whom she proceeded to marry. In Catholic eyes he was next heir to the thrones of England and Ireland after Mary herself. Protestants became alarmed. There were many intrigues and plots. Darnley himself became estranged from Mary; he contracted a nasty disease, and took part in the killing of her Italian secretary David Rizzio, while she was pregnant with the future James VI and I. There is little doubt that her rather cold and calculating temperament was upset by this emotional shock. When the baby appeared she had him baptised by Catholic rites, organized by her Protestant lover, the Earl of Bothwell, though her papalist husband, Darnley, was in the town. In February 1567 the unwanted husband Darnley was strangled, and his house blown up. Three months later Archbishop Hamilton of St Andrews helped on the divorce of Bothwell from his first wife, and promoted his marriage to Mary. Seeing the poor lady was making a mistake, the crafty prelate encouraged it. His aim was to make his nephew Arran King. A coalition of outraged Scots magnates took an army to confront Mary and Bothwell at Carberry. Bothwell's men ran away, and Mary was haled to Edinburgh, amid the curses of the townsfolk, then gaoled in Lochleven Castle. Archbishop Hamilton proposed she should be executed. She abdicated, and on 24 July the baby prince was crowned, by Adam Bothwell, Bishop of Orkney, the precious trimmer who had married Mary to Bothwell six weeks previously. Next summer, 1568, Mary escaped, having charmed the young George Douglas of Lochleven to help her. Archbishop Hamilton had joined a syndicate of magnates to defend her this time, perhaps planning now to marry her to a Hamilton. There took place at Langside, near Glasgow, a scrimmage between 6,000 Queen's men and 4,500 King's men, led by Moray. The minority took the initiative and won. Mary fled to England, where her cousin Elizabeth imprisoned her, and finally, in February 1587, alarmed by papist plots, had her beheaded.

Moray ruled as Regent for the young King till he was shot in 1570 by a Hamilton. The King's grandfather Lennox then became Regent, and was killed at Stirling in a rapid raid made from Edinburgh Castle by Sir William Kirkcaldy of Grange, who was still holding that fortress for Mary. After a short regency of Mar, the government came into the hands of the fourth Earl of Morton, a Douglas. His clansman John Douglas, Rector of the University, had already become Archbishop in succession to Hamilton. He was now in his seventies, and died in the pulpit while attempting to preach, in 1574. Historians write of him as a 'tulchan' bishop: that is, like a stuffed calf's skin set beside a cow to make her give milk, the cow being the Church, and the milk the revenues of the see swallowed by land-owners. But he seems to have been no more of a *tulchan* than his recent predecessors, and had contributed in his day to the Reformation. His successor, Patrick Adamson, appointed in 1576, had a rough ride from the Presbyterian champions, and was let down by the young King James VI: so that he died in penury in 1592, a pensioner of his old opponent, Andrew Melville.

Whatever one may think now about the upsets of the time in State and Church, and the issues on which people fought, one must note that the atmosphere seems somehow to have sharpened the wits of at least some of the students of the 1560s. The greatest talent among them was that of John Napier of Merchiston, who entered St Salvator's in 1563, at the age of thirteen. His invention of logarithms was not published till 1614. Napier also invented a calculating-machine and an early form of tank for land warfare. He improved pumping machinery for coalpits, and developed fertilizers for crops. His commentary on the Revelation of St John, written from a strongly Calvinist and anti-papistical viewpoint, was translated into French, Dutch, and German. Versatility and internationalism were characteristic of the Scots intellectuals of that age.

Latin was still the international language of the sixteenth century, and in Latin no man had a wider international reputation than George Buchanan, who became Principal of St Leonard's College in 1566. Indeed, taking verse and prose together, Buchanan may be thought the finest Latin stylist of all time, for his verse is much better than Cicero's attempts at poetry, and his prose far surpasses that of Seneca. Buchanan was born in 1506, in an area of Stirlingshire where Gaelic was still spoken. He learned it. Latin had recently been made compulsory by the Scots Parliament, in 1496, for eldest sons and heirs of barons and substantial freeholders. They were to be put to it at the age of eight or nine, and 'remane at the grammer sculis quhill [*till*] thai be competentlie foundit and have perfite latyne and thereftir to remane thre yeris at the sculis of art and jure [*Arts and Law*] sua that thai may have knawlege and understanding of the lawis'. When only fourteen Buchanan went to Paris and learned some Greek, before matriculating at St Leonard's in 1524. Two years later he was again in Paris, having as fellow students Rabelais and the founder of the Jesuits, St Ignatius Loyola. Later he became professor at Bordeaux, where Montaigne was a pupil, and in Portugal at Coimbra, where he fell foul of the Inquisition. While in prison he translated the Psalms of David into Latin in thirty-eight different metres, a work that long had an international vogue as Sunday reading for the learned. His Latin history of Scotland is better for style than for scholarly insight, and is not unimpeachable in point of intellectual honesty, as has been well demonstrated by Professor Hugh Trevor-Roper. His work on the constitutional rights of Scots Kings, *De jure regni apud Scotos*, continues the old Scots tradition of constitutional monarchy, seen already in the work of his old teacher, John Major. It had a wide influence, on John Milton among others, and was ceremonially burned at Oxford so late as 1683. Buchanan's attempts to reform the university failed, and he left the principalship in 1570. In his native Scots he wrote a political pamphlet on Queen Mary's secretary, Maitland of Lethington, entitled *Chamaeleon*.

How students lived at that period is well seen from the autobiography of James Melville (1556–1614), who came to St Leonard's in November 1571. His father, Richard Melville of Baldovie, had studied at Wittenberg with Luther's friend Melanchthon, and was Minister of Maryton near Montrose. His mother was Isobel Scrymgeour, of the family of the hereditary standard-bearers of Scotland. Her brother, Henry Scrymgeour, born in 1506, was one of the leading Greek scholars of the age, active in editing classical texts, and became Professor of Civil Law at Geneva, where he witnessed the testament of John Calvin. The young James Melville became a pupil of Mr William Collace, the Regent, who took him through the whole Arts course over four years. At first, faced with Cassander's Rhetoric, he could not understand Collace's Latin, and 'did nathing bot bursted and grat at his lessones, and was of mynd to haiff gone ham agean, war nocht the luiffing cear of that man comforted me, and tuk me in his awin chalmer, causit me ly with himselff, and everie night teatched me in privat, till I was acquented with the mater'. The pastoral care of a tutor could hardly go further. The boy's father was so grateful that he sent Collace two gold pieces in a napkin: 'bot the gentleman was sa honest and loving, that he wald haiff non of his gold, but with austere countenance send me bak with it'.

At school in Montrose young Melville had been 'teached to handle the bow for archerie, the glub for goff, the batons for fencing, also to rin, to loope [*lowpe, leap*], to swoom, to warsell [*wrestle*] . . .'. At the university he had no excess of pocket-money. 'Als I haid my necessars honestlie aneuche of my father, bot nocht els; for archerie and goff, I haid bow, arrose, glub and bals, but nocht a purs for catchpull [*a kind of rackets*] and tavern; sic was his fatherlie wisdom for my weill.' He also learned music, 'wherin I tuk grait delyt, of ane Alexander Smithe, servant to the Primarius of our Collage, wha haid been treaned upe amangis the mounks in the Abbay. I lerned of him the gam [*gamut*], plean-song [*plainsong, the tenor part*], and monie of the treables of the Psalmes, wherof sum I could weill sing in the kirk. . . . I lovit singing and playing on instruments passing weill, and wald gladlie spend tyme whar the exercise thairof was within the Collage; for twa or thrie of our condisciples played fellon weill on the virginals, and another on the lut and githorn [*lute and zither*]. Our Regent had also the pinalds [*spinet*] in his chalmer . . .' Mr Collace taught the boy to play the spinet a bit, but saw he was too keen, and gave it up. 'It was the grait mercie of my God that keipit me from anie grait progress in singing and playing on instruments; for, giff I haid atteined to anie reasonable missure thairin, I haid never don guid utherwayes, in respect of my amorous disposition, wherby Sathan sought even then to deboiche me.' Here we see the incipient Puritanism of the Reformation, which went deeper in the next generation, and restricted many artistic expressions in favour of intellectual soul-searching.

Another diversion of James Melville's student days was listening to the veteran John Knox, 'that maist notable profet and apostle of our nation'. The Queen's Lords having occupied Edinburgh Castle, he thought St Andrews safer in 1571. He expounded the book of Daniel. 'In the opening upe of his text he was moderat the space of an halff houre; bot when he enterit to application, he maid me sa to grew [*shudder*] and tremble, that I could nocht hald a pen to wryt.' The ageing prophet 'wald symtymes com in and repose him in our Collage yeard, and call us scholars unto him and bless us, and exhort us to knaw God and his wark in our contrey, and stand be the guid cause, to use our tyme weill, and lern the guid instructiones, and follow the guid exemple of our maisters. Our haill Collage, maisters and schollars, war sound and zelus for the guid cause. The uther twa Collages nocht sa.' At the 'New College' of St Mary three of the Regents were Hamiltons, named Robert, Archibald, and John, clansmen of the bad Archbishop; and the Law professor, William Skene, disliked Knox's doctrine. The 'Auld Collage', St Salvator's, was ruled by John Rutherford, 'a man lernit in philosophie, bot invyus, corrupt'. These inter-collegiate animosities were to continue.

St Salvator's was the most fashionable college for sprigs of nobility, such as James Crichton of Eliock in Dumfriesshire, son of the Lord Advocate. He arrived in 1569, at the age of nine, and graduated MA five years later. After a period as playmate of the boy King at Stirling, he sought his fortune on the Continent, disputing publicly at Genoa, Venice, and Padua, and received large public awards for his virtuosity. An Italian handbill of 1580 tells that, at the age of twenty, the Scotsman is a master of ten languages:

... Latin and Italian in perfection, and Greek so as to compose epigrams in that tongue; Hebrew, Chaldaic, Spanish, French, Flemish, English, and Scots; and he also understands the German. He is most skilled in philosophy, theology, mathematics, and astrology, and holds all the calculations hitherto made in this last to be false. ... He possesses a most thorough knowledge of the Cabala. His memory is so astonishing that he knows not what it is to forget; and, whenever he has once heard an oration, he is ready to recite it again word for word as it was delivered. Latin verses, whatever the subject or the metre proposed to him, he produces extempore; and, equally extemporaneous, he will repeat them backwards, beginning from the last word in the verse. His orations are unpremeditated and beautiful. He is also able to discourse upon political questions with much solidity.

He was beautiful in person, a finished gentleman, in conversation most gracious, a remarkable gymnast, dancer, horseman, swordsman, as well as thoroughly acquainted with the Fathers of the Church, Greek and Latin, and Aristotle and all his commentators, not to mention Thomas Aquinas and Duns Scotus. The Venetian publisher Aldus Manutius testifies the like in dedicating to him his edition of Cicero's *Paradoxa*. In 1582 Crichton took service with the Duke of Mantua, for whom he designed a system of fortifications. On the night of 3 July, 1582, not yet twenty-two, he was mortally stabbed in a street brawl by the duke's heir, Vincenzo Gonzaga, and buried in the church of San Simone.

The most important St Andrews man of the later sixteenth century was Andrew Melville (1545–1622). Youngest of nine sons of Richard Melville of Baldovie, who was killed at Pinkie, he had been reared by his eldest brother, Melanchthon's pupil, the minister of Maryton, and learned Greek at Montrose school. When he came to St Mary's in 1559 he astonished the professors, none of whom knew Greek, by reading in the original the Aristotle which was the staple diet of their arts course. In 1564 he went to Paris, and heard Turnebus lecture in the 'Royal Trilingual College', and Petrus Ramus, the assailant of Aristotle. Melville amazed the French by the ease with which he could declaim in Greek. In 1566 he went on to the University of Poitiers, and was made a Regent in the College of St Marceon. Its students had a great rivalry with the College of St Pivareau in writing epigrams and declaiming orations. While Melville coached them, the Marceonites always won. Melville studied jurisprudence, but found himself interrupted through the Huguenot Admiral Coligni besieging the city, which the Duc de Guise defended. Melville became tutor to the son of a local lawyer, to whom he taught Greek. One day he found the little boy bathed in blood, having been mortally wounded by a Protestant cannon ball. As he died he quoted the New Testament in Greek, 'Master, I have finished my course.' Because he was always reading the Bible, the young Scot was suspected of being a Huguenot. The city wall had been breached, and an assault was expected. A Catholic captain challenged Melville as a traitorous Huguenot. Small and slight as he was, Melville repudiated the charge, put on his armour, seized a horse, and prepared to defend the breach. The captain was startled into humble apologies.

Leaving Poitiers in 1569, Melville walked to Geneva, with a small Hebrew Bible attached to his belt, and an introduction to the eminent Theodore Beza, Professor of Divinity in the Academy. Beza was so impressed by him that he had his colleagues give him the vacant chair of Humanity, that is Latin language and Roman civilization. At Geneva, where he found his sister-in-law's brother Henry Scrymgeour occupying the chair of Civil Law, he stayed till 1574, studying Oriental languages. After the Paris massacre of 1572 scores of French Huguenots came to Geneva, and it became the bastion of international Calvinism. On his way home, Melville disputed with Jesuits at Paris, where their college was run by a St Andrews graduate, Edmund Hay.

After a stay at Baldovie, he went to see at Stirling the eight-year-old James VI, who was being tutored by Sir Peter Young, son of Henry Scrymgeour's sister Margaret, in a curriculum devised by Buchanan. With Buchanan's advice Melville introduced a new system of arts study in the University of Glasgow, of which he was appointed Principal. Though founded over a century earlier, that seminary had petered out and been shut up. The reputation and zeal of Melville revived it, with a six-year course in Latin, Greek, mathematics, geography, moral and natural philosophy, universal history, Hebrew, Chaldee and Syriac, and divinity according to Calvin's *Institutions*. Andrew's nephew James taught Greek, logic, and rhetoric, being the first Regent in Scotland to read Greek authors with his class in the original. Andrew also revolutionized teaching, by introducing specialist professors, to replace the old system of one Regent carrying his pupils through every branch of a course of years. He also preached as minister of Govan parish.

One of the Principal's duties was corporeal chastisement of erring students, in symbol of which he was invested at his inauguration with a leather strap, as well as the keys of the college. Melville devolved this task on the Regents, but he had to take the lead in maintaining the right of discipline when some hundreds of men-at-arms of the Cunningham and Boyd families gathered in Glasgow to prevent due punishment being exacted from a refractory student named Cunningham. With his habitual intrepidity, the little Principal carried the day.

Melville's intrepidity remained as constantly with him when his views on Church-government brought him into conflict with the Regent, the Earl of Morton. That magnate had seen need to deal with the problem of filling up vacant bishoprics and other prelatical positions, as incumbents were dying off. He held at Leith, in January 1572, a convention of superintendents and certain ministers, who constituted themselves a General Assembly of the Church and appointed a committee to confer with the Privy Council. The joint body then decided that bishoprics should stay as they were till James VI came of age, and that abbacies and priories also should continue, the persons elected to them being of due age and scriptural qualifications, chosen by a chapter of learned ministers, and subject to the General Assembly in spiritual matters, as to the King in temporal. Abbots and commendators were to form, with the bishops, the ecclesiastical Estate in Parliament. Morton's scheme was rejected by a General Assembly at St Andrews in March 1572, and the dispute continued.

Melville first attended the General Assembly in 1571, as a Doctor of Divinity, and was put on a committee, which evolved what became the Second Book of Discipline, the charter of Presbyterianism. In August 1575 Melville gave a long address to a further General Assembly, asserting that prelacy had no foundation in Scripture, and that, as a human expedient, its tendency was extremely dubious. The primitive Christian *episkopos*, or bishop, was, in Melville's opinion, merely a parish minister or presbyter, that is elder. He argued that the Church of England was in a bad way because of its diocesan bishops, and advocated the restoration in Scotland of that parity of ministers which had characterized the original Christian Church. The same, and additional, arguments have continually recurred, most recently during the attempts of persons of œcumenical spirit to bridge the historic and theoretical gaps separating the established Church of Scotland from the established Church of England and other Christian associations. The complexity of the issues is exemplified in the fact that the Regent Morton sent in a paper asking the General Assembly for answers to no fewer than forty-two questions.

Melville was Moderator of the General Assembly at Edinburgh in April 1578, when it adopted its 'Book of Policy', better known as the *Second Book of Discipline*. This in effect put all the historic diocesan episcopal functions into committee, by making Presbyteries responsible for the superintendence of all Church matters in their areas, to the exclusion of persons called bishops, superintendents, or visitors. The Second Book lays down that Jesus Christ has appointed a government in his Church, distinct from the civil government, which is to be exercised in the name of Jesus by the office-bearers authorized by Jesus, and not by civil magistrates. The government of the Church consists of three things: doctrine, including the administration of the sacraments; discipline; and distribution. For these there are needed three types of church-officer: ministers, who preach as well as ruling; elders, who merely rule, which involves visiting people at home, whether well or sick; and deacons, who manage funds and distribute alms. The Scriptures do not allow one man to be a pastor of pastors, or a pastor of many flocks. The Second Book also recognized the 'doctor', who expounds the Scriptures, as in divinity colleges, refuting error and instructing youth. It evolved the hierarchy of Church courts, from the kirk-session of a parish, consisting of minister and elders and deacons; to the Presbytery, of ministers and elders from a group of parishes; to the Synod, a regional grouping; and the General Assembly, of the churches of the Scottish realm. An œcumenical assembly was also part of the scheme, for the whole of Christendom. Each court was to appoint the time and place of its meeting, and elect its own Moderator as chairman.

The Regent Morton grew suspicious of the Presbyterian movement, and sent for Melville to browbeat him into the Episcopalian schemes of the government, modelled on those of Elizabethan England. As they talked Morton exclaimed, 'There will never be quietness in this country till half a dozen of you be hanged or banished the country.' Melville replied, 'Tush, Sir, threaten your courtiers after that manner. It is the same to me whether I rot in the air or in the ground. . . . Let God be glorified: it will not be in your power to hang or exile his truth.'

Melville's moral ascendancy having been manifested to the Regent, that astute nobleman was obliged to give him his head for the meantime. One of the tasks in hand was the reformation of the University of St Andrews, and in 1579 a 'New Foundation and Erection' of the three colleges was carried out, with Melville as the mastermind. He planned it as a propagandist institute of Reformed theology to refute the errors disseminated by Edmund Hay and the Jesuit publicists of the Counter-Reformation. St Salvator's and St Leonard's were to be colleges teaching arts, with a Principal and four 'ordinary professors or regents', each a specialist in one of four subjects: Greek and Latin; rhetoric; logic, ethics, and Politics; and natural philosophy, which meant all the physical sciences. St Salvator's was also to have professors of mathematics and law, and its Principal was to profess medicine. The St Leonard's Principal was to specialize in the philosophy of Plato. Parts of this scheme for the propaedeutic colleges seem to be tailor-made to fit the existence of particular academics who had to be given something to do for their salaries.

The main part of the university was to be St Mary's College, with a Principal professing systematic theology, and a Professor of Hebrew, one of the New Testament, and two of the Old Testament. In 1580 Andrew Melville moved from Glasgow to become Principal of St Mary's, where his arms and initials embellish the South Street front. One of the first steps he took was to offer chairs to two leading English Presbyterian propagandists, Cartwright and Travers, known as 'the head and neck of English Presbyterianism'. They did not come, but the gesture was indicative. From the later 1580s to 1626 St Andrews attracted relatively many foreign students, 159 in all, of whom 47 English, 30 French, 23 Dutch, 12 Danes, 8 Belgians, 5 Poles, 5 Prussians, 4 Germans, 3 Italians, 2 Norse, 1 Welshman, and even 1 Jew, with 18 others of unknown nationality. This afflux was mainly thanks to Melville.

As Principal of St Mary's Andrew Melville taught divinity, Hebrew, and other Oriental languages, and did a good deal of preaching in the parish kirk and elsewhere, besides serving as Moderator of the General Assembly in 1582, 1587, and 1594. During most of this period there were occasional alarms in Scotland about popish plots inspired from abroad. In Scotland itself there were so few priests left that regularly practising Catholics hardly existed; but several important nobles and their wives cherished sympathy for the old ways of worship. In England papalist conspiracies were more significant, and there was sometimes a possibility of major activity from France or Spain, like the Spanish Armada of 1588.

Inside the Protestant camp there were extremists, like Melville, who wished to reform everything in the light of the Bible, and moderates, who were happy enough with the compromise Lutheranism of the 1560s, especially as that fitted in with Elizabeth's England. Soon after 1580 the young King James fell under the influence of his cousin, Esmé Stewart, Duke of Lennox, and Knox's brother-in-law, James Stewart, Earl of Arran, and took a strongly Episcopalian line. Melville protested, and joined in presenting a remonstrance to the King at Perth. Arran demanded, 'Who dare subscribe these treasonable articles?' Melville stepped forward and took a pen to sign: 'We dare.' In February 1584, he was summoned before the Privy Council for treason, in respect of a sermon in which he had compared Queen Mary to Nebuchadnezzar, who was banished and would be restored again. He denied saying so, but, more importantly, rejected the authority of the Privy Council in a matter of religion. He was an ambassador from a King and a council greater than themselves. Throwing his Hebrew Bible on the royal table, he cried, 'There are my instructions and warrant.' He defied them to test him in the Hebrew. The Privy Council sentenced him to be warded in a castle, but he broke his parole, and escaped to England, where the Universities of Oxford and Cambridge honoured him. Next year, 1585, he returned, when James VI forgave some rebel lords of extreme Presbyterian sympathies. Another show-down came in April 1586, when the Synod of Fife excommunicated Archbishop Adamson, who retaliated by excommunicating Andrew Melville and his nephew James.

In the early 1590s Melville was rather well in with King James, writing a tasteful Latin poem for the coronation of Queen Anne of Denmark in 1590, a year in which he became Rector of the University. His great moment came in 1592, when the King and Parliament established the Presbyterian system as the government of the Church of Scotland. The crown reserved the right to fix place and time for meetings of the General Assembly, and to appoint royal commissioners to visit and oversee.

In 1594 Melville put on his armour to join the King in a northern campaign against the Earls of Huntly and Erroll. But next year, when the King allowed the exiled earls to return, Melville's protest was brushed off. Then, with a commission of the General Assembly, he proceeded to Falkland to give the King a good talking-to. When James spoke of sedition, Melville grasped him by the sleeve and called him 'God's silly vassal [*weak dependant*]', going on to expound the doctrine of the Two Kingdoms. 'And now, Sire, I must tell you that there are two kingdoms: the kingdom of Christ, which is the church, whose subject King James VI is, and of whose kingdom he is not a head, nor a lord, but a member; . . .' The civil authority in the temporal kingdom was bound to assist and support those whom Christ had called to govern the spiritual kingdom; 'otherwise they are not faithful servants to Christ'.

King James got his own back when the death of Elizabeth Tudor left the English short of a monarch, and he succeeded to the throne in London. In 1606 he invited both the Melvilles, with others, to confer with him there on the Church of Scotland. A memorable conference took place at Hampton Court on 23 September, when a long and bold speech by Andrew Melville astonished the English prelates. He did not hesitate to seize Archbishop Bancroft's fine linen sleeves and term them 'Romish rags'. It was felt to be more outrageous when he wrote

St Salvator's College from the castle, drawn by James Oliphant in 1760.

Professor J. F. Ferrier's class in Moral Philosophy, 1862–3, with Andrew Lang on the Professor's right (in light trousers).

The funeral procession of Principal Sir James Donaldson
in 1915, approaching the cathedral from North Street.

May Day—students dancing eightsome reels in the castle
courtyard at dawn.

Old Daw Anderson at the Ginger Beer hole, with Old
Tom Morris.

a Latin epigram satirizing a Michaelmas service the King had asked him to attend at the Chapel Royal, where he saw on the altar two closed books, two empty chalices, and two candlesticks with their candles not lit. The epigram's purport was that England was here imitating the 'purple whore [*or scarlet woman*] of Rome'. A spy brought a copy of the poem to the King, who had Andrew thrown into the Tower of London. He amused himself scratching Latin verses on the walls with the tongue of a shoe-buckle. In 1611 he was released, and became Professor of Biblical Theology in the Protestant University of Sedan, where he died, unmarried, in 1622. In private life he was notably witty and hospitable, but his zealous views continually involved him in disputes, including some at St Andrews.

A good specimen of the spirited exchanges of the age is found in 1581, when Andrew Melville 'coming in the pulpit, spak the treuthe of all thingis with grait ardentness and zeall'. In rebuking sin, he spoke such home truths to the provost that in the middle of the tirade that worthy rose and left the kirk, later being taken to task by the Presbytery, and having to beg pardon of the congregation. There was a war of placards. One day the gate of St Mary's College was embellished with a notice in Italian and French, threatening to bastinado the Principal. Knowing it to be by James Learmonth, heir of Balcomie, Melville took it up with him into the pulpit, and, like another Elijah or Amos, denounced the culprit, sitting before him: 'Thou Frenchified, Italianate, jolly gentleman, wha has defyled the bed of sa monie maried, and now threatens with thy bastonados to defyll this Kirk, and put hands on his servants, thou sall never enjoy the fruicts of mariage, be haifing lawfull succession of thy bodie; and God sall bastone thee in his righteous judgements!' The sermon was recalled when Learmonth, having joined with other Fife adventurers in colonizing Lewis, was bastinadoed by Highlanders, and died in Orkney, in 1598.

Another Learmonth, the Laird of Dairsie, had been provost till 1592, when the burghers elected somebody else. Infuriated, because his family had enjoyed the office almost by heredity, Dairsie and his friends began a series of nocturnal depredations. Melville, with a white spear as emblem of his rectorial office, kept Dairsie in order by forming a coalition of rival lairds. They included Lindsay of the Byres, a sound Presbyterian, and George Douglas of Lochleven, who lived in what is now called Deanscourt, the former manse of the archdeacon, opposite the west end of the cathedral. The militancy of the students on this occasion was great, as also in 1584, when they paraded with muskets and menaces at the castle to show their disapproval of the Episcopalian activities of Archbishop Adamson, newly returned from taking lessons in England on how to be an archbishop. One of the Learmonths fired at the Archbishop on the Links. From that family sprang the Russian poet Lermontov.

Republican tendencies among some Presbyterians were expressed most notably by David Black, one of the ministers of St Andrews, when he remarked in a sermon in 1596 that Queen Elizabeth was an atheist and that 'all kings were Devil's bairns'. King James VI felt strong enough to proceed against him, and, for good measure, demoted Melville from the Rectorship of the University, in 1597. Acting on the slogan 'No bishop, no king', the canny monarch began adroitly to buttress his royal position, as he thought, by a gradual reintroduction of bishops.

This modified episcopacy was accelerated once he took over the powers and patronage of the throne of England in 1603. George Gledstanes, a tobacco-smoking businessman who was one of the ministers of the parish kirk, was created titular Bishop of Caithness and then, in 1604, Archbishop of St Andrews. To renew the 'apostolic succession' interrupted by the Lutheran reform, James had three Scots bishops consecrated in England by the Bishops of London, Ely, and Bath. They returned home and consecrated Gledstanes and other prelates in Scotland. No challenge was made by Anglicans to the validity of the Presbyterian orders of these bishops before consecration. In its early phases the restored Episcopalianism did not differ in doctrine or forms of worship from the recent Presbyterianism. There was no compulsory use of a particular Prayer Book, no kneeling at Communion, no altar, no surplice. However, as *ex officio* Chancellor of the University, Gledstanes promoted forms and ceremonies. More to the point, he founded the university library, in 1612, with its handsome, rather Palladian, façade on South Street, with a public hall below, and a long bookroom above. James VI sent it over two hundred volumes, regarding St Andrews as the 'principall fountayne of religione and good letters in Scotland'. He came to see it again in 1617, and was regaled with quantities of Latin verse and prose. Among the Scots who fostered learning in the place at this time were two sons of the king's old tutor, Sir Peter Young: namely, John Young, Dean of Winchester, and Dr Patrick Young, an excellent patristic and Biblical scholar, later librarian to Charles I. Their relative Thomas Young, another graduate of St Andrews, became tutor to John Milton, and Master of Jesus College, Cambridge. Such men called themselves '*Scoto-Britanni*', 'Britons from Scotland', and were among the first to make the Anglo-Scottish cultural and political compromise of which Sir Walter Scott was later the most notable exponent. One of Dean John Young's reforms was that each Scots diocese was obliged to maintain two students of divinity at St Mary's, which was accepted as the main centre of the Scottish Church.

The nobility continued to regard St Andrews as the fashionable place to send their sons for education, so that the leading men of the century were Andreapolitan graduates, including Montrose and Argyll, Lauderdale and Claverhouse, Sir George Mackenzie, founder of the Advocates' Library, and Sir Robert Moray, first President of the Royal Society set up by Charles II at London. Both Montrose and Argyll in their time won the Silver Arrow for archery; and there is a noble series of silver medallions, running from 1618 to 1754, with the arms of the leading nobility and gentry who won the same coveted trophy. They also played golf, and were allowed off to attend Cupar races, a forerunner of the English Derby. They even read and annotated good books.

Archbishop John Spottiswoode, who was translated from Glasgow in 1615, was a cultivated and learned churchman, son of the Knoxian Superintendent of Lothian, and a pupil of Andrew Melville. Soon after he became Primate of the Church of Scotland, he made a notable assertion of its historic independence. The General Assembly had excommunicated the Marquis of Huntly for his popery, and Huntly then posted off to Lambeth and got himself absolved by the Archbishop of Canterbury, Primate of England. Spottiswoode protested, and

King James VI and I tactfully ordained that 'the like should not fall out hereafter'. Spottiswoode proceeded to compose a *History of the Church and State of Scotland, from the year of our Lord 203, to the end of the reign of King James VI, 1625*. It is more objective and critical than some might expect. But the well-meaning cleric ran into great trouble in his later career, thanks mainly to the wrong-headedness of King Charles I and Archbishop Laud of Canterbury.

King James had known the Scots all his life, but when Charles I succeeded him in 1625 he was very out of touch. Sincere in his anxiety to improve the Episcopalian establishment, he sought adequate funds to endow the bishoprics, and began by revoking all grants of Crown property made since 1540, and all deals in church lands since 1560. This at once put almost the whole Scottish aristocracy and gentry against him, even those who were in principle not hostile to the order of bishops. In trying to smooth them down, Charles came up in 1633 for his Scottish coronation, and dished out numerous earldoms and other peerages. The land-owners accepted the honours, and began to plot against the purpose for which they had been granted.

Charles I's wife, Henrietta Maria, was daughter of the turncoat Henri IV of France, who had abandoned his Protestantism because he cynically thought 'Paris well worth a Mass'. When the English clergy appeared in their surplices in Scotland, the pious thought it a fearful backslithering in the direction of popery. Moreover, thousands of Scots soldiers of fortune had been involved as mercenaries, mainly on the Protestant side, in the atrocious Thirty Years' War that began in 1618, and anti-papalist feelings could readily be aroused. Charles further offended the nobles by giving the chancellorship to Archbishop Spottiswoode, in 1635. The occasion for a showdown came in 1637 when a new liturgy, or service book, was introduced to control the form of worship. Though a compromise between what Laud wanted and what the Scots bishops preferred, it was widely felt to be not merely English, but idolatrous and devilish and altogether a hellish production of Antichrist. (The extremism of the controversial language of the period has hardly been exceeded by the wildest utterances of underprivileged insurgents in the twentieth century.)

Edinburgh had recently been created into a separate see, by splitting off the large tract of the archdiocese of St Andrews south of the Forth, whose prelate was compensated somewhat by being given former lands of the Augustinian priory, bought back from the Lennox family. The Edinburgh cathedral was the Hie Kirk of St Giles. Here the new liturgy was to be read for the first time on Sunday, 23 July 1637. A group of anti-clerical nobles, fearing for their inherited lands, decided to force a showdown, and organized with sundry Presbyterians and rabble-rousers, including, very likely, apprentices dressed as women. When the Dean began to read from the new-fangled book, with its printing in both red and black, a person known as Jenny Geddes flung a stool at his head, shouting, 'Dost thou say Mass at my lug?' The mob of the capital pelted Bishop Lindsay, and the Scots Privy Council was inundated with petitions against the liturgy.

The so-called National Covenant was then set on foot. It was drafted by a Fife minister, Alexander Henderson of Leuchars, who in 1642 was to give £1,000 of his own money for the 'perfyteing' of the St Andrews University Library, and by an Edinburgh lawyer, Archibald Johnstone of Warriston. Adroitly, the manifesto renewed an old anti-papalist covenant of 1581, which James VI had signed, and tacked on to it a protest against all sorts of recent innovations. The document was publicly launched on 28 February 1638, in the Greyfriars' kirkyard at Edinburgh, when over a hundred and fifty magnates and lairds signed. The main aristocratic promoter was John Leslie, sixth Earl of Rothes, hereditary Sheriff of Fife. Clarendon records that Rothes was 'very free and amorous, and unrestrained in his discourse by any scruples of religion, which he only put on when the parts he had to act required it, and then no man could appear more conscientiously transported'. Rothes recruited among others the fifth Earl of Montrose.

On the next day the document was made available for signature by ministers, burgesses, and the general public; and copies were signed all over the country, with overwhelming support, except in Aberdeenshire and round about. Rothes brought over his kinsman Alexander Leslie, a reputable Field-Marshal in Germany, and had the Covenant signed by Scots in garrisons throughout Europe. Later in 1638 a General Assembly at Glasgow, with Alexander Henderson as Moderator, refused to allow bishops to sit, and re-established Presbyterianism. Poor Spottiswoode was accused of 'profaning the Sabbath, carding and dicing, riding through the country the whole day, tippling and drinking in taverns till midnight', not to mention 'adultery, incest, sacrilege, and frequent simony'. He was deposed and excommunicated, and died in London next year, being buried in Westminster Abbey, with eight hundred torches in the funeral procession.

The Covenant kindled a flame throughout the British Isles, when Charles I raised an army to suppress it, which quickly had to come to terms with the noble Scots Covenanters. The English Parliamentarians were encouraged to defy the arbitrary acts of the unhappy monarch, and in the upshot the whole evolution of English history was accelerated. In 1641 Charles I accepted the Presbyterian Establishment for the Church of Scotland, and agreed to select the Scots Privy Council and officials in consultation with the Scots Parliament. Here was the model for the later English constitutional monarchy, and that which obtains in such British nation-states elsewhere as Canada and New Zealand. In 1643 the English Parliament, needing Scottish backing to beat the King and his Cavaliers and Irish, made a deal with the Scottish Parliament, entitled the Solemn League and Covenant, whereby it was undertaken to set up Presbyterian Church-government in England, Wales, and Ireland. The Scots army having shifted the balance of power against the King, after the decisive battle of Marston in 1644 Oliver Cromwell and the new English régime went back on the deal, and no attempt was made to install the Presbyterian system. Montrose had meantime parted from the Covenanters, as their policies evolved, and won a series of brilliant victories for the King, ending in a fiasco at Philiphaugh in September 1645. During these years St Andrews was visited with a renewal of the 'feighting and fascherie' of Andrew Melville's era.

The university had at first denounced the illegality of the National Covenant, but the pressure of the local magnates before long induced most of them to change their opinions.

Ministers of Episcopalian leanings were removed, including George Wishart, the future biographer of Montrose. As propagandist engines of the Covenanting magnates were installed Robert Blair, an Ayrshireman, and Samuel Rutherford, a Borderer, who became also Professor of Divinity, and in 1647 Principal of the New College (St Mary's). Rutherford's *Letters* are an astonishing revelation of a certain type of religious experience, apparently common enough in his time, and sometimes since. Most famous of his polemical writings is *Lex Rex* (1644), arguing for the right of the people to control their sovereign in accordance with God's law and their covenant with God. The book runs to some five hundred pages of detailed answers to forty-four questions, with hair-splitting distinctions, elaborately worked-out syllogisms, and abundant quotation of the Bible and all sorts of historical and polemical authorities. Rutherford was not a likeable man as was Andrew Melville, and fiercely intolerant of the very idea of tolerance or liberty of conscience. Principal Tullideph of St Leonard's heard him preach in the Town Kirk, and thought he 'would have flown out of the pulpit. He had a kind of skreigh [*screech*] that he had never heard the like.'

In July 1641 the General Assembly of the Kirk met in St Salvator's, and a parliamentary commission later investigated the university's staff and curriculum. It instituted the Senatus Academicus. The revenues of the archbishopric were largely made over to the university, which at this period had well over two hundred students, many more than previously or for centuries after. The Principal of each college was required to catechize his students each Wednesday. They had to wear gowns in college or out, and talk in Latin all the time. In 1620 a Chair of Humanity had been founded at St Leonard's by Sir John Scot of Scotstarvit, author of *The Staggering State of the Scots Statesmen*, because he was dissatisfied with the way Latin had been taught. In 1644 St Salvator's set up a rival chair. Latin was still the language of international controversy and much else, as witness John Milton's polemics in defence of Cromwell. The Covenanting party was zealous in tightening things up morally. The Presbytery ordered three elders to attend at the Market Cross on market days and keep record of profane swearers. The General Assembly resolved that 'because scholars and students give great scandal and offence in keeping of Yule and other superstitious days, it is unanimously concluded, and hereby ordered, that they, being found guilty, shall be severely chastised therefor, by their masters . . .' The hunting of witches was stepped up. Afrikaner Predikants might have enjoyed the atmosphere.

The war against King Charles hit St Andrews hard in outlays of money and blood. In 1644 the burgh held sixth place among the Scots towns, as a table shows, with the monthly sums of money and the numbers of men they had to raise for service under the Scots Parliament: Edinburgh £5,166 and 574 men; Dundee £1,674 and 180; Aberdeen £1,440 and 160; Glasgow £990 and 110; Perth £990 and 110; St Andrews £540 and 60 men: thereafter Kirkcaldy, Stirling, Cupar, and Dunfermline. Twenty-five householders were killed at Tippermuir. Worse was the casualty list from Kilsyth. It was held to be a bad omen that the Laird of Cambo had led off the St Andrews contingent from the West Port before worthy Mr Robert Blair, the minister, came to pray for them. So many Fifers were slaughtered by Montrose's Highlanders that the presbyteries of St Andrews, Cupar, and Kirkcaldy were spared further levies thereafter.

The Covenanters got their own back somewhat in dealing with eminent prisoners captured at Philiphaugh. Because there was plague in Edinburgh the Scots Parliament met in St Andrews, in what is now called the Parliament Hall, on 26 November 1645. Blair preached from the 101st Psalm: 'I will destroy all the wicked of the land, that I may cut off all wicked doers from the city of the Lord.' The lawyer Johnstone of Warriston demanded that the Parliament itself be purged of 'malignants', for it was like Noah's Ark, 'a harbourer of creatures foul and clean'. The adjournment to deal with the purge produced only two suspects, the Provosts of Jedburgh and St Andrews.

The Parliament sat on till 6 February, the noblemen present including Argyll, Loudon, Errol, Mar, Buchan, Cassillis, Perth, Haddington, Wemyss, Dalhousie, Findlater, Lanrick, Callender, Yester, Cardross, Burghley, and the Earl of Crawford and

Lindsay, who had begun as Lord Lindsay of the Byres, and was, with Rothes, the leading magnate of Fife. There were thirty-nine commissioners of shires and twenty-five of burghs. Most of the work was done in committees. A committee dealt with the aristocratic prisoners taken at Philiphaugh, under promise of quarter. The General Assembly and other religious bodies kept urging the Parliament to execute the 'bloodthirsty rebels'. They were all sentenced to death. But Lord Ogilvy escaped from the castle, by changing clothes with his sister. He was a cousin of Crawford-Lindsay, who was said to have con-nived. Ogilvy was an enemy of Argyll's, since the burning of the 'bonnie hoose o Airlie'; and Argyll got a little of his own back in annoying Ogilvy's friends by arranging a reprieve for the Earl of Hartfell. On 17 January 1646 the first execution took place at the Market Cross, which stood on a pyramid of steps. The instrument was a guillotine, called 'the Maiden'. First to suffer was Colonel Nathaniel Gordon, whose blood drenched the scaffold. On to it was then brought Sir Robert Spottiswoode, the Archbishop's son, a former Secretary of State and President of the Court of Session, gifted in several languages and a man of great integrity and loyalty to his principles. The minister Robert Blair refused to let him address the people, as was the custom. Then came Captain Guthrie, the Bishop of Moray's son. The Earl of Tullibardine, a Coven-anter, tried to save his brother, William Murray, on the ground that he was not *compos mentis*; but he got only a postponement of a few days. The young Evan Cameron of Lochiel, Argyll's ward, had visited Spottiswoode in prison in the castle, and was so impressed by his arguments that he became a lifelong royal-ist and Episcopalian.

Among the other transactions of this St Andrews Parliament was the order, on 2 February, that a school should be started in every parish. This was another attempt to realize the ideal in Knox's *First Book of Discipline*, where one reads:

The children of the poor must be supported and sustained on the charge of the kirk, trial being taken whether the spirit of docility [*educability*] be in them found or not. If they be found apt to learning and letters, then may they not—we mean, neither the sons of the rich, nor yet of the poor—be permitted to reject learning, but must be charged to continue their study, so that the commonwealth may have some comfort by them.

Not long after the Scots Parliament met at St Andrews, Charles I surrendered to the Scots army in England. They asked him to sign the two Covenants, of 1638 and 1643. He refused. They then handed him over to the English Parliament, on their promising not to harm him. In these years an Assembly of Divines at Westminster, with Samuel Rutherford among the Scots present, evolved the Confession of Faith, and the Longer and Shorter Catechisms, which were for generations the backbone of religious teaching in Scotland. While Charles I was gaoled in the Isle of Wight, he was visited by three Scots Covenanting magnates, who engaged to fetch him an army if he would promise to establish Presbyterianism in England for three years as an experiment. Charles agreed, and his agreement split the Covenanters. Only a part marched to England, where Cromwell scattered them. He then had Charles beheaded. The bulk of the Scots were horrified, and the Covenanting magnates rapidly proclaimed his son Charles II King. Eventually he signed both Covenants, and was crowned at Scone, on New Year's Day, 1651. Cromwell dealt with his forces at Dunbar and Worcester, and occupied Scotland, with Monck sacking Dundee.

St Andrews in this period was ruined. What rich inhabitants there were went away for good, to avoid high taxes and the costs of Cromwellian soldiers being quartered on them. An English judge, Colonel Bryan, sat with a Scots colleague in the commissary court that met in St Salvator's church. Cromwellian troopers would go into the parish kirk and amuse themselves by sitting on the stool of repentance, and would pester the ministers into debating with them, on pain of having more troops quartered in their manses. Cromwell shipped thousands of Scots Covenanters overseas as slaves to the plantations—whence some of the Scots names among Negroes in the Carolinas and the West Indies.

From the distresses of Cromwell's Protectorate and Commonwealth the restoration of Charles II in 1660 appeared at first a hopeful relief. But the spirit of religious factionalism soon reasserted itself. Cromwell had abolished the General Assembly, while allowing presbyteries and synods to function. Charles II equally left presbyteries and synods alone, and replaced the General Assembly with a set of bishops, under the control of himself through the Privy Council and Parliament. The man picked for the archbishopric of St Andrews was James Sharp, whom Cromwell dubbed 'Sharp of that Ilk'. He had been bred at Episcopalian Banff and Aberdeen, and his mother was a Leslie of Kininvie, fairly close kin to the Covenanting Earl of Rothes. Sharp had been a Regent at St Leonard's and minister of Crail. When he went to England to be consecrated by the Bishops of London, Worcester, Carlisle, and Llandaff, they first ordained him, not recognizing the validity of his Presbyterian orders. On his entrance to St Andrews he was escorted by the Earls of Rothes and Kellie with nearly eight hundred horsemen. Only two ministers attended his inaugural sermon, which was on the necessity of episcopacy. Though nominally Primate of Scotland, Sharp commanded little money or influence, and became the scapegoat for oppressive proceedings of the Scottish Privy Council, dominated by the ex-Covenanter Lauderdale, against those Presbyterians who remained loyal to the doctrines and forms of Church government and worship in which they had been reared for the past generation. Many well-liked parish ministers had been put out of their kirks, and preached on the moors to 'conventicles' of Presbyterians, who came in arms to keep off the troops sent to police them.

It is curious how women of the Covenanting magnate families remained Presbyterian when their husbands changed their views to suit the King's. The sixth Earl of Rothes had promoted the Covenant of 1638. His son, seventh Earl and first Duke, became chancellor in the government of Charles II that enforced Episcopacy, and Scotland's hardest drinker. But his wife, daughter of the Covenanting seventeenth Earl of Crawford, is said to have given signals out of Leslie House to Covenanting conventicles on the Lomond hills, to let them know what the government's troops were doing.

When the government started fining people for not going to Episcopal services, some thousands of Covenanters from the south-west marched upon Edinburgh. They were dispersed, and many of them tortured and hanged. The repression had become exacerbated in 1679, when on 3 May Sharp drove towards St Andrews on his way from Edinburgh. At Magus Muir, three miles off, his coach was waylaid by nine Covenanters, headed by David Hackston of Rathillet and his brother-in-law, Balfour of Kinloch. Hackston had a private quarrel with Sharp, about money, and merely looked on. The Archbishop was murdered, 'by sixteen great wounds in his back, head, and one above his left eye, three in his left hand, when he was holding it up, with a shot above his right breast, which was found to be of powder'. All his papers, gold, and money were taken. His daughter Isabel escaped, losing a shoe in a bog: her descendants preserve its partner. The Covenanting executioners went to a hut and prayed for several hours.

The Archbishop's funeral on 17 May was a fine affair. As he was aged sixty-one, they set sixty-one old men at the head of the procession from the New Inns in the priory to the Town Kirk. The first old man carried a little *gumphion*, or flag; the others followed two by two, in mourning hoods and cloaks. A horse of state was led out, as for the Riding of the Parliament, led by footmen in His Grace's livery; also a mourning horse, with footmen in mourning. Then came the great *gumphion*, borne on a lance. After the professors, with the three university maces, judges, noblemen, heralds, and so on, the coffin came under a canopy borne by six moderators of presbyteries, followed by the Archbishop of Glasgow and other bishops, and 'The bloody gown in which His Grace was slain'; then the fatal coach, with the coachman, horses, and postilions, all in deep mourning. Sir William Sharp of Scotscraig, the Primate's son, was a merchant trading with the Netherlands, whence he brought to the parish kirk an imposing monument in the taste of the times, showing the scene of the murder in relief, with the martyred prelate receiving the crown of martyrdom, and a falling church being buttressed by his rectitude. Perhaps it is symbolic that the other great sculptural tourist attraction in St Andrews is also funereal, the Pictish sarcophagus. The archbishop had given to the parish kirk a splendid silver baptismal basin and Communion cup.

Much as Achilles appeased the angry ghost of Patroklos, the

Episcopalians took five Covenanters caught at Bothwell Brig in June 1579, who were obdurate in refusing to swear not to rebel again, and hanged them at Magus Muir, leaving their bodies to rot in chains at the scene of the murder. Hackston of Rathillet was captured next year at Airds Moss, and executed in Edinburgh, after which one of his quarters was displayed to the public at St Andrews.

Sharp, as Chancellor of the university, induced Charles II to found Regius Chairs of Hebrew and Mathematics. For the latter they appointed James Gregory, the most talented of a celebrated family. He corresponded with Isaac Newton, and anticipated him in some of his discoveries. As he was the only non-collegiate university professor, he worked in the upper library, where his meridian line was carefully preserved. Enlivened by his *avant-garde* views, his students ridiculed the pedestrian dictations of their other preceptors; but he only stayed six years, leaving for Edinburgh in 1674. The notable advance at this time of the university and other learned institutions in Edinburgh, within easy distance, was a major reason for the decline of St Andrews in the next century.

After the Catholic King James VII forfeited the crown in 1689, and William of Orange agreed to the re-establishment of the Presbyterian Church-government in 1690, a parliamentary commission came in and turned out almost all the senior masters of the university, who were showing a staunch Jacobitism, loyalty to the king 'owre the watter'. Though various enlightened projects for improving the curriculum were mooted, no money was bestowed to do anything. In the 1640s the archiepiscopal revenues had largely been used for the university by the Covenanters; but the triumphant Presbyterians of the 1690s handed them over to Dutch William. The loss of the trade brought by the archbishops and their local establishment further embarrassed the little city. Add to all this the series of bad harvests that hit Scotland in the 1690s, aggravated by the commercial upsets of Louis XIV's aggressive wars with the Netherlands. Moreover, the new Presbyterian Ascendancy sought to reinvigorate religious life in the parishes, and to develop schools in every one of them, so that parishes became less inclined to pay to the colleges in St Andrews the teinds long ago allocated to them by popish prelates like Kennedy and Betoun. Financial problems became acute. Then there occurred a major quarrel with the burgh.

In 1696 one of the servants employed by the university assaulted a townsman and refused to appear in the burgh court. He was fined for contempt. The university denounced this as a violation of its privileges, conferred by Bishop Wardlaw in 1412. To secure backing, the Senate appointed as Chancellor and Conservator of Privileges the current Secretary of State for Scotland, John Murray, Marquis of Atholl, later first Duke. This Perthshire grandee proposed that the university should simply remove to Perth. Negotiations began, and the burgesses of Perth got the length of offering the Gowrie House site for a divinity college, with twenty 'convenient fashionable rooms', a brewhouse and 'other apertinents necessary', and a philosophy college with sixty rooms. The Andreapolitans demanded a second philosophy college and common university buildings, meaning simply to reproduce in Perth the collegiate structure at St Andrews. Atholl fell from power, and the scheme fell with him.

Most illuminating is the eloquent memorandum by Professor John Craigie in supporting the shift to Perth. He argued *inter alia* that it would contribute much to the civilizing of the Highlands. He complained about St Andrews that:

> The victuals are dearer here than anywhere else, viz. fleshes, drinks of all sorts. This place is ill provided of all commodities and trades, which obliges us to send to Edinburgh, and provide ourselves with shoes, clothes, hatts, &c; and what are here are double rate. This place is ill provided of fresh water, the most part being served with a *stripe* [the mill-lade] where the foul clothes, herring, fish, &c., are washed, so that it is most pairt neasty and unwholesome.

The place had, moreover, 'a most thin and piercing air, even to an excess', which caused nitre to grow on rooms facing north where fires were lit, and 'old men coming to the place are instantly cut off'. Infectious diseases were very bad, as in 1640 —which seems rather far to go back—and, in the previous year, 'a most malignant flux, whereof dyed upwards of two hundredth persons in a few weeks, which much prejudiced the universitie'.

Craigie's eighth point was grave:

> This place being now only a village, where most part farmers
> dwell, the whole streets are filled with dunghills, which are
> exceedingly noisome, and ready to infect the air, especially at
> this season [*September*] when the herring gutts are exposed in
> them, or rather in all corners of the town by themselves.

In fact, the dysentery of 1696 had been epidemic all over the
country. Incidentally, the worst epidemic recorded at St
Andrews was in 1585, when over four thousand persons are
said to have died there.

The Craigie indictment asserts that the non-academic
townsmen of St Andrews had 'a great aversion to learning and
learned men'; that the rabble of the place were much given to
'tumultuate', having broken the new mill owned by the
university, and once, in 1690, chased the students into the
colleges and brought up cannons to bombard them. One
suspects that the citizens might have had some counter-
accusations to bring; otherwise why were undergraduates
compelled to wear conspicuous red gowns, 'that thereby the
students may be discurraged from vageing [*wandering round*]
or vice'? The students might also have had accusations to make
against the system to which they were subjected by the academic drones and dotards who ran the Regenting system, still
persisting in spite of such enlightened teachers as Andrew
Melville. Students slept two to a bed, in 'box-beds', cubicles in
the wall, in rooms where the chimneys smoked so vilely that
the boys preferred to keep warm by wearing gloves and plaids.
Wealthier 'Boarders' dined and supped at the High Table with
the Regents, on better fare than the bursars, portioners, and
servers, each duly graded. At 5 a.m. they were aroused by a
bell, and at 9 p.m. the Regent in charge for the week, the
'Hebdomadar', went his rounds to see that all were inside and
the lights out.

Not want of money alone could excuse the way the colleges
were run. In 1723 John Macky found St Salvator's church and
cloister 'entirely neglected'. He saw 'very good Apartments for
the Masters and Scholars, all built of Free-stone, but un-
accountably out of repair, they being hardly at the Pains of

keeping out the Rain or mending the Windows'. Daniel Defoe in 1727 commented that if only St Salvator's were repaired 'there would be few Colleges in England go beyond it for Magnificence'. Meantime it seemed to him 'looking into its Grave'. Defoe found the city:

> . . . a most august monument of the splendour of the Scots Episcopal Church in former times; remarkable for a fine situation, surrounded by extensive corn-fields, and the pleasant downs, the Links, lying on the sea-side towards the north. The famous physician Cardan esteemed it the healthiest town he ever lived in, having occasion to experience it some months, when he came over from Italy at the request of the Pope to prescribe to Archbishop John Hamilton.

In 1707 a Treaty of Union between Scotland and England came into force, as a result of which the Scots Parliament ceased to meet, and the government was more than ever centralized in London. The main motive of the treaty on the Scots side was the desire to secure a Protestant prince's succession to both Kingdoms: commercial motives weighed with some, but the imagined commercial advantages were by no means apparent in the early decades of the political amalgamation. The east-coast ports, like St Andrews, had a specially thin time of it immediately after the Union, which may have disposed the academics and townsmen of St Andrews to welcome exuberantly the landing in 1715 of the Old Pretender, the Jacobite challenger to the Hanoverian George I. At least half the gentry of Fife, though Protestant, were willing to fight for the direct Stuart heir in that Rising. By 1745 very few were interested, and the university made the 'Butcher' Duke of Cumberland their Chancellor, even after Culloden.

Little as the English governments might do for Scotland's oldest university, an individual Englishman, the first Duke of Chandos, was good enough to bestow on it a Chair of Medicine and Anatomy, in 1721, in thanks for a service done to his son. Having since 1414 had the right to give degrees in medicine, the university had occasionally taught the subject, and since 1696 had been selling doctorates of medicine without teaching it. The Chandos chair enabled them to do so with less false pretence, and the trade in MD degrees remained a useful source of income till after 1850.

One finds at this time a marked decline in the teaching and examination for the ordinary degree, and an increased bestowal of doctorates in different faculties. And yet the numbers of students went on declining. In 1738, therefore, Professor Thomas Tullideph set on foot negotiations to unite the three colleges, pool their resources, and rationalize their educational system. St Mary's soon withdrew; but in 1747 an Act of Parliament was passed bringing into existence 'the United College of Saint Salvator and Saint Leonard in the University of St Andrews'. St Mary's people referred to it as 'the North College'. There is a tale of a Divinity professor at St Mary's saying to one of his theological students who had blundered in interpreting the New Testament, 'Is that the kind of Greek they taught you in the North College?' The United College had a Principal, a Professor of Greek, one of Humanity, one of Mathematics, one of Medicine, one of Civil History—created as a sinecure for William Vilant, the St Salvator's Humanist—and three of Philosophy: of whom one for Logick, Rhetorick, and Metaphysicks; one for Natural and Experimental Philosophy; and the third for Ethicks and Pneumaticks, a branch of science nowadays replaced, more or less, by psychology. Having carried through the union of the colleges, Principal Tullideph seems to have ceased to be energetic. In his younger day an officer in the Swedish Dragoons, he would now lie in bed all day and spend his nights inditing a laborious commentary on the Gospels. He ended up a hypochondriac. The salvation of the university came from quite another source than a mere academic desire for reform, namely from the addiction of certain gentlemen to the royal and ancient game of golf.

10

SALVATION THROUGH GOLF

The year 1754 is symbolic for St Andrews. In that year for the last time the students of the university shot arrows in their historic competition for the coveted Silver Arrow, and in that same year was founded 'The Society of St Andrews Golfers', which became the world-renowned R & A in 1834, under the patronage of the Duke of St Andrews, better known as King William IV (properly III of Scotland). In 1837 His Majesty was graciously pleased to present to the Club a Gold Medal and Green Ribband, the medal bearing to be presented 'to the Royal and Ancient Golph Club of St Andrews'. Some have suspected a misprint for 'Guelph'. But spelling seems not to have been quite the strongest point then, for the original Minute Book of the Club lists the twenty-two original subscribers, and then goes on:

The Noblemen and Gentlemen above named being Admirers of the Anticient and healthfull Exercise of the Golf, and at the same time having the Interest and prosperity of the Anticient City of St Andrews at heart, being the Alma Mater of the Golf, Did in the Year of Our Lord 1754 Contribute for a Silver Club Weighing — pounds — ounces and having a St Andrew engraved on the head thereof, to be played for on the Links of St Andrews upon the 14th Day of May said year, and yearly in time coming Subject to the Conditions and Regulations following vizt.

1. As many Noblemen or Gentlemen or Other Golfers from any part of Great Britain or Ireland, as shall book themselves on, or before the day appointed for the Annual Match, Shall have the priviledge of playing for the said Club, Each Signer paying Five Shillings Sterling at Signing in this Book, which is to lye in the house of Mrs Williamson in St Andrews, or in the Custody of Robert Douglas Merchant there, Who is Appointed Clerk, ad vitam, Aut ad culpam. . . .

In effect, the R & A started as a touristic promotion stunt by some patriotic local lairds and other gentlemen. It generously invited 'Other Golfers', as well as Noblemen and Gentlemen, to compete annually, for so modest a fee as Five Shillings

Sterling, with no formality but signing up with a local shop-keeper, or maybe tavern-keeper, if Mrs Williamson had a 'pub'. And how well the touristic promotion paid off! In the end it gave a much more healthful look to the 'Anticient City'. As witness the judge Lord Cockburn, writing about 1844, ninety years later. The natives, he says:

> . . . have a pleasure of their own, which is as much the staple of
> the place as old colleges and churches are. This is golfing,
> which is here not a mere pastime, but a business and a passion,
> and has for ages been so, owing probably to their admirable
> links. This pursuit actually draws many a middle-aged gentleman
> whose stomach requires exercise, and his purse cheap pleasure,
> to reside here with his family; and it is the established recreation
> of all the learning and all the dignity of the town. There is a
> pretty large set who do nothing else, who begin in the morning
> and stop only for dinner; and who, after practising the game,
> in the sea breeze, all day, discuss it all night. Their talk is of
> holes. The intermixture of these men, or rather the intermixture
> of this occupation, with its interests and hazards and matches,
> considerably whets the social appetite. And the result is, that
> their meetings are very numerous, and that, on the whole, they
> are rather a guttling population. However, it is all done quietly,
> innocently, and respectably; insomuch that even the recreation
> of the place partakes of what is, and ought to be, its peculiar
> character and avocation.

Already in 1691 the place had been written of as 'the metropolis of Golfing', by one of the professors, Alexander Munro, when sending to John Mackenzie of Delvine 'ane Dozen of Golfe balls' and some clubs, 'viz. ane play club, ane scraper, and ane tin fac'd club'. He prudently adds, about the balls, 'I am told they are good, but that will prove according to your play and the fields.' Apparently bad golfers were apt to blame the balls for not going the way intended.

The new Club founded in 1754 for golf was very much a carry-over from its old rival of archery, and some of the initial members had won the Silver Arrow in their day: the fourth Earl of Wemyss, then Lord Elcho, in 1716; the Hon'ble James Leslie in 1720; Sir Robert Henderson of Fordell in 1738; and the fifth Earl of Elgin in 1751. There were two Members of

Parliament subscribing, Lt-Gen. James St Clair and James Oswald of Dunnikier, a schoolmate of the economist Adam Smith, and friend of the philosopher David Hume. There were two university dons, David Young, Professor of Natural and Experimental Philosophy, and his brother John, Professor of Ethicks and Pneumaticks. David Young took a lead in another promotional stunt, giving the honorary doctorate of Laws, LL.D., to Benjamin Franklin, in 1759.

The promoters of the 'Anticient City' included several names famous in its history, with two members of the family of Cardinal Beaton, the head of the Bruces, several Wemysses, a Scot of Scotstarvit, and a Spens of Lathallan, kinsman to the 'skeely skipper' Sir Patrick Spens: while the Provost of St Andrews who signed was James Lumsdaine of Rennyhill, a descendant of Archbishop Sharp. His forebear Sir James Lumsdaine was a Scots soldier of fortune, who took command of the Swedish army in the Battle of Lützen, after the death of Gustavus Adolphus, the Lion of the North. Since those days the economic situation of the Fife lairds had changed so much for the better that they could afford to start a golf club in a derelict village with a view to making it a holiday resort for people with assured incomes and plenty of time on their hands.

The economic basis for the incipient R & A was the boom in land-values created by the agricultural revolution of the eighteenth century, which was largely caused by belated application of the intelligent methods used in the seventeenth century by the frugal and industrious Dutch. Scots Law was based, as was Dutch Law, on Greco-Roman Law, and many Scotsmen went to study at the Universities of Leyden and Utrecht, as Boswell did for a time. In the Netherlands they learned modern farming, and applied the lessons on their family's estates, nowhere more keenly than in the counties near Edinburgh, the seat of the Scots law courts, preserved under the Treaty of Union in 1707. By 1754 there were many landed families able to afford town houses in Edinburgh, which helped to promote the Golden Age of that city, with its exemplary New Town and highly progressive university, a centre of the international Enlightenment. Families who might not rise to Edinburgh living could perhaps afford a house in St Andrews, especially if they were near-by lairds; and there were scores of rather fine houses from the sixteenth and seventeenth centuries, mostly towards the east end of the Southgate, which could be bought or rented. There was also a good inn, the Black Bull, facing the top of Abbey Street, now occupied by a Co-operative Society, which has ruined the fine old façade with a well-intentioned piece of modernity.

Besides the lairds who owned the lands, there were swarms of younger brothers and cousins and wives' fourth cousins five times removed, who, in the clannish Scots way, helped one another on in the world, which, for Fifers, often meant in government jobs in the colonies. Already by 1754 there was some hostility to Scots on the part of Americans for their in-group wangling there. Not long after 1754 the great field of opportunity lay in India, conquered from the French largely by the hardy Scots. Civil or military jobs with the East India Company became a great thing for lads o' pairts with connections, and many a handsome fortune was realized from the East, sometimes not very respectably. A noted militarist from the East Neuk of Fife, General Scott of Balcomie, was reputed to have made his pile largely from rubies, diamonds and so forth, showered on him by an amorous Begum. Incidentally, horrifying as it may be to some, there is documentary evidence that some Fife gentlemen of high standing ran a club to compare notes on the subtler minutiae of fornication, with as much zeal and precision as others, or indeed they themselves, might devote to the finer points of Calvinist theology or the varieties of fossils and ferns.

One of the finest fortunes made in India was that of the Rev. Dr Andrew Bell, who was born at St Andrews in 1753 and studied in the university. After American travels, he became chaplain to the Honourable East India Company in Madras, and was given charge, among other things, of an asylum for soldiers' orphans. He hit on the scheme of mutual tuition by the schoolboys themselves, which proved extremely efficacious and stimulating. In 1797 he came back to Britain to propagate what came to be called the Madras System of elementary education. By 1833 there were ten thousand schools in Great Britain operating it, as well as many overseas. Dr Bell gave the burgh of St Andrews £10,000 for its purposes, and set up a trust with a further £50,000 to start the Madras College. Founded in 1832, by 1838 it had 800 pupils normally attending—probably four times as many as there were students at the university then. Till about 1900 the Madras College by itself was sufficient to bring many families to live in St Andrews for the education of their children. There was a specially strong connection with India, and one may compare St Andrews in Victorian times to Cheltenham, as a residential town with a strong educational component.

The golfing club formed in 1754 to promote the 'Anticient City' did in fact contribute powerfully to its economic development, and may be said to have rescued it from utter decay. In the 1750s there were fewer than four thousand people, existing in squalor along grass-grown streets embellished by dungheaps. One-fifth of the thousand or so houses were roofless and empty. There was only one small ship in the harbour. In 1728 William Douglass, MD, claimed in a pamphlet, 'By Nature this Harbour is the most conveniently situate for Trade of any in this Country; but particularly for that of the Cod and Herring-Fishing. It has a natural Bason Land-lock'd, and capable to contain above an hundred Ships: it has a Brook running through it, which, with the help of Flood-Gates, is sufficient to scour and clean it on any occasion.' But there had been a series of disasters by encroachments of the sea. In 1655 a crisis arose about the long breakwater, and authority was given to use the stones of the castle to rebuild and extend it. Tradition tells how the work was largely done by Dutchwomen. Apparently Dutchmen were content to spend the winter smoking their pipes, and shipped their wives to Scotland to build harbours. Crail is another in Fife that is said to have been laboured upon by Dutchwomen. Imagine them heaving across the North Sea in their little brigs or schooners, with countless petticoats and Bibles and bottles of gin, while the decadent Andreapolitans took a look at them and returned to their idle ale-drinking— or maybe golf! Though it had but one ship, the St Andrews of the 1750s had forty-two ale-houses.

To come back to the early days of the Society of St Andrews Golfers, it is notable that their code of rules is copied from that in use by the Company of Gentlemen Golfers who played at Leith Links. It even includes a reference to 'Soldiers' Lines' on the links, which made sense at Leith, but not at St Andrews. But the Society also borrowed from the old tradition of academic archery, where silver medals were affixed by winners to the Silver Arrow. After the annual golf match the victor had to attach a silver ball to the Silver Club. Before long a jolly little initiation rite evolved, whereby new members had to kiss the silver balls. This is a reminder of the enthusiasm shown at that time in Scotland for Freemasonry, which had just become a kind of mass movement among the intelligentsia and the gentry, categories far from mutually exclusive in Scotland then.

The first subscriber of the Society of Golfers was the fifth Earl of Elgin, who in 1761 was installed Grand Master of Scotland, being already Master of St Regulus Lodge, at Cupar, the county town of Fife. In 1761 this Cupar lodge resolved that their drink should, in time coming, be whisky punch, as expressive of 'their love to their country and public spirit'. They also contributed to the repair of St Regulus' tower at St Andrews, and sixty years later, on 20 May 1821, there is a record of the Cupar brethren proceeding to the 'chapel of St Regulus at St Andrews' to hold a lodge there in memory of their patron saint. It is maybe worth mentioning that the cult of St Andrew's Day, 30 November, was also promoted by this Earl of Elgin. The architect Robert Adam was in Rome that day in 1756, and found the Earls of Elgin and Rosebery entertaining, with a sea of liquor, such compatriots as came to the Caledonian Club, which, incidentally, used 'our ain Mither tongue', the old Court Scots. This is the social background in which the Gentlemen of the Caledonian Hunt subscribed with enthusiasm for the poems of Robert Burns, and the Scots aristocracy, as well as everybody else, went wild over Sir Walter Scott's Waverley novels.

In 1754, the first time the Silver Club was played for, it was won by Bailie William Landale, Merchant in St Andrews. He was probably kin to Alison Landale, mother of James Wilson, son of a farmer at Carskerdo near Cupar, who came to the university in 1757. Later he became a lawyer in Pennsylvania, signed the American Declaration of Independence, and was a chief theorist of the American Constitution and justice of the Supreme Court. Wilson was uncommonly far-seeing, and some proposals of his that were rejected at the start were put into the Constitution by later amendments. Similarly, the founding fathers of the R & A did not achieve perfection right off in their rules. An early addition was in 1771, when it was decreed that any man tipping a caddie more than sixpence would be fined two bottles of claret.

The first score recorded was 121 strokes for twenty-two holes, returned by the victor of 1764, William St Clair of Roslin, then aged sixty-four. Next day it was decided to reduce the course to eighteen holes, by converting the first four holes to two. Over the new standard course of eighteen holes St Clair won again in 1766 with 103, and in 1768 with 106. The most fantastic performance was in 1767, when James Durham of Largo returned 94, a record not broken till 1853. With the balls and clubs of the time, and the whins and the rough grass and the cart-tracks and rabbit-scrapes, and the lack of smooth shaven greens, it is most impressive. In 1770, for further touristic promotion, the Society advertised in the Edinburgh papers a competition for a Gold Medal valued at seven guineas. It was won outright by a Mr Beveridge with 101. Then a Silver Cup, value eight pounds, was put forward, but the competition restricted to members of the St Andrews and Leith Societies. In 1780, a uniform was devised, by the sixth Earl of Balcarres, a red jacket with yellow buttons; and in 1784, a red tail coat with a blue velvet cape. By 1820, this seemed too fancy, and the uniform became a plain blue coat. But the mere fact of having a uniform indicated how the Society had become restricted to Noblemen and Gentlemen, and was no longer for 'Other Golfers'.

In 1785 there was a surprise visit from Vincent Lunardi, the Italian balloonist, who was more of a sensation in his day than an astronaut now. He flew off from Edinburgh and landed near Cupar. Next day he was elected a member of the Club and given the Freedom of the City. He wrote: 'All these ceremonies over, I was conducted to the Ball Room, where I found upwards of 100 beautiful Ladies already assembled. The Town of St Andrews is respectable on many accounts, and abounds with antiquities . . . and it was with regret I took my leave, after having amused myself for some time with the Gentlemen Golfers, at their diversion.' He would be entertained in the old Town Hall or Tolbooth at the west side of the Market Square, taken down in 1862. The ladies and gentlemen were conveyed to balls in sedan chairs, because the ordure in the ill-paved streets was so oppressive to their footgear.

It seems that the Golfers had made no attempt to entertain Dr Samuel Johnson and his faithful Boswell when they visited the town in August 1773, after a dreary drive in a dusky light. A supper of 'rissered' haddocks and mutton chops revived the lexicographer agreeably, at Glass's Inn, otherwise the Black Bull. They stayed with Professor Robert Watson, who had bought the buildings of St Leonard's College, except the church, and its tower. The tower was demolished, and the church made into a picturesque ruin. But Watson's house afforded Johnson 'very comfortable and genteel accommodation'. In touring the town next day he vented indignation against John Knox, and said St Salvator's chapel was 'the neatest place of worship he had seen'. In the street they saw what Boswell terms 'a remarkable proof of liberal toleration: a nonjuring clergyman [*i.e., an Episcopalian*] strutting about in his canonicals with a jolly countenance and a round belly, like a well-fed monk'. Johnson later wrote that 'in the whole time of our stay we were gratified by every mode of kindness, and entertained with all the elegance of lettered hospitality'. He pronounced the University Library 'not very spacious, but elegant and luminous'. His general verdict was:

> St Andrews seems to be a place eminently adapted to study and
> education, being situated in a populous, yet a cheap country,
> and exposing the minds and manners of young men neither to
> the levity and dissoluteness of a capital city, nor to the gross
> luxury of a town of commerce, places naturally unpropitious
> to learning; in one the desire of knowledge easily gives way to
> the love of pleasure, and in the other is in danger of yielding
> to the love of money.

Dr Johnson did not mention the golf links as an added inducement for the studious to congregate.

In 1797 the Town Council did an odd thing. They sold the

Golf Links to two merchants, Gourlay and Gunn. There had been a long course of municipal mismanagement. Even though, in 1774, the Town Clerk complained that his office had had no increase of salary for more than three centuries, the Council's outlays always exceeded its revenues. The outlays largely consisted of drinks to celebrate the royal birthday, drinks on the occasion of an election, drinks to persuade naval officers not to pressgang fishermen, drinks on admitting a burgess, and just drinks. Anyway, the Links were sold, and passed through various hands to the Messrs Charles Dempster and Son, who were interested in exploiting commercially the philoprogenitive propensities of the rabbit. As the little quad-rupeds multiplied the golfers became more and more frustrated to see the balls they had so carefully aimed disappear down unexpected burrows. In 1803 the Society began to raise a fund to raise an action in the Court of Session at Edinburgh, found-ing on a reservation in the articles of sale, whereby the Golf Links were 'to be reserved entirely, as it has been in times past, for the comfort and amusement of the inhabitants and others who shall resort thither for that amusement'. Enthusiasts as far afield as the West and East Indies sent in their guineas to swell the fund. The Court of Session found that the Dempsters were bound to 'suffer no damage to the Golf Ground'. They appealed to the House of Lords, but the case never came on there, for in the meantime an epidemic had carried off the rabbits. In 1832 the course was made longer and broader, with a separate green for each of the eighteen separate holes: so that duplication was avoided of out-going and in-coming players working towards the same hole at the same time, as had hap-pened till then.

The golf went from strength to strength, with King William's royal patronage in 1834. Curiously enough, there was a revival in the same year of the old rival, archery. A Silver Arrow, with a gilded point and feathers, was bought for six guineas, and duly shot for in the old Bow Butts, the hollow between the Martyrs' Memorial and the Witch Hill, just east of the present R & A clubhouse. It was won by the Professor of Mathematics, Jackson, who duly affixed his medal, and the next year by the Professor of Greek, Alexander. Later the competition was shifted to the College Lawn, north of St Salvator's; but eventually succumbed to the more fashionable game of lawn tennis.

The Links and Town were then subjected to the sweeping influence of a new broom, Lt-Col Sir Hugh Lyon Playfair. His father had been Principal of St Mary's. Hugh served in India as an artillery officer, with distinction, finally retiring with a fortune in 1832, having purchased the buildings of St Leonard's, which he proceeded to embellish with a pagoda and other curiosities. It annoyed him to see dunghills around the grass-grown streets, with pigs and cows grazing, as if it were a benighted Bengali village. But his first reforming efforts were given to the Links. Getting the golfers and archers to agree, he started a Union Club, where later was the red stone Grand Hotel, now called Hamilton Hall, in honour of the university's Chancellor, the fourteenth Duke of Hamilton, and consecrated to the accommodation of studious young gentlewomen. As a touristic promoter Playfair welcomed all and sundry, so that in 1850 the *Fifeshire Journal* described the Links as 'every evening populated by hundreds of all sexes, sizes, and grades, to witness or participate in what is going forward'. Bowls, tossing the caber, putting the stone or iron ball, quoits, skittles, hammer-throwing, football, even cricket, were all going on at once, and tending to get mixed up with the golfers, and put them off their aim. Add that ladies would take an airing in their carriages across the Links, and older golfers would even ride ponies between strokes on the fairway.

In 1842 Playfair became Provost, and served till his death in 1861. He was rather adroit in getting the town paved and generally cleaned up; but one regrets his removal of the picturesque old outer stairs of the South Street mansions, which led up to the first-floor entrances where the gentry went in and out, while the fishwives and message boys gossiped at the street-level kitchen door. As a specimen of Playfair's propagandist line consider his world-wide New Year's Day appeal of 1846:

The great interest which has been excited throughout Scotland for the preservation of her antiquities, has been particularly felt in St Andrews. As the seat of her oldest University, and the ancient ecclesiastical metropolis of Scotland, the city is entitled to some regard even from those who were neither born nor educated within its walls; but when we view it as the theatre of many of the most important and exciting events in the history of Scotland, as the cradle of the Reformation itself, as well as the grave of its earliest martyrs, we may claim for it the sympathy and liberality of every Scotchman.

During the last twelve years, St Andrews has acquired additional importance by the establishment of the Madras College, an institution equally open to all denominations of Christians, and where upwards of 900 youths—many of whom come from various parts of the world—receive a cheap and excellent education under the first masters.

An anonymous poet in the *Fifeshire Journal* celebrates the reform:

> Where yawning jaw-holes late were known to lurk,
> A broad paved street proclaims the Provost's work;
> The friendly gas lights home the drucken body,
> Primed to his lips with many an eke of toddy.
> No longer Neptune, with insidious sway,
> Steals bit by bit our bonnie Links away . . .
> Our rising harbour wears a busy air;
> New streets are planned, Reform moves everywhere. . . .

The neighbouring nobility and gentry were so gratified with Playfair's work that they treated him to a Public Breakfast in the Town Hall on Saturday, 10 April 1847, at—mark this— *nine* o'clock a.m. A couple of years later he was presented with an address of thanks by fifty-eight ship-owners and ship-masters connected with the River Tay, who had reason to bless his improvement of the harbour, and provision of a warning-light in a tower of the old priory precinct wall.

Odd as it may seem, for half a century St Andrews was without fishermen. In 1765 the five yawls then operating out of it were all lost in a storm, with few survivors, and the local men all took up land work instead. A new fishing community was brought in from Shetland in 1803, and quite a lot of coastal carrying trade was done from the harbour as well. To keep the sea from carrying away the links near the first tee, Playfair built an embankment. When the present R & A clubhouse was begun, in 1854, the sea came very close to its windows on the north. Then in 1893 a leading local improver, George Bruce, put down a line of old boats, and began the Bruce Embankment, which furnishes a putting-green, protects the clubhouse and links, and makes the sea come further up on the West Sands. There are those who say, however, that it is not enough to preserve the golf-courses from the sea: they also need protection from the greenkeepers with their chemicals!

This brings us to the technological revolutions of the past generations as they have affected the 'Anticient and healthfull Exercise of the Golf'. And first of all the gutta percha ball, first made in 1845 at St Andrews. It ended the two-century-old reign of the old 'feathery', and ruined a local craft, which had been turning out about ten thousand featheries a year. A good workman could make fifty or sixty a week. Half the production was needed, say the reverend authors of the *New Statistical Account*, in 1838, 'for the use of the cultivators of the amusement in St Andrews'. Others went to Calcutta and Madras. But the actual ball-makers found it an unhealthy form of skilled labour. The leather was cut into two, three, or four pieces, and stitched together, leaving a small hole for insertion of the feathers. The incomplete skin was then turned inside out, and feathers were stuffed into it with a special stuffing-iron pressed by the chest, which was bad for the lungs. The feathery was easily damaged, and not many makers could turn out balls that would fly and roll truly. Yet a good ball, well propelled, could fairly fly.

Gutta percha is the evaporated milky fluid tapped from a type of tree grown in the Malay archipelago. A quantity of it was used to wrap round a statue of Vishnu, in black marble, sent in 1843 from Singapore to Dr Paterson in St Andrews. The family used the wrappings to sole their footgear. Then one day the student son, Robert, formed a bit of the 'guttie' into a sphere, painted it white, and, in April 1845, drove it out on the Old Course. After a few strokes it collapsed on him. However, his brother experimented further, and in 1846 marketed some, called 'Paterson's Composite Golf Ball'. It was an imitation feathery, even having lines to suggest the sewn seams of the leather. Experience showed that it flew better after being hit a bit to roughen the surface. Further experiments were made to produce dimpled or brambled surfaces.

At first there was great controversy about the new 'gutta' or 'guttie'. H. B. Farnie, in his *Golfer's Manual* of 1857, writes: 'The first flight of *Guttas* was hailed with a burst of joy financial by everyone except the old monopolists of the feather manufacture.' Allan Robertson was at that time the leading St Andrews player. Such was his skill that, on the narrow fairways and coarse putting-greens of 1846, he did the Old Course in 95 with only one club, a wooden driver—a feat that would probably baffle most Open Champions today! He was also a clubmaker and supplier of featheries, for making which he had some employees. He and his partner, Tom Morris Senior, decided not to deal in or use 'gutties'. Then one day John Campbell of Saddell, who was playing with Morris, used 'gutties', and Tom also tried his hand with one, having run out of featheries during the round. Allan was told, and nursed his wrath. When they got together in their shop, says Old Tom, 'We had some words about it; and this led to our parting company, and I took to making balls on my ain account.'

From 1848 the gutta held the field till 1901, when Walter Travis won the US Amateur Championship with a rubber-cored ball, originally invented by Coburn Haskell, of Cleveland, Ohio. The gutta was much cheaper and more durable than the feathery, and thus brought the game within reach of far more people than could afford featheries. A good feathery would hardly do more than one round, barring accidents; and caddies normally took out six or eight with them for their employer's use on a round, each feathery costing one shilling and eightpence as supplied by Allan Robertson. When new, good featheries flew further than the gutties, according to Mr Robert Browning. He notes that 'in 1786 a player named John Gibson made a series of measured drives with a feather ball, the distances ranging from 182 yards to 222 yards'. The alleged record for a feathery was a drive of 361 yards by a Swiss, Monsieur Samuel Messieux, modern languages master at the Madras College. In 1836, on a frosty day, he drove a tee'd-up feathery from the Hole o' Cross green coming in, the thirteenth, into the Hell bunker, with a favourable wind. Some sceptics will tell you that the feathers came through the seams of the ball and flapped. The record drive for a gutta was made in 1892

by Edward Blackwell, with a swipe from the eighteenth green
that struck the R & A clubhouse steps 366 yards away, and
rebounded an unspecified short distance. But these are exceptional strokes. In general, to judge from later nineteenth-century
comment, there seems to have been no marked difference in
the length that the feathery and the gutta could be sent. Where
the gutta won was in durability and cheapness. Its effect
on the game was largely social, that it brought in many new
devotees. In St Andrews, as Balfour notes, the gutta and the
railway 'destroyed the patrician and rather exclusive tone of
the game'.

Already in 1832 there had been enough additional devotees
to cause the R & A to make two holes on each green, except the
first and the last as then reckoned, that is the eighteenth and
ninth in modern parlance. The proposer was a highland chief,
Aeneas Ronaldson MacDonell of Glengarry and Clan Ranald.
Outgoing players used the eastern, or right-hand, holes,
incomers the others. The 1832 decision led to a gradual widening of greens and fairways, with much eradication of whins
and reduction of rough grass and heather, and some suppres-
sion of yawning bunkers. The last wholly new green to be
created, not merely remodelled, was the Burn Hole (first), in
1870. In the earlier part of Tom Morris's régime from 1864 he
used to alternate the system week about, making outgoing
players keep to the left one week and to the right the next. Thus
each fairway gained variety, and the bunkers fluctuated in
their significance according to the direction from which they
were approached. The last championship played on the left-
hand course was in 1886, but it is sometimes used in winter to
give some respite to parts of the sward that are much hashed
about by irons. It is perhaps a tribute to the thrift of the Fifers
that for so long they aimed at the same hole on the same green
in both their goings-out and their comings-in. It struck the
English enthusiast Bernard Darwin as droll that 'the two processions of golfers, outward and inward bound, pass close to
each other, not without some risk to life and much shouting of
Fore!'.

During the 1880s the afflux of golfers increased, and the
R & A members found themselves being crowded out. The

regular and the irregular caddies enjoyed an intermittent sellers' market. Hugo Everard, the English historian of the R & A from 1754 to 1900, comments on the exorbitant rates then demanded by caddies, and describes how 'the guileless wayfarer was beset by hordes of ragamuffins at St Andrews station; how, in despair at their battle-cry, *Kairy for you, sir? Kairy for you, sir?*, he would surrender, as it were, body and soul, being 'deaved' out of all his wits by the insistent clamour; how, ultimately, in too many cases, he was unconscionably fleeced. Again, a resident would engage a caddie by the month or by the year; clothe him, feed him, perhaps help him through the dark winter months when work otherwise and pay are scanty and precarious—all for what? To be thrown over at the first opportunity, if there appeared a chance of making an extra shilling from the unsuspecting stranger.' The R & A solved the problem by forming a register of caddies, appointing a caddie-master, fixing tariffs, and arranging a benevolent fund for caddies. Incidentally, clubs were carried loose till about 1890, when canvas bags were devised to carry them in. The first man to use a caddie-car on the Old Course was an Anglo-Irishman, Lord Brabazon of Tara, in 1949. Maybe caddie-cars will be computerized some day; but meantime they cannot replace the advisory function of the old-style St Andrews caddie, who could tell a visiting competitor in a championship just what club to use and how to use it, as many grateful champions have testified.

Congestion on the Old Course in late summer led to the contemplation of ways and means to establish a New Course, in the later 1880s. The whole area of the Links was then owned by Mr Cheape of Strathtyrum, and the R & A sought to make a purchase from him. The Town then entered the market. After negotiations, with occasional acerbities, the R & A became proprietors in 1893, but transferred their ownership to the Town in 1894, an operation that required an Act of Parliament. The R & A agreed to maintain the Old Course and to construct and maintain a New Course, and to keep up the short Ladies' Course, for putting, provided that the ladies paid them a reasonable rent. The management was vested in a joint 'Green Committee of St Andrews Links', with five R & A members and two from the Town Council. The New Course was formally opened on 10 April 1895. The presumption is that Old Tom Morris was its architect. There was no ceremony at the opening. Old Tom took part in a foursome with local amateurs. The *St Andrews Citizen* reported: 'The players state that they did not get so many bad-lying balls as was expected. The putting-greens are in very good condition, although some are a little soft.' Bernard Darwin in 1910 found the New 'soft, slow, and easy', with not nearly so many good natural greens as on the Old.

There was an interesting development in 1896, when the Green Committee formed a circular course out of Old and New, by closing the first eight holes of the New and the middle section of the Old, during reconstruction of the High Hole green. For some time before and after this there was keen debate on the long-term desirability of some such circular system for the courses in perpetuity; but currently that issue is dead. In 1896, also, work started on a further course between the New and the sea, which was opened on 22 June 1897, to commemorate Queen Victoria's Diamond Jubilee. A procession of the Town Council, headed by a pipe band, and followed by crowds waving red, white and blue flags, marched to what the local paper termed 'the third golf course, which is specially intended for ladies'. Provost McGregor delivered an oration, stating that 'golf and education are the backbone of St Andrews' (Applause). Mrs McGregor drove the first ball, with a club decorated with red, white and blue ribbons. The twelve-hole course cost £400, and was for long regarded as 'the duffers' course'.

On 2 July 1914 Provost Herkless opened the Eden Course, lying to the south of the Old, partly on former school playing-fields: 'Mrs Herkless then struck off the first ball in a graceful manner amid the loud plaudits of the gathering.' The architect of the Eden was H. C. Colt. Its fifth, sixth, and seventh holes were not ready till 1915, making its then total length 6,130 yards. In 1919 the Eden Tournament was instituted, and became one of the most popular amateur competitions in Great Britain. The Eden now runs to 6,250 yards, but has been made easier in the last thirty years, by rooting out whins and filling in bunkers. For example, there used to be a mass of whins at the short sixteenth hole, which compelled the player to keep on the straight and narrow between the whins and the railway, which was out of bounds. By uprooting of the whins the hole has been made harmless. Likewise, since about 1938, the New has been subjected to a beauty treatment, which has made it easier, by cutting whins at the outgoing holes and by a great bulldozing of hummocks on the last five fairways. In the 1930s the New was often considered more difficult than the Old; but that is not now the general opinion. The record for the New is 63, by Frank Jowle in 1954.

In 1945 the R & A found the upkeep of its courses too costly, and another Act of Parliament was promoted, whereby the R & A pays no more than £4,000 for upkeep, and the Town Council is liable for the rest, being empowered to make the ratepayers pay for their golf. Up till 1913 the courses were free to everybody, native or visitor. Since 1953 the management has been vested in a joint Links Committee of ten, half from the R & A, the other half from the Town Council. Since 1888, when it issued a set of Rules of Golf to all then known clubs, the R & A has had something of a formally recognized international authority to legislate for the 'Anticient and healthfull Exercise'. In 1951 its clubhouse was the venue for the unification of the British and American codes, whereby the stymie was, after generations of controversy, abolished. That year Mr Francis Ouimet was chosen Captain of the R & A, the first American to be so honoured; and Bobby Jones presented a portrait of him to the Club.

Reclamation of land from the sea has proceeded apace since the 1830s. The Bruce Embankment putting-green was opened in 1913. By a shift in the currents a fresh tract of ground arose between high-water mark and the dunes fringing the original Jubilee Course. During the 1940 invasion scare concrete anti-tank obstructions were erected, which have proved an additional instrument of reclamation. The Town Council built a road on top of them, and added materials for which the citizens had no further use. Already in 1938 a reconstruction of the Jubilee was set on foot, under the direction of Willie Auchterlonie, the Open Champion of 1893. He designed a course of some 7,000 yards; but his scheme was not finally executed in detail, and the length of the modern Jubilee, opened on 1 June 1946, is not much over 6,000. The desire for a modern long championship course, to be constructed out of the New and Jubilee courses, was voiced by Burgh Treasurer Howe on 18 July 1938, when he proposed to the Town Council a course of 7,400 yards. The point is that the modern rubber-cored ball flies and runs about a third further than the old featheries and gutties for which the courses were originally designed, and has thus made them all relatively about a quarter less long than they used to be.

The technological revolution in golf started with the gutta ball. It is a problem how far its relative solidity caused changes in the design of clubs; but its durability certainly encouraged the evolution of iron clubs, instead of the thitherto usual wooden spoons, baffies, and brassies, employed for the midfield long game. With the feathery ball track-irons and cleeks were used to get it out of rough lies, or run it up cannily onto undulating greens; the application of mashies and niblicks tended to split it at the seams. The much-enduring gutta percha allowed harsher treatments. Young Tom Morris was the first to use a niblick not simply for exploding the ball out of bunkers, but also for lofted approach shots. Tom Kidd, champion in 1873, the first Open played on the Old Course, put ribs on the face of an iron to spin the ball so that it would stop on the ice-rink greens of the period. The St Andrews club-makers were keenly experimental all along, till the growth of a mass-production industry in America and elsewhere altered the conditions of business. The rubber-cored ball of the twentieth century enabled good players to drive some sixty or seventy yards further as a rule, and rendered all existing courses more or less obsolete, with their old bunkers now irrelevantly sited. At St Andrews many of the terrors of my boyhood have been much diminished, like the narrow approaches to glassy greens between forests of whins and yawning bunkers—though the vexing crosswinds usually provide hazards of another type. The greens have been doctored and watered to stop a ball lofted up onto them with any one of about ten graded iron clubs.

One wonders what the Victorian giants of the game, like

the Tom Morrises, Old and Young, would think if they saw the vast batteries of clubs trundled round today in caddie-cars. The last of the Victorian veterans was Willie Auchterlonie, who died at the age of ninety in 1963. He had won the Open Championship seventy years before, in 1893, at Prestwick, with only seven clubs, of which he used only five. Modern golf he reckoned, latterly, to be just a kind of 'ping-pong, played with an ironmonger's shop'. One cannot, however, see a new Scottish Parliament renewing the statute of 1458, and ordaining that the Golf should be discontinued in favour of the much more exacting sport of archery. Willie Auchterlonie's son, Laurie Auchterlonie, who succeeded his father in the dignified position of Honorary Professional to the Royal and Ancient Golf Club, has recently been laying out, so far as the terrain allows, a replica of the Old Course, with the Swilcan burn and Hell Bunker and all, for the American Golf Hall of Fame Association, in Foxburg, Pennsylvania. There has been in transatlantic parts some discontinuity in the pursuit of the 'Anticient and healthfull Exercise' since 1779, when a New York newspaper advertised 'excellent CLUBS and the veritable Caledonian BALLS'. But now that the cult has taken root all over America, with some 10,700,000 players in the USA in 1967, playing 190,000,000 rounds there on 9,336 courses, with annual maintenance costs of 255,000,000 dollars, it rather looks as if the same profound truth may remain valid for golf as Groucho Marx promulgated in regard to sex. It has come to stay.

11

A ROUND OF THE MODERN OLD COURSE

You are standing, eager Pilgrim, on the first tee of the historic Old Course, with your driver in your hand, having flown with it, perhaps, from Los Angeles or Melbourne, or more humdrumly motored from Manchester or Milngavie. Eager as you are, you are not without a certain queasy feeling at the thought of the many critical eyes converging on that famous first tee, under the big window of the Royal and Ancient clubhouse of 1854. You are dimly conscious of the many illustrious predecessors you have had here or hereabouts, like Bobby Jones and Young Tom Morris, Mary Queen of Scots and the Duke of Windsor and Bing Crosby and Joyce Wethered, and Peter Allis, the first to go round in 66. The par score is 72, and the normal course totals about 6,545 yards. For championships most of the tees are put back somewhat, and the total length runs to about 6,936 yards. Quite many local golfers do the round inside 80, but many others consider 90 quite a respectable figure. As a local businessman expressed it, 'If you go round in less than 90 you must have been neglecting your business; if you go round in more than 90, you must have been neglecting your golf.'

Compared with a century ago, the course is now very easy, and the first hole notably so. Before the first green was made in 1870 the first hole lay on the present seventeenth green, a small plateau between a bunker and the road. The golfer teed up within eight club's lengths of the last hole, which lay roughly in the Valley of Sin, a small residue of which remains just west of the present eighteenth green built by Old Tom Morris. The fairway was narrow, because the broad Bruce Embankment, with its putting courses, had not yet been reclaimed from the sea. The salt waves in storm would blow spray onto the north windows of the R & A clubhouse, which overlooked the then usual bathing place. If one sliced a drive from the first tee it might well go for a bathe in the briny. Today, about 130 yards from the first tee, a metalled road runs across towards the sea, debouching from the narrow street called Grannie Clark's Wynd. A century ago that was known as the Sandy Track, and

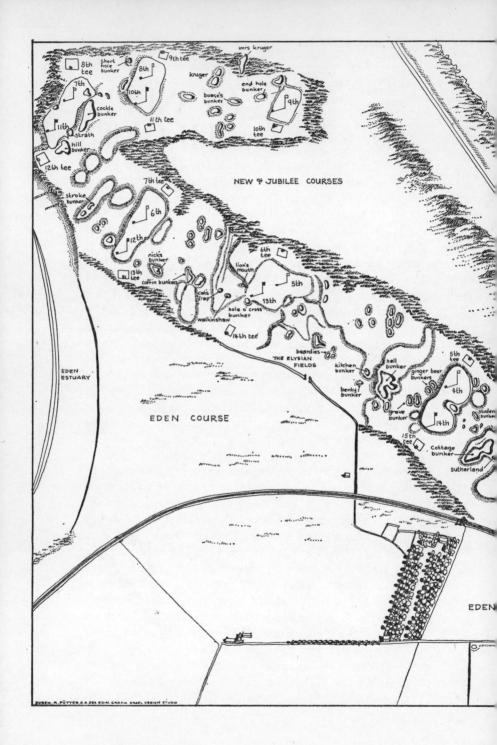

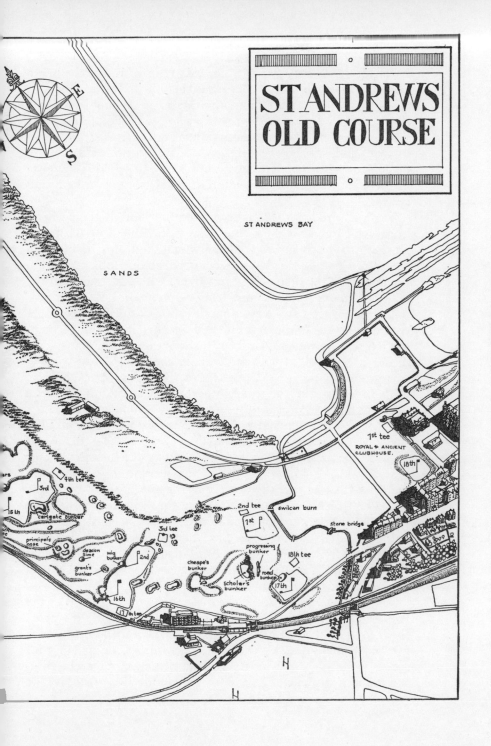

it constituted a considerable hazard. West of it, on the north side of the fairway, was a large bunker called Halket's Bunker, from John Halket, Rector of the Grammar School, who won the Silver Cup twice, in 1773 with a score of 114, on a rainy day when there were pools at many points on the course, and again in 1774, and in 1780 was appointed Chaplain to the Society of St Andrews Golfers. The large bunker that kept his memory green was turfed over in Victorian times to make a beautiful sward.

The principal hazard today at the first hole is the Swilcan burn, which gives it the name Burn Hole, now duly displayed on the square box at the tee from which sand may be taken to tee up the ball for the drive. A century ago one took sand from the bottom of the hole on the last green, with the result that the hole became very deep, and it was troublesome to get a ball out. Sandboxes at tees were an innovation of the early 1880s. A century ago the Swilcan wandered whither it willed, through sandy banks that were frequently altered by occasional spates. Today it is canalized between vertical banks, at widths varying from about five feet to about twelve. The hump-backed stone bridge over the burn on the eighteenth fairway is some centuries old now, and still handsome. The several wooden bridges are discreet. In 1821 the first hole was called Bridge Hole, because the drive was made towards the stone bridge. It is so described in the survey made in 1821 by A. Martin for the then proprietor of the Links, Mr James Cheape of Strathtyrum. But in the plan made by Chalmers in 1836 one finds the alternative name Hole of Leslie, which is unexplained. It was in those days 361 yards, which few players could reach in two strokes, because the gutta and the feathery ball travelled as a rule somewhat less than 200 yards, even for the strongest hitters. Today, with a ball that flies roughly a third further than those of a century ago, most golfers can reach the first green with their seconds.

Today the drive off from the first tee should be aimed at the footbridge over the railway just at the end of an unsightly brick shed, somewhat to the left of the white flag on the first green, 367 yards away. If you slice a longish drive, or foozle your second, you may land in the Swilcan, which Horace Hutchinson found a distasteful streamlet. 'A muddy little dribble,' he terms it, 'worming along ignominiously at a crawl, between little stone-built walls, as if it would never get to the sea.' Sometimes there is hardly any water in it. I recall Cyril Tolley's ball landing in the burn on a spit of gravel. With great *sangfroid*, and smoking a cigarette, he clambered down with a niblick, stood in the burn, and played out near the pin. What made the feat more impressive to my juvenile eyes was that he was wearing the type of variegated footgear known in the Naughty Twenties as 'Co-respondent Shoes'. They were probably ruined, but he saved a stroke.

A more singular episode at the first hole I recall from September 1927, when the town was full of visitors and a great many spectators were hanging about the first fairway. A foursome was on the tee, ready to drive off, when there debouched from Grannie Clark's Wynd an elderly white-bearded man, wearing a top hat, and pedalling a tricycle. He progressed sedately across the fairways towards the sea. Everybody shouted at him, 'Fore!'—a monosyllable very salutary for filling the lungs with salt-laden air. But the veteran paid no attention. Perhaps he was deaf. Finally, one of the foursome swung his club and drove. The ball was hooked somewhat, and impinged upon the tricyclist's lum hat, knocking it off. With astonishing agility the old man dismounted, his white beard bristling. After grasping the lum hat with one hand, and brandishing the clenched fist of the other, he re-mounted and rode off towards the sands, amid loud cheers. Not many golfers in future are likely to run a risk of dislodging the top hat of a white-bearded tricyclist. It is doubtful too if any will repeat Major Chiene's feat of killing a swallow on the wing. He had the poor bird stuffed, and mounted on the ball that slew it, to sit as a talking-point in the clubhouse.

Nor will any golfer be likely to emulate the feat of Captain Maitland Dougall of Scotscraig, afterwards Admiral, at the R & A Autumn Meeting of October 1860. He was about to play off, in a gale of rain, when word came that a yawl was in distress in the bay, and the lifeboat was called for. It had been housed since 1824 in a shed where now Rusack's Hotel stands. The storm was so great that many of the fishermen thought it madness to put out to sea. Some of the R & A members began

offering sums of money for volunteers for the crew. When
Maitland Dougall heard of this, he postponed his drive and
took the stroke oar of the lifeboat. His brother-in-law, James
Balfour, recorded in his *Reminiscences of Golf on St Andrews Links*
(1887), 'The men were rescued, and the lifeboat came ashore in
the afternoon. The play for the medal was begun after the
arrival of the lifeboat. The wind was still furious. It was to
Maitland Dougall's credit that, though his arms were sore, and
he was stiff and all wet, he gained the Club gold medal at 112
strokes.' Indeed, such is the resource of naval officers, the
Admiral solved the problem of keeping his ball somewhat on
course by boring a hole in the gutta percha and loading it
with lead pellets from a cartridge.

Compared with a century ago, the player of the first hole
today will not have his eyes regaled by the spectacle of clothes
bleaching benorth the first green after having been washed in
the Swilcan by barefoot girls, whose charms were celebrated in
a stanza that appeared in *Blackwood's Magazine* for September,
1819.

> It is in sooth a goodly sight to see,
> by east and west, the Swilcan lasses clean,
> spreading their clothes upon the daisied lea,
> and skelping freely barefoot o'er the green,
> with petticoats high kilted up, I ween,
> and note of jocund ribaldry most meet.
> From washing tubs their glowing limbs are seen
> veiled in an upward shower of dewy weet.
> Oh, 'tis enough to charge an anchorite with heat!

Today such notes of 'jocund ribaldry' as are to be heard around
the Links will be more likely to proceed from transistor radios
of the less golf-minded holiday-makers, whose cars are happily
parked somewhat out of earshot of the Old Course.

Having got your par four at the Burn Hole, you proceed
to tee up at the second, called the Dyke Hole today, though
Chalmers in 1836 names it 'Hole of Bafield'. The ballfield in
question was probably south of the present seventeenth fairway.
Martin's Survey in 1821 erroneously calls Chalmers's Hole of
Bafield the Cunnin hole, and applies the name Ballfield Hole to
the present fourth hole, which Chalmers calls Hole of Cunnin

Links. There is little doubt that the football field would be the nearest suitable tract on descending from the town, and that is at the seventeenth fairway. We learn also, from evidence given by the old ball-maker William Robertson in the 'Rabbits Case', that around 1760 the rabbits were thickest round the Shepherd's Cottage, on the level of the present fourth and fifteenth fairways: so that the Society formed in 1754 is likely to have called that area the 'Cunnin Links'.

When you tee up for the Dyke hole (403 yards) you may see some ladies to your right on the Ladies' Putting Course; but do not be distracted by them. There are also on your right, in the rough, quite many whins, prickly shrubs that in some places are called furze or gorse. Though the yellow flowers smell agreeably, that is not much compensation for the pain and trouble of searching for a ball among them: therefore be careful not to slice your drive. At St Andrews it is always safer to hook than to slice. At this second hole you will get a mild initiation into the system of bunkers of the Old Course. There is a tale of a golfer playing the round for the first time, who remarked to his caddie at the end of it, 'This is a terrible course for bunkers.' To which the knowledgeable porter of clubs retorted, 'Ay is it. And there's a twa three o' them you haena been in yet.' Bernard Darwin once wrote: 'St Andrews never looks really easy, and never is really easy, for the reason that the bunkers are for the most part so close to the greens.' At the Dyke Hole there are three shallow bunkers that can catch a sliced drive, and another that can trap a long hook, known as Cheape's Bunker. In 1836 Chalmers named it 'Cheape's Dyke Bunker', and the Hodge plan of 1875 calls it 'Corner of Dyke Bunker'. There is a group of four near the green on the right, and two near it on the left, besides two eating into the edges of the green, of which the one at the far side is called the Wig. Unlike most greens on the Old, the second lies in a hollow.

After having got your par four, you proceed to tee for the third hole, called Cartgate, because there is an old track through the rough on the right, by which people had a right of way to the mussel scaups on the Eden, and still have it. There are five bunkers on the right and four on the left, not counting the large Cartgate bunker eating into the edge of the green, and the pin is 342 yards away, on a backward-sloping green. To avoid the whins you drive left, but only a little left, of the flag, but to the right of the round bunker in a hillock about 150 yards away. There were formerly bunkers named Tam's Coo and The Calf, which were filled up by Old Tom Morris, who was chief greenkeeper from 1864 to 1904. A curious legend is still to be heard that Tom Morris filled up Tam's Coo because he had been discovered in it as a foundling baby. This legend is the more improbable that in 1836 Chalmers calls the bunker 'Thom's Coo', and in that year Old Tom Morris was only fifteen, at which age no bunker is likely to have been named for him. After The Calf had been turfed over, George Glennie, a notable Victorian figure, who was Captain of the R & A in 1884, found his ball lying on the site. He took a snuff, and solemnly observed, 'Ma guid auld freen', ye're awa!' The grassy hollow where Tam's Coo lay is sometimes called 'Tom Morris's Coo' by locals.

The fourth hole (424 yards) has been called the Ginger Beer Hole since at latest 1836, before which it was the Hole of Cunnin Links. The reason why is explained by James Balfour in 1887, recalling his early golfing experiences from about 1842. He writes:

> When I first visited St Andrews there were only a few resident gentlemen who played, and some occasional strangers from a distance, from Musselburgh, Leith, and Perth. The custom then was to meet in the small Union Parlour in Golf Place about twelve o'clock, and arrange the matches. Parties at once proceeded to play, and if the match was finished two or three holes from home they immediately turned and played their second round, taking a glass of ginger beer at the fourth or 'Ginger-beer' Hole.'

That accounts for the location of the refreshment near the end of the course but not at it. The second round must have been, by common consent, less than eighteen holes. Balfour does not mention that the ginger beer was commonly fortified with brandy. He goes on:

> If, however, they finished their first round, they came into the Union Parlour only for ten minutes; did not sit down to lunch,

but took very slight refreshment, and finished the second round a little after four. The dinner hour was then five. How different now [in 1887], when matches are made a week, or even a fortnight, in advance; when places are taken early in the morning, and a man is kept with a record to start each in his turn, and so prevent disputes about the order of play; when play is begun a little after nine, and fifty or sixty matches start between that hour and twelve; when parties have to wait a quarter of an hour at the 'high hole' [the eleventh]; when an hour or an hour and a half is devoted to lunch, and the second rounds are not begun till between two and half-past three! The dinner hour is half-past seven, to give time to have a putting match on the Ladies' Links with the fair and enthusiastic devotees of the game!

Nowadays, if you wish for ginger beer at the fourth hole, you must bring it along with you. Beware of slicing into the whins on the right, or the two bunkers on the edge of the rough. You do not run much risk of hooking into Sutherland's bunker on the left, a nasty wee pot in a hillock, where a Victorian Mr Sutherland is alleged to have spent as much time as in his own home. He is commemorated also by a bunker at Musselburgh. A much more likely destination for a pulled stroke is the large Cottage bunker on the left. But if you land in that one, take heart from the experience of Bobby Jones in 1930. He played out so accurately as to sink the ball in the hole 160 yards away for an eagle two. During another of his rounds in 1930, when playing Tolley in the Amateur, Bobby Jones sliced his second into the wind. After hanging in the wind, the ball plumped down on the bald cranium of a spectator, and rebounded ten feet, to near the edge of the green, instead of falling into the rough—a most providentially favourable 'rub o' the green'.

There are two small bunkers on the right near the green, and the shallow Students' bunkers on the left, then a round bunker on the edge of the green, and the two Ginger Beer bunkers beyond it, where old Daw Anderson used to dispense that refreshing fluid. There is an awkward humplock in front of the green, which spreads widely and wavily. In his book *The Golf Courses of the British Isles* (1910), Bernard Darwin observes that the St Andrews greens 'are for the most part on beautiful pieces of golfing ground, which by their natural conformation, by their banks and braes and slopes, guard the holes very effectively, even without the aid of the numerous bunkers.' Darwin continues:

> Providence has been very kind in dowering St Andrews with plateau greens, and they are never easy to approach. A plateau demands of the golfer that a shot should be played; it will not allow him merely to toss his ball into the air with a lofting iron and the modest ambition that it may come down somewhere on the green. Again, a plateau never gives any undeserved help to the inaccurate approacher, as do the greens that lie in holes and hollows. Even in a more marked degree than at Hoylake, the ground is never helping us; in its kindest mood it is not more than strictly impartial. Finally, the turf is very hard, and consequently the greens are apt to take a keenness that is paralysing in its intensity.

This last feature noticed by Darwin is much mitigated nowadays by the much more extensive watering of the greens, so that lofted approach shots may stay on the green near where the ball falls. But there are still many good exponents of the old St Andrews style of running-up approach, such as Allan Robertson used to perform with a cleek. The subtle undulations of greens, whether plateau-type or not, continue to make it difficult for the inexperienced to 'read the green' at most holes on the Old.

The fifth hole, of 522 yards, is mysteriously known as the 'Hole o' Cross', though there cannot have been a cross visible about it since the Reformation of 1560. Can it possibly preserve a memory of the game of *Crosse* from which, in part, golf evolved? You will find eight bunkers in the fairway near the direct line to the white flag. Of these the first is called the Pulpit, though it is merely a pot in a hillock; the rest are anonymous, like over two-thirds of the Old Course bunkers. Avoid them all by aiming to the left, on a ridge that runs out from the escarpment of the Elysian Fields on the fourteenth fairway. In front of the green there is an undulating ridge with two bunkers in it, and a gully beyond. Balfour in 1887 found the fifth hole 'sadly destroyed' compared with the fifth hole of the 1840s, which was known to many as 'Hell'. He complains:

'There is hardly any hazard; there are no bunkers of any consideration, and the approach to the green is a blind stroke without any bunker between. The hole is altogether much tamer, and less interesting, as well as easier." In fact, he recommended 'the young laird of the Links' to plough it up, or honeycomb it with bunkers! Balfour's advice was not taken; but even as things are most players find it hard to make their par five here.

You would notice some heather on the left as you came to the fifth green, and now the sixth is called the Heathery. In 1821 it was known as Muir Hole, in 1836 as Hole of Shell. Balfour explains that formerly the putting green had no turf, 'but was merely earth, heather, and shells'. This sort of information makes it all the more admirable that Allan Robertson in 1846 did a round of the course in 95 with no other club than a wooden driver! In front of the sixth tee there are deep gullies and steep ridges, covered with heather and grass. The white flag, 370 yards off, is just visible from the left edge of the tee, being nearly hidden by dense whins on a long ridge to the right. If you try and drive over the edge of the nearest mass of whins you may land in one of five bunkers: so aim left of the direct line, on the rightmost of the hangars of Leuchars aerodrome, visible across the Eden estuary, unless there is too much of an East Fife *haar*, the North Sea mist which occasionally saves the Andreapolitans from excessive sunburn. As you come near the green a rise in the ground hides from you the dip on your side of the green, which, moreover, slopes away from you. These problems are less when the green is soft, and should not prevent your getting a par four.

Now let us move on to the seventh or High Hole (359 yards), which in 1821 was intelligibly termed the Eden Hole, because its green overlooks the Eden estuary, but in 1836 was mysteriously called Hole of Rhi. Just as the Doo Craig is sometimes spelt Dhu Craig, to indicate the etymologist's acquaintance with Gaelic, the spelling *rhi* may be Chalmers's fanciful way of spelling the Scots word *ree*, sometimes *reegh*, which means, *inter alia*, 'An inclosure from a river, or the sea, of a square form, open only towards the water, for the purpose of receiving small vessels', according to the lexicographer Jamieson. It can also mean a sheep-pen. There may well have been at one time some such structure adjacent to the seventh hole. Be that as it may, there is nothing problematic about the contemporary presence of whins, which stand in a menacing phalanx on the right and advance near the tee so as to make the hole a dog's leg. It is best to drive well clear of the whins, aiming not at the white flag of the seventh hole itself, but at the red flag of the eleventh hole, which shares the double green. The approach to the hole is guarded by the large Cockle or Shell bunker, to the right of which are three smaller traps, one of which seems to be that called the Green Pot by Hodge in 1875. Balfour knew the seventh green originally as very small, and surrounded by thick bent grass, which caused bad lies. G. F. Stout, an eminent psychologist in his day, who was for many years the local Professor of Logic and Metaphysics, remarked about golf that 'it is a game where the ball invariably lies badly and the golfer well'. From the High Hole green you may observe the great variety of shore birds that throng the mudflats when the tide is out. At full tide the estuary brims like a sea, which induced Sir Peter Scott Lang, a Regius Professor of Mathematics more distinguished for his amateur militarism, to exclaim, in the phrase of Xenophon's Greeks when they came down from the mountains of middle Asia to behold the Black Sea, '*Thalassa! Thalassa!*' (This mysterious cry caused one caddie to remark to the other, 'A dinna see onie lassie.')

Having got your par four at the seventh you address yourself to the task of securing a par three at the eighth, or Short Hole Out (161 yards). You will notice now that you have changed direction. Hitherto you have been going in a generally north-westerly line, along the straight shaft of a course of which the general design is like a shepherd's crook. At the eighth tee you have reached the inward turn of the crook, and you now face south-east, with a fine view of the broken castle and cathedral and the other vertical projections of the town. The difficulty of this hole depends even more on wind than most. Almost in the direct line of the hole is a hillock with a deep bunker in its side, the Short Hole Bunker. Behind and to the left of this bunker the ground is such as somewhat to funnel balls into the hazard. Unless, therefore, you can be sure of putting your shot straight onto the green and stopping it there, you may be better advised

A mid-Victorian foursome on the 18th tee: Old Tom Morris (2nd from left), Cathcart of Pitcairlie (4th from left), Allan Robertson (3rd from right) and Wemyss of Wemyss Hall (far right).

Hell Bunker.

The funeral of Old Tom Morris in 1908—on the left is
the old Toun Kirk in process of reconstruction.

bby Jones receiving the Freedom of St Andrews from
Provost Robert Leonard, 1958.

The most famous links in the world. Left to right: the Eden, starting left of the railway and continuing across it to the Eden estuary; the Old Course, from the R. & A. clubhouse across the Swilcan Burn to the Eden; the New Course, to the right of the Old; the Jubilee nearest the West Sands.

to play a bit to the right, aiming at the College Tower, which is the highest piece of architecture on the horizon. There is another wee bunker on the right of the fairway, but it takes a very bad stroke to find it. This eighth hole was named Hole o' Turn in 1821, when the ninth was called End Hole, as it still is. But in 1836 Chalmers called the ninth the Hole of Return or Last Hole, it being the last hole outward.

When Balfour first knew it the ninth was mainly heather; and there is still plenty of heather on the left, mixed with whins. But Old Tom Morris turfed most of the fairway. About the time of the Boer War he put in the turf a couple of bunkers to catch drives, naming them for the Boer President Kruger. I suppose one of them represents Kruger's celebrated top hat. Further on, to the left, amid the bonnie blooming heather, he set the bunker called Mrs Kruger. Nearer the green, on the right, is Boase's bunker, a pot in a hillock, commemorating W. Norman Boase, who served both as Provost of the city and as a leading office-bearer of the R & A, and helped to reconcile their conflicting interests at a period when passions had run high. Beyond Boase's is the End Hole bunker, another pot in a hillock; and there is a wee trap in the rough on the left beside the green. But, by and large, the End Hole is a dull one; and so is the next.

The tenth seems not to have had any other name, and it is not a memorable hole (314 yards). From the tee you are facing north-west again, retracing the crook part of the shepherd's crook. There are three rather irrelevant bunkers in the whins to your left near the tee, and four more on the left of the fairway to catch your drive, so you aim to the right of the red flag. Red is used instead of white to mark the incoming holes. Further on, there is a small bunker on the right, and another behind the green, where also lies a gully. It is a plateau green with a backward slope.

After the dullish ninth and tenth holes, the eleventh administers a great stimulus or a demoralizing shock to most venturers. It is the High Hole In, of only 170 yards, but described by Bernard Darwin as 'the most fiendish short hole in the world'. Oddly enough, the American devotees of golf, gluttons for punishment, allowed Charles Blair Macdonald, who had been a student at St Andrews, to copy it on Long Island at his so-called National Links of America. You drive about due west, to a high-set green, rather narrow, with a slope towards you. Behind it is a tract of rough bent grass, falling to the Eden shore. The fairway crosses the seventh fairway, and on the right of the line to the hole is the Cockle bunker. Eating into the sloping green from below is the deep pit called the Strath bunker, for the famous trio of brothers, Davie, Andrew, and George, the third of whom was the first St Andrean to become a professional golfer in the USA. Even more horrid is the Hill bunker to the left of the line of approach. The wind makes a lot of difference at this hole. If it takes your ball too far, you may have a bad lie; and even if you have a good one it is enormously risky to propel the ball back onto a green that slopes towards two nasty bunkers. Even to land your drive on the green above the hole is hazardous, if the green is at all dry and hard, when it turns into a sort of inclined ice-rink, on which it is hard to stop a downward putt that misses the hole. The cannier types of old used often to play their drives short, so as to putt uphill. In the Open Championship of 1921 a nineteen-year-old enthusiast from Atlanta, Georgia, Robert Tyre Jones, Jr, came to play. For his first two rounds he took 151, which was good enough; but on the third round he came to grief at the High Hole In. His tee-stroke landed in the Hill bunker. He hit two explosive strokes to try and lift it out, but it still stayed in the bunker: so the young Georgian tore up his score-card and left the competition. His revenge came in 1930.

When you stand on the twelfth tee above the Eden, for the Heathery Hole Inward, of 316 yards, you are once again facing south-east, to come back along the shaft of the shepherd's crook. This fairway has six bunkers, none of which is visible from the tee. Particularly large is the Stroke bunker, some 170 yards on the direct line to the flag. Therefore you aim to the left, onto the right edge of a whin-covered ridge. There is a nasty pot in a hillock as you approach the green, which is rather narrow at the end where the hole is cut.

You move on to another par-four hole, the thirteenth, or Hole o' Cross Inward, 409 yards, where Balfour noted that more medals had been lost than at any other. Seven bunkers lurk to the left of the direct line, the first rejoicing in the name of Nick's, which means Auld Nick's, the Devil's. Then there are the three Coffins, not very sinister to look at. After that you have a steepish ridge, with the Cat's Trap on the near side at the left, and Walkinshaw's Grave on the far side at the right. This is named for the veteran Sutherland's most habitual partner, a left-handed enthusiast who spent much time in it. One presumes that these names were mainly given and transmitted by the old corps of caddies, father to son. Nearer the green on the left is the Lion's Mouth, an innocuous little pot, to look at anyway. On the right hand, in the near corner of the green, is the Hole o' Cross bunker, and there is another that eats into the further right corner of the green. For your drive it is advisable to keep left of the whins near the tee on your right, but somewhat to the right of the red flag of the hole. Then your second, all being well, should usually be played towards the white flag of the fifth hole, which shares this double green.

The thirteenth fairway was the scene of a celebrated drive in 1892 by Freddie Tait, son of the Edinburgh professor P. G. Tait, who used to spend his summers in St Andrews, playing up to five rounds a day, starting at 6 a.m. He once organized a nocturnal match, with the balls painted with phosphorescent paint. It was abandoned at the second hole, when Professor Crum Brown noticed that his glove was on fire. Professor Tait had made many theoretical calculations, and reckoned that no human being could drive a ball so as to carry more than 190 yards. His son Freddie hit a ball at the thirteenth tee that carried for 250 yards, and completed a distance of 341 yards and 9 inches, ending within ten feet of Walkinshaw's Grave. Moreover, the ball so driven was of gutta percha: so that the effort was equivalent to driving a modern ball well over 400 yards. Besides winning the Amateur and other competitions in his dashing style, Freddie Tait was a keen player of the bagpipes, even at midnight through the town's streets; and he was universally mourned when he was killed in the Boer War in 1900, as a Lieutenant in the Black Watch.

Coming to the fourteenth, or Long Hole In, you may find it difficult to see the red flag some 513 yards distant, and quite difficult to achieve the par five. From the tee you see heather

and whins to your left, and a stone wall on your right, everything to the right of which wall is out of bounds. You play your
drive towards the steeple of the Hope Park Kirk, which is the
farthest steeple to the right of those in your view. But you must
not play your second stroke on the same line. Hope Park was
originally a Free Kirk, which occasioned a comment by an
Auld Kirk caddie in Victorian times: 'Noo play on the Toun
Kirk. If ye play on the Free Kirk ye'll land in Hell.' Hell was
the name given to a large bunker lying athwart the direct line
to the hole. Local ministers sought to get the caddies to call it
Hades, or even Sheol, which proved too highbrow for them.
Balfour uses a periphrasis, 'the big bunker with the uncouth
name'. A Bishop of London once got into 'Hell', and rose to the
occasion by getting his ball out again with a dexterous blow of
the niblick. His caddie too rose to the occasion, and advised his
lordship, 'Mind noo whan ye dee tae tak your neeblick wi ye.'

The beautiful tract of greensward from the fourteenth tee to
the Hell bunker is called the Elysian Fields. On its left is a
group of bunkers, one large and three small, called the Beardies,
still sometimes frequented. Further on is Benty, a crescent-
shaped sandpit, which used to be called Dunny, or Willie Dunn,
because the Musselburgh champion of that name once drove
into it from the Hole o' Cross green, some 250 yards, which was
about fifty yards beyond the norm for a first-class player with a
gutta or feathery. Further on you come to the Kitchen bunker,
originally Hell's Kitchen or the Deil's Pat (Devil's Pot), then
to Hell, and beyond it to the Grave, a couple of small pots. For
over a century, remember, the present fourteenth fairway was
the fourth fairway going out: so that one encountered the Grave
before getting to Hell, and Hell's Kitchen was in the back
premises of Hell. Nowadays, the fairway is played only south-
eastwards. In that direction, if one avoids the Grave, one may
still run into the Ginger Beer bunkers, which are no more
exhilarating.

After contending with the long fourteenth it is a comparative
relief to face the fifteenth, or Cartgate Hole In, with its 404
yards. To keep clear of the long bristle of whins on the right
people usually drive left of the line to the flag, somewhat to the
right of the big Cottage bunker on the fourth fairway, and

aiming for the Hope Park spire. The drive should land in a gully, from which there is a clear approach onto the green, avoiding the three Rob's bunkers on the left.

At the sixteenth, or Corner of the Dyke Hole, the railway line comes very close on the right, and it is now out of bounds, though the Victorian stalwarts thought nothing of playing iron shots off the tracks. There is a narrow gap between the railway and the three bunkers called the Principal's Nose; which Principal's nobody seems now to know. Unless you are very certain of driving accurately, it is well to keep left of the Principal's Nose by aiming for the left edge of the new Old Course Hotel, erected by the British Railways organization for reasons best known to themselves. Beyond the Principal's Nose is Deacon Sime, a pot in a hillock, then the little bunker called Grant's, and finally the Wig, cutting into the green on the left. The green has an awkward slope towards the railway. It was the scene in 1929 of a great example of determined concentration by a leading lady golfer, Miss Joyce Wethered, afterwards Lady Heathcote-Amory, when fighting Miss Glenna Collett for the Ladies' Championship. She had to sink a putt to win a crucial hole, and did so while a train thundered past ten yards away. When asked why she had not waited for the train to pass first, she asked, 'What train?'

Miss Wethered, you see, was not one of those sensitive players who explain their missed putts and foozled drives by the disturbance caused by a damnable lark singing half a mile away.

Last hole but one is the famous Road Hole, also sometimes known as the Stationmaster's Garden Hole. It shared with the Eleventh the honour of being copied on Long Island for the National Links of America. It is a dogleg of 466 yards. Till 1967 there were black sheds on the right of the tee which the bold drivers used to carry, aiming to soar over the second letter *d* of the name *D. Anderson*, which was painted there till 1940, when the prudent citizens obliterated it, for fear that Adolf Hitler might parachute in and realize he was at the seventeenth hole. If one could not drive over the sheds, it was a problem how to pass to the left of them without entering Cheape's bunker. If one drove too far into the fairway past the left of the sheds the second shot was liable to enter the Scholar's bunker; and if one lofted the ball out of the Scholar's bunker it might well fall into its neighbour, the Progressing bunker, a narrow sandpit with a sharp ridge on the side towards the green. Moreover, even if a tiger driver could soar over the black sheds with his drive he might find difficulty in keeping his second shot on the green, a narrow plateau, with a bunker on its left and a road on its right, nowadays with a decent strip of sand between the hard surface and the turf. In the great competitions this hole has of late ceased to be so formidable, as, in the interests of crowd control, the tee has been set thirteen yards forward, and somewhat to the left. For a golfer new to the course, perhaps the best advice is to drive on the Hope Park spire again. It is a par five, and easier than of yore, or at least less difficult. With the forward tee for competitions it is a par four, of 453 yards.

The seventeenth green is celebrated for a feat by the great Allan Robertson, recounted by the Rev. Principal Tulloch of St Mary's in his life of Tom Morris. With Mr Erskine Wemyss of Wemyss little Allan, with his red side-whiskers and red jacket, was playing a two-ball match against Willie Park and Mr Hastie, a Member of Parliament. In their second round Robertson and Wemyss were one down with two to play at the seventeenth. A prominent R & A member, Mr Campbell of Saddell, offered three five-pound notes to one on the Park–Hastie combination. His bet was taken by Mr John Blackwood, the publisher. The result of the long game was that Park had put the ball on the plateau green for Mr Hastie to putt, and Wemyss of that Ilk had landed Allan with an approach shot from the hard high road, playing 'two more' at that. Taking his broad-bladed iron, nicknamed 'the Fryingpan', Allan studied his shot, going back and forward from road to hole several times. Old Daw Anderson, his caddie, whispered to him, 'Ye can dae it, Allan.' With a dexterous application of the 'Fryingpan' Allan lofted the ball from the road to the top of the green, whence it trickled down into the hole, amid tremendous cheering. By the way, caddies often discountenanced cheering, and still more any occasional booing, asking Victorian spectators the rhetorical question, 'Wad ye dae that i' the kirk?' Such reverence was attached to the solemn sport a century ago. Mr Hastie lost his parliamentary sangfroid, and sent his putt past the hole. Park was so demoralized that his putt came short, violating the great maxim, 'Never up never in.' Thus Allan and Wemyss won the hole to square the match, with only the Home Hole to play. Allan sent off a superb drive, but Park plopped his into the Swilcan. Blackwood took three fivers off Campbell of Saddell. Allan Robertson, to be sure, could have his off days too. When he started a famous match at North Berwick in 1849 a local critic was heard to state, 'That wee body in the reid jaicket canna play gowf.'

Finally, you take your stance on the eighteenth tee for the Last Hole, or Home Hole, nowadays called Tom Morris, because he made the present green, which faces his shop. Its earliest name was Hole o' Hill. But the hill in question has been reduced, both absolutely and relatively. The present Valley of Sin west of the green is a residue of a much bigger hollow in which Old Tom elevated the present green. This last hole is 356 yards, and has no bunkers. There is a sinister S-bend of the Swilcan about ninety yards ahead, but you disregard it, aiming the ball for the Martyrs' Monument, an obelisk to the right of the R & A Clubhouse. That keeps you well to the left, so as not to go out of bounds by landing on the road in front of Rusack's Hotel. It is not hard to get onto the green in two, but this does not end your problems, for the eighteenth is the most awkward green on the course to read correctly for putting. It slopes up to its right-hand corner, at the junction of two fences which are commonly draped with idle spectators, who have nothing better to do than look down their noses at the wretches trying to hole out for a par four. Never mind, after the eighteenth hole comes the nineteenth, for which St Andrews offers a variety of agreeable locations, in which pilgrims may recuperate from 'the Anticient and healthfull Exercise of the Golf'.

12

THE GROWING UNIVERSITY

Of the trio—Religion, Golf, and Learning—the third was a poor third till quite late in the nineteenth century, at any rate as regards secular learning. Religion, or at least theology, was dominant, even over golf. When Sir Walter Scott first came to St Andrews, in 1793, and cut runes into the turf by the castle gateway to spell out the name of the lady who had rejected his addresses, Williamina Stuart Belshes, a third of the undergraduates were students of Divinity, and most of the professors were also Ministers of the Church of Scotland as by law established. There were forty-eight students in St Mary's, a hundred in the United College. Almost till Queen Victoria's death the divinity students dominated the social activities of the little university. After all, they pursued their studies for more years than those reading for the degree in arts. It was only the 'divines' who reached an age at which whiskers and beards could luxuriate, and whose muscular development became capable of disciplining the entire local police force by throwing him into the harbour at the start of the Martinmas Term in autumn.

Typical, in his interests, of the nineteenth century is Thomas Jackson, born in St Andrews in 1797. He held chairs of divinity at St Mary's and Glasgow from 1836 to 1874, and then returned to St Andrews to write his great work, designed to settle all the controversies of the centuries and bring discordant Scots into unanimity. He had one of the big houses on the south side of South Street, with its 'lang rigg', at the foot of which was an elegant garden-room, with a table and a chair. Hither daily the septuagenarian resorted, garbed in his ecclesiastical frock-coat, took off his shiny top hat, and grasped a quill pen to set down his great thoughts on the virgin white folio quire daily laid out on the table. After several hours he would tear it all up and go back to the house. After four years they found him dead, aged eighty-one, and the garden-house yielded a single written sheet with the sum of his wisdom: 'Theology is everything, and everything is theology.'

Professor Jackson is described as 'a mystic of the highest order, and one of the kindliest of men'. In this he was not so typical of the Andreapolitan religionists, many of whom could be quite worldly and waspish. For example, in the mid-Victorian 'revival' promoted by the American evangelists Dwight L. Moody and Ira D. Sankey, when the rest of the Andreapolitans began confessing their sins in public, Principal Shairp of the United College went round confessing to various hearers the sins of his colleague John Tulloch, the Principal of St Mary's. Religious disputes were, of course, not all just about theology, but very often about Church government, and who would have what job, and what should be the architectural style of a church, or the mode of its worship. In considering the evolution of these activities it is perhaps most convenient to make the development of the university, small as it was, the core of the narrative. In recent decades, indeed, the university has become the economic and social core of the town.

The later eighteenth century saw the Church of Scotland dominated by the so-called Moderates. In contrast to the minority of 'High-Flyers', the Moderates cultivated elegance and urbanity in deportment and utterance, and inclined to rationalism in the defence of Calvinist orthodoxy. Earlier in the century Archibald Campbell, a St Andrews professor, asserted that the Apostles had been 'no enthusiasts'. Of this breed was George Hill (1750–1819), son of a St Andrews Minister. He got the Greek chair at twenty-one, and became Principal of St Mary's in 1791. Not only did he dominate the General Assembly of the Church, but before long it was found that, of the thirteen members of the academic Senatus, six belonged to the Hill family. Worshippers came to relish the 121st Psalm in its metrical version: 'I to the Hills will lift mine eyes, From whence doth come mine aid.' A cosy academic job of that period was the sale of St Leonard's College to Professor Robert Watson, for £200 and a £10 annual feu duty. He demolished the bonny bell-tower, and removed the roof of the chapel to make it a greenhouse. The shrubs did not thrive, but the professor did well by taking in aristocratic boarders into the old college buildings, now his private house. Maitland Anderson, sometime University Librarian, found in the margin of a book a comment by a student of this period: 'Every kind of dissipation was carried on openly, and never checked by any professor.'

The vandalism at St Leonard's College was paralleled at St Salvator's, where the original Gothic roof had a rather flat arch, and there was an echo that made every sermon seem twice as long. After a report in 1773 by James Craig, planner of the New Town of Edinburgh, the professors had the roof cut away at the wallheads and dropped bodily into the church, wrecking the elaborate Gothic tomb of the pious founder. However, a spirit of improvement was stirring in the cultural climate, and reached even St Andrews, as manifested in the careers of Andrew Bell and Thomas Chalmers.

Andrew Bell was son of a local bailie and hairdresser, who experimented in type-founding with Alexander Wilson (1714–86), later Professor of Astronomy at Glasgow, where he designed types for the Foulis Press. At the age of eighteen, in 1781, the young Bell set out to the Witch Hill one morning to fight a duel with an English student: being short-sighted, he fired at the seconds instead of the antagonist. No harm was done; and Bell took to religion, ending up as a canon of Westminster Abbey, where he was buried in 1832, after endowing the Madras College, which put St Andrews on the Victorian educational map. Thomas Chalmers was born in 1780, along the coast at Anstruther; he came to college at the age of eleven, and was good at football and handball. His main bent was mathematical, but through family influence he became in 1803 Minister of Kilmany parish, about ten miles away, riding over to lecture as assistant to the Regius Professor of Mathematics, Nicolas Vilant. At the oral examination the two preceptors disagreed, and Chalmers delivered a long invective, which led to the ending of his assistantship. Nothing daunted, Chalmers ran a class of his own in the next session, with numerous students attending. He defied the Presbytery to stop him, maintaining that 'after the satisfactory discharge of his parish duties a minister may enjoy five days in the week of uninterrupted leisure for the prosecution of any science in which his taste may dispose him to engage'. Around the same time William Ferrie, Minister of Kilconquhar, held the chair of civil history for eighteen years (1808–26), and gave only two lectures. Chalmers had an illness in 1810, during which he experienced a religious conversion; his sermons began to attract crowds to Kilmany from far afield. In 1814 he was called to the Tron kirk in Glasgow, and began to campaign for the rescue of the poor folk in industrial cities. In 1823 St Andrews made him Professor of Moral Philosophy, where he lectured mainly on political economy; and in 1828 he removed to Edinburgh as Professor of Divinity, taking a leading part in the movement that led to the Disruption of the Church of Scotland in 1843, of which anon.

As rebuilt in 1754 St Salvator's had rooms for only some forty resident students, and most of them lived in the town, sometimes boarding with professors. As Chancellor (1765–88), the eighth Earl of Kinnoull encouraged gentlefolk to settle with their families for golf and education. So did his successor, Harry Dundas, first Viscount Melville (1788–1811), called 'the uncrowned king of Scotland' for his Tory political management. His son Robert was also Chancellor (1814–51), and got the Government to give some money for rebuilding the decrepit quadrangle of St Salvator's. In 1828 Robert Reid, the King's Architect, erected a large Jacobean structure, providing only four classrooms, all too big. He also did some restoration and alteration at St Mary's and the University Library, more intelligently. Then the Whigs succeeded the Tories, and, as the Rev. Dr Grierson lamented in 1838, 'the funds which had been honourably pledged for the completion of the United College were unceremoniously and unjustly given for the rebuilding of Marischal College, Aberdeen. Hence the United College of St Andrews stands a hideous compound of mean and gorgeous architecture, a proof of the faithlessness of public men. . . .' Many times since 1838 not only St Andrews but other universities could lament likewise.

In 1826 the Government appointed a Royal Commission, which reported in 1830; but nothing was done to implement its proposals till the Act of Parliament of 1858. In 1827 a new nine-subject Master of Arts degree curriculum was introduced; Humanity (Latin), Greek, Logic, Mathematics, Moral Philosophy, Natural Philosophy (Physics), Natural History, Chemistry, and Political Economy. But few graduated. For example, in 1845 three men graduated BA, three MA, one DD; but 106 bought the MD degree, which cost them twenty-five guineas a head, of which the Government took ten pounds for stamping the academic diploma. This paucity of graduates is the more curious that by 1845 the Madras College had about nine hundred pupils, and the town was still enjoying a boom as a 'watering-place'. There had been some nice Regency building, such as Pilmuir Links (1820), convenient for the golf-course and the sea. These elegant houses, writes Grierson, 'are generally well filled during that season when invalids and hypochondriacs lave their limbs in the briny deep'. In similar style he writes of the Lammas Fair in August, where farm-servants struck new bargains for the next year's feeing, and the visitor could enjoy 'the unrestrained jollity of these unsophisticated children of the land'. Since 1810, also, there had been baths on the clifftop west of the Castle, with hot water and showers for those who funked the North Sea. An annual event was the carters' race, run by the Whiplickers' Society, from the Blue Stane, oldest sacral object in the burgh, now behind the railing of the Windsor and Station Hotel.

The religious and political movements that came to a head in the Disruption of 1843 had been simmering for generations. By a religious settlement annexed to the Treaty of Union of 1707, the Church of Scotland, as established on its Presbyterian basis in 1690, was guaranteed a monopoly for all time coming in Scotland. But in 1712 the recently created Parliament of the United Kingdom of Great Britain passed two Acts which were constitutionally beyond its powers as derived from the international treaty. A Toleration Act pretended to authorize Episcopalian worship in Scotland, and a Patronage Act gave local land-owners the power to present ministers to parish churches, whether the local congregation liked the presentee or not. After a series of General Assembly protests, a number of ministers seceded in 1733, and formed an Associate Presbytery. In 1747 these 'Seceders' split into 'Burghers', who accepted an oath imposed on new burgesses in certain burghs, to uphold 'the true Protestant religion presently professed within this realm', and a rival body of 'Anti-Burghers'. The Burghers then split into 'Auld Lichts', who upheld the Solemn League and Covenant of 1643, and 'New Lichts', who thought it obsolete. By another split, there arose 'Lifters', who allowed ministers to raise the bread and wine when consecrating them for a communion, and 'Anti-Lifters', who prohibited such 'papistical backslitherings'. Gradually, however, the fissiparous sects began to coalesce again, and in 1820 arose the 'United Secession' Church. In the 1820s a spirit of religious revival spread through much wider strata, and in 1824 the General Assembly of the Established Church adopted an overture to institute foreign missions. Famous among the missionaries was a St Andrews graduate of 1829, Alexander Duff, who went to India in 1830, being shipwrecked twice. His Bible, rescued from the waves, keeps company in the University Library with the Koran of Tippoo Sahib, and the Bible of Donald Cargill, the Covenanter, who was captured in 1681, in Charles II's 'killing times'. Another St Andrews alumnus, the dissolute Duke of Rothes, who had signed the two Covenants as a student, threatened Cargill with extraordinary torture and violent death, to which Cargill retorted, 'Die what death I will, your eyes will not see it.' The debauched duke died suddenly the night before Cargill was hanged. It was by a revival of interest in such Presbyterian martyrs as Cargill that people subscribed to erect in 1842 the obelisk at the west end of the Scores commemorating four of the sixteenth-century Protestants executed by the Papalists.

With the revived evangelical stirrings, more and more people began to rebel against the imposition of presentees on parishes by land-owners, many of whom were themselves Episcopalians or indifferent in matters of religion. A series of litigations arose in the 1830s, but the law courts invariably upheld the right of land-owners to intrude ministers of their own choice whatever a congregation might wish. Finally, in 1843, at the annual General Assembly, a massive minority of ministers and elders walked out, in protest against the refusal of the government and Parliament to remedy the grievance. In all, 451 out of about 1200 ministers and a third of the communicants left the 'Auld Kirk' to found the Free Church of Scotland. Thomas Chalmers used his mathematical ability to organize a sustentation fund, which soon was able to pay five hundred ministers £150 a year. Within four years the Free Kirk had seven hundred churches, and many schools, and its own colleges and overseas missions, including those founded by Alexander Duff. At the same time the ministers who had stayed in the Auld Kirk began to exert themselves to compete. Chalmers's chief opponent was his successor in the chair of moral philosophy, George Cook (1828–45), leader of the Moderates in the Assembly. A majority of the academics seem to have been Auld Kirkers, and they made life unhappy for the United College Principal Sir David, Brewster (1838–59), who was a Free Kirker. He was also hostile to the cosy jobbery of the Hill and Cook type, and always looked for the best man for any vacant chair. Himself a distinguished scientist, he wished the university to teach civil engineering and such social and economic studies as would be useful to bankers, merchants and manufacturers. Aided by the Presbytery of St Andrews, Brewster's colleagues tried to have him deposed; but they failed on a technicality, that he had not personally signed the deed of demission of office in the Established Church. He was glad to move off to be Principal of Edinburgh.

The Christian spirit of the 1840s is exemplified in the prayer of a Divinity student for a professor about whom he had his doubts: 'Lord, have mercy on our Professor, for he is weak and ignorant. Strengthen his feeble hands, confirm his tottering knees, and grant that he may go out and in before us like the he-goat before the flock.' Architects at least benefited from the rivalry of sects. In 1849 Dr Charles Roger noted the seating capacities of churches in St Andrews thus: the Toun Kirk, largely rebuilt in 1797, could seat 2,500; its overflow St Mary's (1839: now the Victory Memorial Hall) held 630; the Martyrs' Free Kirk, opposite the College Kirk in North Street, built in 1844, held 870; and the United Presbyterian edifice at the east end of North Street (1826) could seat 450. An Independent Church in Market Street, enlarged in 1824, held 340; and the Baptist Church west of Madras College (1841) had 250. The small Episcopalian community, having long met in private houses, had built a smallish chapel in 1825 in North Street. They had 108 members in 1836, at which time there was only one Roman Catholic family, of Irish immigrants; not till 1884 could the Papalists afford a church, when they erected what Andrew Lang called 'a corrugated place of worship', more vulgarly a 'tin tabernacle', on the clifftop, just east of the Martyrs' Memorial. An old fisherman in 1930 told me how he had broken in, with others, and thrown the tall candles into the sea. In 1910 Reginald Fairlie was architect of the fine St James's Church on the same site. Today the Roman Catholic Society is the largest of the students' clubs; the oldest is the Theological Society, started in 1760. There was by 1849 seating accommodation for over 5,000 worshippers at a time, rather more than the total population of the burgh.

A tourist commented to his coachman, 'There must be a great deal of religious zeal in this town: there are so many churches.' To which the cynical Jehu replied, 'It's no religious zeal ava. It's juist cursedness o' temper.' Somewhat similarly I recall a chat with a chauffeur waiting on his mistress to emerge from a Buchmanite or 'Oxford Group' meeting in the Town Hall in the 1930s. He thought it 'juist a kind o' Salvation Airmy for the gentry'. One effect of the Disruption in the university was that attendance at the College Kirk ceased to be compulsory. Till 1904 it was also the church of St Leonard's Parish, since the disuse of St Leonard's Chapel. From 1844 to 1904 there was intermittent wrangling and litigation between the St Leonard's congregation and the university, which ended with the removal of the St Leonard's people to a massive new Romanesque church in the opulent western suburban thoroughfare, Hepburn Gardens, put up at the cost of the feuars there, who grudged sorely the expense. One of them decided to get his money's worth by sending his wife to sit in the new church.

More building of the 1840s included the West Infant School (1844), in its day a new model Kindergarten for the Madras College; William Nixon's North building of St Salvator's quadrangle, in Jacobean style like Reid's East building; and the start of Mr Hope Scott's scheme to rival the New Town of Edinburgh, with Hope Street a straight terrace, Howard Place a convex one, and Abbotsford Place a concave, all set round a park. It took half a century to complete. 1854 saw the substantial clubhouse erected for the Royal and Ancient, and the new Town Hall was built in 1861 in Scotch Baronial style. The railway came to St Andrews in 1854, and wealthy *rentiers* began to put up Scotch Baronial dream homes, like Kinburn, Edgecliffe, and Westerlea (now Wardlaw Hall). In 1859 a new

Principal came to the United College, James David Forbes, an excellent geologist, son of the famous banker, Sir William Forbes, and of Walter Scott's first love, Williamina Stuart Belshes. A High Churchman, Forbes put stained glass into the College Kirk. He also sought to restore the residential system for students, and to make the undergraduate body truly representative by attracting boys from the old peerage families. In this he was aided by the chancellor, the eighth Duke of Argyll (1851–1900), who sent his son, who later married a daughter of Queen Victoria. A Marquis of Breadalbane and an Earl of Aberdeen were other alumni of this time; but the best known today was a scholar and writer, Andrew Lang.

Andrew Lang, a Borderer related to Walter Scott, came to St Andrews from the Edinburgh Academy in 1861, aged seventeen, his uncle, W. Y. Sellar, being Professor of Greek. He stayed in the College Hall, newly set up by Principal Forbes in a rented house on the site of St Leonard's College. He remembered it as:

> . . . something between an Oxford Hall and a Master's House at a public school, rather more like the latter than the former. We were more free than school-boys, not as free as undergraduates. There were about a dozen of us at first, either from the English public schools, or the Edinburgh Academy. Fate, and certain views of the authorities about the impropriety of studying human nature in St Andrews after dark, thinned our numbers very early in the first session.

The last Marquis of Breadalbane recalled:

> The two rules the students of the Hall most objected to were, that they were not to enter the billiard-rooms of any of the hotels in St Andrews, nor were they to accept an invitation to dinner or a party except on Friday and Saturday nights. Another bitter complaint was that the gas supplied was so meagre that it only made darkness visible.

In spite of all, the Hall throve enough for Forbes to have a new one specially built in 1868, which, however, failed in 1874. In 1877 the valuable site was sold to St Leonard's School for Girls, a new venture that has since acquired great renown. Already in 1836 the New Statistical Account had told of two boarding-houses for young ladies, in which 'all the usual branches of education that are required for females in the higher ranks of life may be attained'.

The most popular teacher in Lang's time was J. F. Ferrier, Professor of Moral Philosophy. Lang writes:

> There was I know not what of dignity, of humour, and of wisdom in his face; there was an air of the student, the vanquisher of difficulties, the discoverer of hidden knowledge, in him, that I have seen in no other. His method at that time was to lecture on the History of Philosophy, and his manner was so persuasive that one believed firmly in the tenets of each school he described, till he advanced those of the next! Thus the whole historical evolution of thought went on in the mind of each of his listeners.

Another student remembered Ferrier's series of variegated waistcoats, and his habit of arriving late and leaving early; and his ability to give students more to think about in fifteen minutes than any other teacher could give in an hour. Mrs Ferrier was less impressed, being a daughter of 'Christopher North', of *Noctes Ambrosianae* fame. Of her husband's philosophy she said: 'It makes you feel as if you were sitting upon a cloud with nothing on, a lucifer match in your hand, but with no possible way to strike it!' Her brother-in-law, the poet W. E. Aytoun, spent a week with them and returned to Edinburgh asserting that Hell was 'a quiet and friendly place to live in compared with St Andrews'.

Forbes was succeeded as Principal by John Campbell Shairp (1868–85), who objected to innovations lately made in the College Kirk, such as kneeling at prayer and standing at praise. He desired the students to wear blue bonnets with red tassels, instead of square mortar-boards, and wrote: 'Anglicized Scotchmen are generally poor creatures, and an Anglicized Scotland will be a contemptible country.' Shairp founded the Cottage Hospital, in memory of his mother-in-law, Lady William Douglas of Dunino (1864). It could not have pleased him that the historian J. A. Froude, elected Rector by the students, said of them in 1869, 'These youths are exactly like Oxford undergraduates.' By the Act of 1858 the undergraduates were allowed again to elect an extrinsic Rector, and the post has been filled by some most distinguished personalities. The longest rectorial address so far is that of J. S. Mill in 1867, 140 minutes. The judge Lord Neaves was Rector in 1873, and sang to the Senate his own songs, including 'Let us all be unhappy on Sunday'.

Building of this period includes Queen's Gardens, and the Episcopal church of St Andrew at the foot of it (1869), and the Victorian Gothic Hope Park Church for the United Presbyterians (1865). The first 'kist o' whistles' (i.e., organ) in a St Andrews Presbyterian church was installed at St Mary's in 1874, amid violent controversy, such as greeted also the first weekday Christmas service in the Toun Kirk, in 1872. Old scandals got a new breath of life in 1873 when the demolition of an old public-house at the north-east corner of Church Street revealed a child's skeleton beneath a hearthstone. In Archbishop Sharp's lifetime somebody published a book about him in which Sharp was said to have lodged in a St Andrews change-house, before becoming a Regent in the university, and to have gotten with child one Isobel Lindsay, under promise of marriage, she being the innkeeper's sister-in-law. Sharp was said to have strangled the subsequent child and buried it beneath the hearth-stone. When he was Archbishop Isobel Lindsay stood up in the kirk and denounced him, more than once: for which the Provost personally put on her the 'branks', or scold's bridle, still to be seen; and Sharp made her stand, thus bridled, at the Tron. But such old tales did little to moderate the goodwill of Victorian St Andrews to the first resident bishop of the Episcopalian diocese for a century and a half, Charles Wordsworth, a nephew of the poet. He is best remembered as founder of the Oxford and Cambridge Boat Race, and he also played cricket for Oxford. In 1853 he became Bishop of St Andrews, Dunkeld, and Dunblane, and from 1876 lived in the city, where he was invited to dine with the Presbytery, and even to preach in the Toun Kirk, in the spirit that has since been termed 'ecumenical'. A further departure from the Andrew Melville tradition was the institution of a Christmas party for old folks, in 1879, by Bailie McIntosh, father of the pioneer marine biologist W. C. McIntosh.

When St Leonard's School started in 1877, the university

itself had only 130 students; but attempts were being made to promote it with modern publicity methods, largely organized by William Knight, Professor of Moral Philosophy (1876–1903). A Chair of Education was founded, and degrees of Bachelor and Doctor of Science introduced, and a curious diploma titled *L.L.A.*, usually thought to mean 'Lady Literate in Arts'. It was granted to women successful in examinations held up and down the island, and overseas; and proved widely popular. Meantime a public-spirited Dundee lady, Mary Ann Baxter of Balgavies, was promoting the idea of a university college in Dundee, an old city which had recently expanded vastly in population through the boom in jute-manufacturing. She gave £120,000 to found University College, Dundee, which started teaching in 1883. Her hope was that others would give generously, as had happened with university colleges in England, where, if one magnate gave £100,000, his rival would put down £150,000. Not so the Dundonians. Other local plutocrats said, 'Well, if the Baxters want a college, let the Baxters pay for it.' And, it is said, the other Baxters thought to themselves, 'One fool in a family is enough.' So Dundee did not grow as rich as Manchester; but still it was richer than St Andrews; and once again academic pundits here and there were saying, Why not suppress St Andrews, and distribute its endowments, such as they are? In the end money talked, most unexpectedly: for St Andrews received a windfall of £100,000 in 1889, from Australia. Alexander Berry, a former student, when emigrating to Australia, had been shipwrecked. His shipmates were eaten by cannibals; as he was too thin, the cannibals fed him on frogs in the hope of fattening him up; but before he was fat enough he was rescued, and lived long enough to gather a lot of wealth. Knowing his wishes, his surviving brother David sent along £100,000, a great sum in 1889. Quite apart from this windfall, the university had been generating some new energy in competition with its new rival across the Tay.

In 1882 W. C. M'Intosh, Professor of Natural History (1882–1916), started work in an improvised laboratory consisting of a timber fever-hospital by the East Sands. In 1896 he was provided with the Gatty Marine Laboratory, through the generosity of an Englishman, Dr C. H. Gatty, and much valuable work was done for fisheries. St Andrews still had about a hundred fishermen with fourteen boats in mid-Victorian times. M'Intosh was born in 1838, the year when the small medieval red gown was lengthened and sleeved to make a student's cloak. He died in 1931. Even in his nineties he was to be seen working at the Gatty, wearing his old red gown, and sometimes with his feet in a hay-box to keep them warm. His successor, Sir D'Arcy Wentworth Thompson, went to Dundee as professor in 1884, aged twenty-four, and held the Chair of Natural History at St Andrews from 1917 to 1948, when he died, having been sixty-four years a professor. Best known for his epoch-making book *Growth and Form*, D'Arcy had the widest-ranging of interests, and wrote, *inter alia*, glossaries of ancient Greek birds and fishes. When a hoopoe was shot on the golf-course in autumn 1930, D'Arcy took it about, wrapped in a silk handkerchief, and discoursed to his classes on Aristophanes' *Birds*. At graduations, when Principal Irvine made false quantities in his Latin, D'Arcy could be heard making strange whoops and whistles from behind his majestic beard, a beard the prickliness of which was attested by pretty bejantines with whom he danced in the 1930s, when he was in his seventies.

The principalship of the Aberdonian Classical scholar Sir James Donaldson (1886–1915) saw the university attaining a respectable position among the older universities. The Universities (Scotland) Act of 1889 had given increased powers to the University Court, a mainly non-academic body set up by the Act of 1858. For example, the Court could now institute new departments, with lectureships in default of professorships, and could appoint assistants, who had hitherto been privately hired by professors as they thought fit. A parliamentary annual grant of £6,300 was made, which in 1892 became £10,800. In 1892, also, Andrew Carnegie's Trust for the Scottish Universities was set up, which lent money to students for their tuition fees. In the same year women were admitted as graduating students. Then, too, the third Marquis of Bute was elected Rector, and served from 1895 for a second term. A wealthy and polyglot papalist peer, Bute was eager to make Blairs College, an Aberdeen seminary for priests, form part of the university of St Andrews; but the Vatican finally came down against him on this. Bute was also hostile to the affiliation of University College, Dundee, to the university, which had taken place in a half-baked fashion in 1890. Others for various reasons agreed with him, and, after wrangling and litigation, the union was dissolved in 1895, only to be re-made in 1897. In 1898, a Conjoint Medical School was established. Bute's munificence allowed the construction of fine buildings for natural sciences at St Andrews, and the inception of a Chair of Anatomy (1900). The Chandos Chair was specialized for physiology (1908), and it became common for intending medicoes to do their pre-clinical courses in old-world St Andrews before going to Dundee for their clinical years. Bute also donated largely for the extension of the Students' Union, which in 1892 secured the old house west of the College Tower, part of which is traditionally associated with the Admirable Crichton. In 1889 the brightest of undergraduate periodicals, *College Echoes*, began its career; and the Nineties produced that delightful Scots-American poet, Robert Fuller Murray, of *The Scarlet Gown*, and the *Scottish Student Song-book*, largely promoted by the Andreapolitan enthusiast Millar Patrick.

In 1897 a separate Science Faculty was instituted; and around that time chemistry flourished under Professor Purdie, whose opulent aunt, Mrs Purdie of Castlecliff, gave fine laboratories, which he extended. There was a good deal of private money about St Andrews up till the Kaiser's War of 1914, and some dozens of wealthy people built fine houses in the western suburbs. During what was called 'the Great South African War' imperialistic jingoism was in fashion, and an effigy of the Boer President Kruger was driven round the town to be burnt at the site of the old Mercat Cross, near the fountain in memory of the local novelist George Whyte Melville, killed in a hunting accident in 1878. Till the 1930s it was traditional to fling the President of the Union into it on Raisin Monday, the day when first-year students pay to their senior man or woman a pound of raisins, as fee for moral tutelage, and receive a Latin receipt specifying '*unam libram uvarum siccarum*'. On the same site a Covenanting mob had battered to pieces the coach of Archbishop Spottiswoode, after driving it round the streets with the burgh hangman inside.

257

The millionaire philanthropist Andrew Carnegie, a native of Dunfermline in West Fife, served as Rector from 1902 to 1908, and gave a fine sports park. In this connection the tongue of scandal tells how Principal Donaldson pulled a fast one. St Leonard's College had owned lands in the western suburbs, which in 1747 had passed to the United College, and were now vested in the University Court. Donaldson got Carnegie to sign a large cheque to enable the University to buy a tract that it already owned. When Carnegie said it seemed a high price, Donaldson replied that wealthy Dundee men were buying land for villas. Again, Carnegie wrote a cheque to build a modern indoor swimming-pool for the students. The Regius Professor of Mathematics, Sir Peter Scott-Lang, whose appointment had been a Tory political job in 1879, insisted on spending the money on an armoury for the cadet corps. When Carnegie asked to see his new swimming pool, Donaldson escorted him to the armoury door, and then the resourceful Coutts, the janitor, suddenly found he had mislaid the key; and they took Carnegie off to tea in University Hall, the womens' residence built in 1896. Coutts the janitor was a power in those days. Percy Theodore Herring, who died in 1967, told how he applied for the Chair of Physiology in 1908 and put on his top hat and frock coat for the interview. When he reached the Hebdomadar's Room he saw a rival candidate with a short jacket and bowler hat. Coutts looked at them both, and showed in Herring to see Principal Donaldson, with the remark: 'Here 's the gentleman for the physiology chair. Ye'll no be wantin' tae see the ither man.' On taking possession of his lab., Herring found only about two test-tubes, and complained to the Principal. 'Och,' said Donaldson, looking down again at his Byzantine history tome, 'go and see Coutts about it.'

In spite of a certain academic roguery here and there, and some insouciance, the Donaldson régime marked a new high point, and at the quingenary celebrations in 1911 for the university's foundation the staff included many men of world-wide distinction then or later, such as D'Arcy Thompson and Patrick Geddes, John Burnet in Greek and W. M. Lindsay in Humanity, A. E. Taylor and G. F. Stout, R. K. Hannay and J. D. Mackie and W. L. Lorimer, and the future Principal Sir

James Irvine (1921–52), a distinguished chemist who proved a capable promoter and administrator. A surviving participant in the 1911 celebrations remembers one incident most vividly: at the chief banquet Hermann Diels, historian of Greek philosophy, launched out into a very long speech, during which the waiters, who were all German, stopped serving and drank so much that their locomotion was impeded. The lecturer in German, Dr Georg Schaafs, started swearing at them, but was overwhelmed by a relevant vocabulary more copious and sustained than his own. The quingenary service was held in the Toun Kirk, beautifully rebuilt in 1910 by Macgregor Chalmers. The generation before the 1914–18 War was characterized by somewhat ostentatious living by the small class with secure private incomes from investment, some scores of whom dwelt in St Andrews, with large domestic staffs to cater for their creature comforts. At the other end of Fife was a large coalfield, where the miners were notably militant, headed by Miss Jennie Lee's grandfather, Michael Lee, who won the Eight Hour Day campaign. His campaign song was: 'Eight hours' work, eight hours' play, eight hours' sleep, and eight bob a day'—making forty-eight shillings for a six-day week. In one of their agitations, in 1912, the West Fife miners sent a squad of muscular colliers, equipped with stout sticks, to go round the mansions of the St Andrews *rentiers* and ask for contributions to the strike fund. The comfortable denizens of Hepburn Gardens and elsewhere mostly handed over some golden sovereigns, rather than risk having their lawns dug up at night or their conservatories bombarded with stones. Andrew Lang had been living largely in St Andrews since 1891, and was growing old. The advent of the miners terrified him. He buried all his coined gold in the garden, and fled to Banchory on Deeside, where he succumbed to a heart-attack. His wife testified, 'It was really the strikes that killed him.' It is said that nobody ever found his hidden cash.

During most of the 1914–18 war, in which 185 men of St Andrews were killed, the Principal was Sir John Herkless, formerly Professor of Church History. He was succeeded in 1921 by Sir James Colquhoun Irvine, whose work on the chemistry of sugars had been highly valued. One of his ambitions was to develop residences for men students, and he started with Chattan House, at the east end of Abbotsford Crescent, in 1921. Largely filled with ex-Servicemen, it proved hard to discipline. In 1927 Irvine secured a benefaction of £100,000 from an American Scot, Dr E. S. Harkness, with which he built a much larger residence for men, St Salvator's Hall, facing the castle (1930). Meantime the university had been dubiously embellished by the Younger Graduation Hall (1929), an eclectic structure by Paul Waterhouse, whose signature appears at the east end of the south front, the letters *P* and *W* above and below a Noah's Ark on stylized waves. Waterhouse also completed All Saints' Church (1924), an Episcopalian 'High' Church, containing now the best modern sculpture in the city, a Virgin and Child by Hew Lorimer of Kellie Castle. The Martyrs' Kirk was rebuilt in 1927, with a more imposing crowstepped outline, not long before the reunion of the main Presbyterian bodies in 1929. The College Kirk was refurbished internally, with the addition of a stone screen between ante-chapel and nave, by Reginald Fairlie (1930). St Leonard's Chapel was restored in 1952 by Sir David Russell, in memory of a son killed in the war, Ian Lindsay being architect. There are some fine modern stained-glass creations in various St Andrews kirks now, by Douglas Strachan, Lewis Davis, William Wilson, and others: the best organ is that of the Toun Kirk as reconstructed in 1966. It has also a fine peal of fifteen bells (1926).

In 1926 Principal Irvine allowed the revival of the Kate Kennedy procession. This student pageant started as a 'rag' in the quadrangle in the 1840s, became a scurrilous and riotous public demonstration, and was finally suppressed after Saturday, 5 March, 1881, when a specially outrageous display coincided with a heavy snowstorm and a nautical disaster. The three-master *Merlin*, of Sunderland, struck on the rocks at the Witches' Lake. A rope was thrown out to the crew of eight, who raised a cheer. A moment later, the ship slid off the reef, and all eight, in their stiff yellow waterproofs, drowned within sight of a thousand spectators on the fifty-foot cliffs. The Kate Kennedy procession, each April, includes the heroic Divinity student, John Honey, who in 1800 rescued, single-handed, seven men from a wreck in the East Bay. As a memorial to him, it is said, the students started their walk from the College Kirk to the pierhead after Sunday services. Another student who died untimely was the poet Robert Fergusson (1750–74), whose work in the Scots tongue inspired Robert Burns, who used his first royalties to erect a headstone on Fergusson's grave in Edinburgh's Canongate kirkyard. He too walks in the Kate Kennedy procession, with the French revolutionary Jean Paul Marat, who bought his MD from St Andrews, as did such unlikely alumni as Edward Jenner, the champion of vaccination against smallpox, and Dr Bowdler, who made Shakespeare fit reading for the Victorian family circle.

Principal Irvine also revived, in 1927, the 'Regenting' system, as a type of moral tutorship of undergraduates: since when St Andrews has become rather noted among Scottish headmasters for its familial pastoral care of volatile youth. During the 1930s that remarkable literary partnership, Edwin and Willa Muir, made their home in the town; and Edwin used to walk daily over the Links, meditating his imaginative poems, a very different reaction to the historic greensward from that manifested by the novelist Anthony Trollope. While staying at Strathtyrum in 1868 with the publisher John Blackwood, Trollope tried his hand at the Gowf, and his resultant vociferations were heard all over the Elysian Fields at the fourteenth hole. After a particularly atrocious stroke, he fainted with grief and collapsed upon the turf. Even to the greatest golfers of this century, to be sure, the Old Course has sometimes proved troublesome.

The 1920s and 1930s saw the growth of a 'New Town' south of the Kinness burn, mainly of housing schemes undertaken by the municipality, a leading figure of the time being Provost Norman Boase, who also was influential in reconciling the Town and the R & A, bodies which had for decades been at loggerheads. A group of enthusiasts between the wars founded the St Andrews Preservation Trust, to protect and restore the rich and varied heritage of houses from the sixteenth century on. Another enthusiast, Mr A. B. Paterson, himself a playwright, took the lead in converting an old cow-house into the lively Byre Theatre, which seats about seventy persons and has done dramatic wonders on a shoe-string budget. Theatrical activity has been somewhat discontinuous in St Andrews since John

Knox graced with his presence a play the happy ending of which was the hanging of a papalist garrison-commander. In 1939 two major dramatic events occurred: Hitler invaded Poland, and the Royal and Ancient Golf Club admitted professionals for the first time. At that period the university had about eleven hundred students, some five hundred of them in Dundee, and about two-fifths of them women. Of the young ladies at St Andrews a high proportion were English, often from higher income-brackets than their Scots partners in student dances and ensuing romances, which added to the social comedy of the town—a comedy, by the way, not yet exploited by a novelist. Not in many Scottish burghs could one ever have heard a church-going lady remark, 'It is such a set-off to the service to have the lessons read by a Baronet.' Before 1939, though English girls were frequent, an English male student was rarer than a Negro; and indeed the most conspicuous outlanders were American Jewish medicals, many of whom were splendid pugilists, and put St Andrews ahead in Scottish inter-university boxing matches. But after 1945 Englishmen began to invade the place in great numbers, St Andrews having for some years a 'priority' in the pecking order next to Oxford and Cambridge. This was in part a reflection of the fact that Scotland had relatively many universities compared with England in 1945; and, to be sure, many of the men from English schools were ancestrally Scotsmen, sons of Scots physicians and bureaucrats and executives engaged in 'spoiling the Egyptians'. One result of the new pressure on university places was a re-opening of the problem of the relations between University College, Dundee, and the University of St Andrews, with which it had been partially united in 1897. After extensive argument and a Royal Commission, a more thorough unification was enacted, the academic activities benorth the Tay being grouped in Queen's College, Dundee, incorporating University College, the Conjoint Medical School, and the Dundee School of Economics. The Principal appointed in 1953 to run the unitary scheme was Sir Malcolm Knox, a painstaking administrator with a devotion to Hegelian philosophy and vintage clarets. After he had conscientiously carried out the government's intentions for a decade, rationalizing activities to avoid needless duplication in each college, the government policy switched, and it was decided, for political window-dressing, to set up a separate University of Dundee, which came to pass in 1966. Scotland's senior university thus lost, with much else, its clinical medical school, one of the finest in the United Kingdom. To secure clinical teaching for the pre-clinical students, St Andrews asked Dundee for a block booking of places, but this proved to be impracticable. The University of Manchester in England promptly made a block-booking: so that St Andrews medicals will henceforth emerge with the M.B., Ch.B. of Manchester, an institution well placed for clinical material.

In the 1950s the target of the unitary university was 3,400 undergraduates, half in Queen's College, Dundee, and half in St Andrews. For the 1970s Dundee aims at about 6,000, and St Andrews at 4,000, which will still leave it a relatively small and intimate university. The historic city is still small and intimate also, with some 8,500 permanent residents. There is no university city in Europe so truly dominated by its university as St Andrews—not Uppsala or Heidelberg, Urbino or Poitiers. More than a quarter of the earned incomes in St Andrews depend directly on the university. Undergraduates from the big cities usually relish the privilege of studying in a seaside holiday resort without bustle or vulgarity, and with fine opportunities for the well-balanced life. Some have been known to come primarily for the Old Course, of which Peter Thomson, multiple winner of the World Open Championship, declared in 1955, 'It is the best course in the world, and there is none like it. I am the more convinced of that the more I play it.' Other students like the possibilities of pottering about in small boats, which have multiplied around the harbour as the full-time professional fishing-boats have shrunk to a half-dozen. Others fancy the championship tennis courts, or the excellent hill and shore lands for cross-country running. Those who ski bless the belated erection of a Tay road bridge giving swift access to snowy tracts of the Highlands; and more culture-loving types find the Forth road bridge handy for popping up to shows in Edinburgh. If any student has a taste for undergraduate curricula or post-graduate research there are lots of first-class offerings, and there will be more as plans develop, whether the inquirer's mind runs on low temperature physics or the higher textual criticism of the New Testament, philosophy or Classics or Romance philology, history or astronomy or marine biology, or all sorts of other specialist studies undreamt of by Bishop Wardlaw, the pious founder, and far off St Kenny in his hermitage and the ready-handed Pictish High King Angus. There are now some five million Scots in Scotland, but it has been estimated that there are twenty million people overseas who claim Scots ancestry and have some interest in their ancestral homeland. Among those from this Scottish *Diaspora* who have been benefactors of St Andrews in the past one thinks especially of Andrew Carnegie and Edward Stephen Harkness. One American Scot, Dr Russell Kirk, fell so much in love with St Andrews that he wrote a delightful book about it. It may be that, as air travel becomes commoner, expatriate Scots in Texas or Ontario or New South Wales will increasingly send their young hopefuls to take undergraduate or post-graduate courses in Scotland's oldest university, to realize the ideal set up by Principal Steven Watson, on taking office in 1966, that of making St Andrews, *par excellence*, 'Scotland's International University'.

© Cassell & Co. Ltd, 1969